STARTING & RUNNING

A FOOD TRUCK BUSINESS

BY ALAN PHILIPS

ALPHA

Penguin
Random
House

Publisher: Mike Sanders
Development Editor: Janette Lynn
Art Director: William Thomas
Copy Editor: Rick Kughen
Cover Designer: Jessica Lee
Book Designer/Compositor: Ayanna Lacey
Proofreader: Monica Stone
Indexer: Celia McCoy

This book is dedicated to all of you out there working hard every day to create and share something you deeply believe in. When you are ready to give up, keep going. Your time is too short to spend living someone else's dream.

First American Edition, 2020
Published in the United States by DK Publishing
6081 E. 82nd Street, Indianapolis, Indiana 46250

Published in the United States by Dorling Kindersley Limited.

International Standard Book Number: 978-1-4654-9011-7
Library of Congress Catalog Card Number: 2019946241

Note: This publication contains the opinions and ideas of its author(s). It is intended to provide helpful and informative material on the subject matter covered. It is sold with the understanding that the author(s) and publisher are not engaged in rendering professional services in the book. If the reader requires personal assistance or advice, a competent professional should be consulted. The author(s) and publisher specifically disclaim any responsibility for any liability, loss, or risk, personal or otherwise, which is incurred as a consequence, directly or indirectly, of the use and application of any of the contents of this book.

Trademarks: All terms mentioned in this book that are known to be or are suspected of being trademarks or service marks have been appropriately capitalized. Alpha Books, DK, and Penguin Random House LLC cannot attest to the accuracy of this information. Use of a term in this book should not be regarded as affecting the validity of any trademark or service mark.

DK books are available at special discounts when purchased in bulk for sales promotions, premiums, fund-raising, or educational use. For details, contact: DK Publishing Special Markets, 1450 Broadway, Suite 801, New York, NY 10018 or SpecialSales@dk.com.

Printed and bound in USA.

Reprinted from *The Complete Idiot's Guide to Starting and Running a Food Truck Business*

A WORLD OF IDEAS:
SEE ALL THERE IS TO KNOW

www.dk.com

Contents

Part 1 Food Truck Basics 1

1 The Food Truck Revolution 3

What Is a Food Truck? 4

How It All Began 5

What's Driving the Growth? 6

Technology 7

The Great Recession of 2008 6

Foodie Culture and Social Media 7

The World of Food Trucks 8

Taco Trucks: The Original 8

Pizza Trucks: It's All About the Ovens 9

Dessert Trucks: Nighttime Sweet Spots 9

Ice Cream Trucks: Good-Bye, Good Humor 10

Dumpling Trucks: Simply Delicious 11

Burger Trucks: Look Out Mickey Ds,
We're the Burger Kings! 11

Mediterranean Trucks: New York's Taco
Truck 12

2 Secrets of Food Truck Success 13

Success 15

Embracing Uncertainty and Fear 15

Understanding the Business Model 17

Projecting Food and Labor Costs 17

Estimating Average Sales 18

Estimating Labor Costs 19

Determining Whether You Pass the Test 20

Testing Your Production Time 20

Hitching Your Truck to Three Revenue Streams 21

Estimating Commissary Costs 21

Choosing an Authentic Concept 22

Making Sure You Have Sufficient Start-Up
Capital 22

Generating Volume, Volume, Volume 23

Identifying Your Spots 23

Creating an Assembly Line 24

Getting from Place to Place Efficiently 25

Achieving Consistency 26

Perfecting Your Recipes 26

Sampling Your Food 27

Training Your Staff 27

Taking Charge 27

Hiring Great People 28

Adding Value 29

Creating an Emotional Attachment 29

Turning on the Personality 29

3 The Right Concept and Food 31

Staying True to Who You Are 32

Picking Your Niche 33

Determining Your Cultural Perspective 35

Knowing Who You're Feeding 36

Profiling Your Food Truck Clientele 37

Meeting a Demand 38

Matching Your Menu to
Your Concept 39

Making the Proper Selections 39

Presenting Your Menu 40

Pricing to Your Market 41

Calculating the Price-Value Relationship 41

Ensuring Profitability 42

Downplaying the Price for Customers 42

Defining Your Purpose   42

    Purpose Exercise #1: The Ultimate Question   44

    Purpose Exercise #2: Self-Discovery Q&A   45

    The Result: Your Defined Purpose Statement   45

Creating Your Brand   46

    Step #1: Define Your Concept   46

    Concept Exercise   48

    Step #2: Define Your Brand   49

    Brand Exercise #1:   50

    Brand Exercise #2:   50

Testing Your Concept with
a Focus Group   52

4   The Right Truck   55

Types of Trucks   56

    Chevy Step-Vans   56

    Sprinters   58

    Prefabricated Trucks   58

Calculating Truck Costs   59

Finding Your Truck   59

    eBay and Craigslist   60

    Truck Dealers and Auctions   60

    Customizers   60

Redesigning an Existing Truck   61

    Choosing Your Equipment   62

    Powering Your Vehicle   63

Budgeting for Fuel and Maintenance   64

Finding an Off-Truck Kitchen (Commissary)   65

5   The Right Location   67

Being Mobile: The Pros and Cons   68

Identifying Where You Should Park   69

    Office Buildings and Office Parks   69

    Residential Buildings   69

    Large Events   70

    Dorms and College Buildings   70

    Seasonal Locations   70

    Nightspots   71

    Food Truck Lots   71

Determining Where You're
Allowed to Park   71

Considering Traffic   73

Knowing Locations to Avoid   73

    Low-Traffic Areas   74

    Restaurant Rows   74

Looking at Other Local Businesses   74

Building Your Spots   75

Part 2   The Mobile Food Mogul   79

6   Preparing Your Business Plan   81

Why a Business Plan Matters   82

Describing Your Concept, Brand, and Market   83

    Your Identity   83

    Your Market   84

    Your Competition   85

Forecasting Sales   85

Forecasting Expenses   87

Determining Your Breakeven   88

Estimating Profits   89

Choosing Your Business Structure   89

    Sole Proprietorship   89

    Partnership   90

    Limited Partnership   90

    Corporation   90

7 Finding Financing 93

Knowing How Much Money
You Need 94

  Calculating Your Start-Up Costs 94

  Calculating Operating Capital 95

Determining Your Contribution 96

Identifying Investors 97

  Potential Partners 97

  Silent Partners 98

  Family and Friends 98

What You Need to Show Potential Investors 99

How to Structure an Investment 99

Getting a Loan 100

  What You Need to Show the Bank 101

  Small Business Administration Loans 102

Other Ways to Increase Liquidity 102

  Supplier Credit 102

  Sponsorships 103

8 Regulations and Licensing 105

Knowing Your Local Laws 106

Getting Permits and Required Licenses 107

Following Health Codes 108

Obtaining Health Inspections 109

Staying on Top of Evolving Regulations 111

Buying the Insurance You Need 112

  General Liability Insurance 113

  Commercial Auto Insurance 113

  Finding an Agent and Asking the Right
  Questions 113

Establishing a Domain Name and Trademark 114

9 Creating Your Marketing Plan 115

Marketing Your Truck 116

Designing Your Brand Logo 116

Finding a Graphic Designer 117

Creating Your Online Presence 118

  Website 118

  Instagram and Twitter 119

  Facebook and Foursquare 120

Planning a Launch Event 121

Reaching Out to Bloggers 122

Working with the Mainstream Press 123

Treating Every Day As an Event 124

Making Social Media Your Friend 125

Creating Strong Product and Personal
Relationships 126

10 Setting Up Your Office 127

Deciding Where to Put Your Office 128

Creating a Communications Hub 130

  Telephone 130

  Internet Services 131

  Fax 131

Handling Payroll and Records 132

Keeping Records 133

Getting Outside Help 133

Part 3   **Getting Road Ready**   135

11   Setting Up the "House"   137

Understanding Your Unique Situation   138

Designing the Exterior of Your Truck   138

Paint   139

Vinyl Wrap   140

Window   141

Awning   141

Drink Fridge   141

Exterior Menu Holder   142

Menu Board   142

The Point of Sale System   142

Tablet Systems   144

Credit Cards   144

Setting Up the Kitchen   145

Organization   145

Job Assignments   146

Creating an Efficient Workflow   147

12   Hiring and Managing Staff   149

How Many and What Positions?   150

Getting the Right People On Board   153

Prep Cook   153

On-Truck Cook   154

Cashier/Greeter   154

The Hiring Process   155

Training and Educating Your Staff   156

Setting the Right Tone   156

Training   156

Teaching the Importance of Customer
Service   157

Scheduling   158

Setting Policies   160

Motivating and Retaining Your Staff   162

13   Inventory and Maintenance   165

Purchasing and Managing Supplies   166

Understanding the Role of the Purchasing
Agent   166

Researching Your Product Options   167

Determining Preparation Time   167

Locating Suppliers   168

Comparison Shopping   170

Negotiating   170

Inventory   171

Inventory Counts   172

Preventing Theft   172

Minimizing Waste   173

Truck Maintenance   174

14   Food Preparation and Safety   177

Your Food Truck Responsibilities   178

Working with Your Chef   179

Keeping Your Kitchen Clean and Safe   181

Battling Illness   182

Preventing Cross Contamination   184

Food Safety On the Truck and Off   185

Cleaning Supplies   185

Shift Cleaning Schedule   187

Weekly Cleaning   187

Monthly Cleaning   188

Semiannual Cleaning   188

Emergencies   188

Part 4 **Growing Your Business** 191

15 **Protecting Your Business** 193

Financial Reviews 194
Playing by the Numbers 194
Calculating Your Breakeven Report 194
Reviewing Daily Sales and Expenses 195
Generating an Income Statement 197
Performing a Cash Flow Analysis 198
Evaluating Operations 199
Reviewing Your Menu Mix 199
Reviewing Purchasing and Inventory 201

16 **Building Your Clientele** 203

Feedback: Listen to the People Who Feed You 204
Truck Conversations 205
Feedback Cards 206
Online Dialogue 206
Responding to Criticism and Praise 207
Gathering and Listening to Employee Feedback 208
Understanding Your Customers 208
Observing and Listening 209
Anticipating Their Desires 209
Exceeding Expectations 210
Making Amends: Service Recovery 211
Strategies for Earning Customer Loyalty 212
Gathering Contact Information 212

17 **Expanding Your Marketing Efforts** 215

The Myth of the Food Business 216
Strategic Sharing 217
The Creative Element 219
The Distribution Element 219
The Experiential Element 221
Storytelling 222
The Compounding Cycle 223
Determining Your Message 224
The Campaign 224
The Steps 225
Social Media 226
Doubletree CAREavan 227
Made for Mexicue 227
Chil'lantro BBQ 228
Publicity 228
Community Outreach 229
Advertising 230
Repetition and Consistency 231
Trust 231
Believe 232

18 Food Truck Events and Opportunities 235

Festivals 236
    Getting Noticed 237
    Getting Involved 237
    Covering Costs 238
Food Truck Lots 238
Television 240
    The Great Food Truck Race 241
    Top Chef 242
    Throwdown! with Bobby Flay 242
What's Next 243
Off the Truck 243
Concept Testing and Promoting 244
Community Building—Your Part of Something Bigger 244
Food Trucks in the Classroom 245

19 One Truck or More? 247

Is Expansion Right for Your Food Truck Business? 248
The Lifecycle of a Hospitality Business 249
    Stage One: Market Introduction 249
    Stage Two: Growth 250
    Stage Three: Maturity 250
    Stage Four: Decline 251
Making a Living from a Food Truck 251
Am I Ready to Expand? 252
    Demand 253
    Capital Resources 253
    Staff 254
    Systems 254
    Adding a Bricks-and-Mortar Location 254
Identifying the Benefits of Expansion 255
Watching for the Pitfalls of Expansion 256
Selling Your Business 256
The Myth of Success 258

Appendixes

A Glossary 261

B Resources 267

C Truck Tales 273

Index 281

Introduction

As I write this, I'm sitting on a plane flying to Hawaii for a consulting project. I can't help but be amazed at how I arrived here. I started out much as I envision you: filled with passion and chasing a dream. I've earned the right to spend my days pursuing my passion to serve, feed, and entertain people in the most creative ways I can imagine. My arrival at this nirvana manifested through countless hours of hard work and commitment to my personal vision. At one point, I was so obsessed with my dream, I wrote countless letters to celebrity chefs and restaurateurs begging them for jobs. I wrote so many letters and made so many phone calls that I recall one luminary welcoming me to his office under the moniker "Mr. Persistent."

Following your passion for food and hospitality will be hard work, but it will take you on a spectacular journey, teach you countless lessons, and expose you to amazing opportunities and people. The key is to recognize the opportunities, seize them, and enjoy every moment along the way. Your enjoyment will directly affect the experience you provide to your customers.

At the core of the food truck business and its current revolution is the chance to open doors and expose your talent. If you're passionate about food and hospitality, a truck can be your entry into this world. Trucks provide a platform for the next generation of foodies, entrepreneurs, and chefs to turn their love into a business—at half of the traditional investment. Blogs, social media, and press can then potentially turn you into the newest sensation faster than you can fill up your tank. Just look at the venerable Kogi BBQ truck. It started out as a drunken late-night conversation but wound up igniting a revolution and, along with that, a Los Angeles–based empire.

The journey you're about to embark on is your chance to contribute your voice and talents to the conversation. It's a ticket to the game with front-row seats because of the media hype surrounding trucks. But with great power comes great responsibility. The truck you choose to create will be an extension of you and your views, and in turn, your reputation. You only get one reputation, so protect it with your life. Just as you can establish yourself as a player in the food business, you also can negatively impact your future with unsavory practices or a low-quality product.

The most important advice I can give you is to be authentic, and honest, and always put the customer first. Create a truck that speaks to who you are and what you love. Customers will know if you're being true to yourself, and it will directly affect people's enjoyment of your product. Don't cut corners or try to take advantage of anyone in your business affairs. Treat everyone as you would treat your mother or grandmother. And never forget that your customers are the most important part of your truck business. Make sure, no matter what, that your customers leave your truck happy. Sometimes that might mean losing money or swallowing your pride, but word of mouth and buzz will determine your fate. A customer is 10 times more likely to talk about a bad experience than a good one.

Welcome. You are about to become the proud owner of a food truck, which is the most exciting opportunity in the modern hospitality business and also, quite possibly, the most delicious. Ladies and gentlemen, start your engines and fire up those stoves; it's going to be an extraordinary journey.

How This Book Is Organized

Our journey is divided into four parts. That means you have four major steps to complete before becoming a food truck entrepreneur.

Part 1, Food Truck Basics, provides a breakdown of the fundamentals of the business. You'll learn the history of the revolution to give you a feel for the marketplace and the business behind creating your rig.

Part 2, The Mobile Food Mogul, takes that knowledge and begins to put it into practice. You'll take your ideas and put them into a plan, get your financing together, and understand the regulations that affect your day-to-day operation.

Part 3, Getting Road Ready, shows you what to do with your truck, from staffing it with the most incredible employees ever to hit the road to laying out your kitchen and making sure your food is not only delicious but safe, too!

Part 4, Growing Your Business, helps you protect your truck business like the newborn baby it is, growing it so it can expand through marketing efforts, building your clientele, and monitoring your financial performance.

Acknowledgments

Appreciating your blessings and sharing your gifts are fundamental elements to a living a fulfilling existence. Nothing is possible without the support and guidance of others.

Thank you to Rita Battat Silverman and Leap Over It Productions, my literary agent and agency.

Thank you to everyone who gave me constructive feedback and positive reinforcement along my journey.

Thank you to Jason Mizrahi, Isaac Mizrahi, Gilda Mizrahi, and Farraj Mizrahi for welcoming me into your family and sharing an amazing bounty of delicious food and never-ending love with me.

Thank you to my brother Jason Philips; his wife, Nicole Philips; my sister, Claudia Borg; and my amazing nieces and nephews, Brody, Luke, Kylie, Holly, and Tyler.

Thank you to my mother, Diane Cohen; my stepfather, Jerry Cohen; my father, Frank Philips; and my stepmother, Mona Philips for their unconditional love and support.

Thank you to my beautiful wife, Gelareh Mizrahi, and my sons, River and Teddy. As always, everything is for you. Love you always. Never stop helping others and sharing your endless love with the world.

Trademarks

All terms mentioned in this book that are known to be or are suspected of being trademarks or service marks have been appropriately capitalized. Alpha Books and Penguin Random House LLC cannot attest to the accuracy of this information. Use of a term in this book should not be regarded as affecting the validity of any trademark or service mark.

PART 1

FOOD TRUCK BASICS

Mobile food carts have been around longer than you might think; when engines started purring, so did appetites. The modern food truck revolution is a gourmand's fantasy with no limits. From french fry trucks to mobile meatball meccas, food trucks are here to stay!

In this part, I explain what caused the tremendous growth of the modern food truck and give you a brief sampling of the types of trucks out there. Then I talk about the business behind the trucks, from choosing the right concept and food to selecting a type of rig. After that, we can get busy with what to look for when purchasing and customizing your truck. Finally, I discuss where you can park your truck once you have it. You can't park anywhere you want anymore, and building your spots is crucial to your success.

So, buckle up, get focused, and let's get busy making your ideas and passion into a deliciously profitable enterprise.

The Food Truck Revolution

My first experience with food trucks was a delectable dose of Americana. I was four years old and playing in the park with my friends. As I played on the swings, slide, and jungle gym, I patiently waited for the bell—the bell of the ice cream truck!

That jingle was the highlight of my many days at the park. Who cared about slides and swings when you could taste the succulent sweetness of vanilla soft serve? I thought for hours about what combination or special treat I would choose. I became partial to Creamsicle Push Ups and King Cones, usually with a side of Nerds and watermelon Big League Chew. We are all creatures of habit. Though I wanted to venture off into the latest Teenage Mutant Ninja Turtles green ice cream creation, I was tied to what I knew and loved. Who could bear the thought of wasting a hard-earned allowance on some second-rate ice cream treat? Not me, not then, and not now.

But more than the food, there was something out of this world about the experience of the ice cream truck. Nowadays, marketers might call it *aspirational,* but the ice cream truck made my day magnificent. Waiting for the truck to show up, watching its arrival, eating my goodies in the grass, and the truck's eventual departure was about far more than just an ice cream cone. The colors, sounds, and interactions with friends and neighbors made the ice cream truck an unforgettable food experience.

That's the same type of experience you can create with a food truck business. As you find out about the nuts and bolts of inventing, operating, and marketing your very own food truck business, always keep in mind the most important factor between being moderately and wildly successful: creating an emotional connection between the customer and your food, which leads to an unforgettable experience.

Fast-forward to the present day and urban centers teeming with food trucks. They're the hottest food trend of the decade and the most exciting new segment of the food industry. The ice cream truck remains, but now it's the Van Leeuwen Ice Cream truck in downtown New York City, serving homemade Red Currant ice cream prepared with fresh cream and oak barrel–aged vanilla.

Not only has the ice cream truck evolved into a gourmand's dream, but it sits alongside a virtual street-side food court serving Korean tacos, souvlaki, falafel, schnitzel, waffles, pizza, dumplings, and every other type of food imaginable (and some even unimaginable). Gone are the days of candy bars, ice cream cones, and prepackaged sandwiches at construction sites. In this chapter, I explore the food truck phenomenon and how to find the right truck to begin your business.

What Is a Food Truck?

A food truck is a mobile kitchen, canteen, or catering truck that sells food or drinks. Some trucks, such as ice cream trucks, sell mostly frozen or prepackaged food, but many restaurants-on-wheels have full kitchens with equipment specific to the creation of their specialties. Many cater to individual items or particular meals, such as breakfast, lunch, or late-night grub. The trucks usually park in high-traffic zones in urban centers or at events like carnivals, festivals, and football games. Many trucks move to different locations throughout the day in order to maximize business. Food trucks are a beacon of experimental cuisines and new ideas. The low barrier to entry makes a food truck the perfect testing ground for the newest and most exciting concepts in the food business.

A food truck revolution is underway, and not only does it taste incredible, it's an opportunity for entrepreneurial magic. So, let's take a look at where this revolution began.

How It All Began

Los Angeles was ground zero for the food truck revolution. The mobile food business began there with taco trucks back in 1910, thanks to the influx of Mexicans into California, with east L.A. receiving the highest concentration of immigrants. The taco truck became a staple of the SoCal landscape over the years, with an estimated 7,000 trucks operating in 2010. But it wasn't until 30-year-old Mark Manguera, a self-described failure, had his "aha" moment, that the modern food truck revolution was officially born.

Manguera's story begins after a late night of drinking. Mark and his sister-in-law Alice Shin, decided to head to one of Los Angeles's many taco trucks. As he enjoyed the greasy goodness, a thought popped into his mind: combine Korean BBQ and tacos.

This simple idea, the fusion of these Korean and Mexican staples, was a match made in food truck heaven. Many people would have abandoned the idea along with their hangovers the next day, but Manguera didn't. He believed in following his dream. He was willing to put his money, hard work, reputation, and everything else he had on the line to follow his passion and become his own boss.

Mark partnered with the incredibly talented Roy Choi, a local chef, and purchased a taco truck. The truck took a while to catch on. After several weeks of parking in different locations, including the busiest part of West Hollywood, and not getting any customers, they began going to clubs and giving free samples to the bouncers, who helped spread the word. Their first big break came when they got the idea to contact food bloggers about the tacos. This led them into the world of social media and an eventual use of Twitter to announce the truck's location.

The outcome of Mark's passion and hard work is the Kogi Korean-BBQ taco truck. Kogi is a Los Angeles food phenomenon that inspires rabid dedication from its fans. Every time the truck reaches its destination, people line up to taste their standard menu items and Chef Choi's rotating specials. Kogi set the example for many entrepreneurs to jump into the food truck business. They've even garnered nationwide attention among foodies both on social media and on more traditional food media.

Kogi chef Roy Choi was named to *Food & Wine* magazine's best new chefs in 2010 and was honored by *Bon Appetit* in 2009. Currently, Kogi has four food trucks, a restaurant and a taqueria. Kogi's massive buzz on social networking services, including its 149,700 Twitter followers, led *Newsweek* to call Kogi "America's first viral eatery."

For our purposes, the most powerful thing about Kogi is that they showed the potential of the food truck industry to many incredibly talented people. Not only that, they also formulated a blueprint for the industry. The floodgates had opened, and the revolution was just beginning.

As we begin this journey together, there are a couple of questions I'd like you to ponder. How did this Kogi phenomenon come to life? Was it the food—Spicy Pork Tacos, Kimchi Quesadillas, and Short Rib Sliders? Was it the marketing from a family of Twitterers posting truck locations combined with trendy downtown Los Angeles slang? Was it the design? The trucks are actually pretty simple for the world of food trucks—white with a fairly tame Kogi logo. Was it the culture? Kogi involved their fans in the naming of their trucks and sometimes brings along a DJ to spin for those waiting to dine. Was it connections? Manguera's wife, Caroline, was a food, beverage, and hospitality specialist with Four Seasons hotels. Was it the combination of high-end food at street-level prices?

What's Driving the Growth?

Food trucks have been around for a century, satiating the need for food far and wide, but why the revolution now? What happened that took the lowly food vendor from street meat and dirty water dogs to the top of the culinary food chain? Here are the factors that lit the food truck afire.

The Great Recession of 2008

The hospitality/food business is one of the largest industries in the world. It's filled with some of the hardest-working and most creative minds around. When the economy tanked in 2008, a couple of things happened to the industry. First, many people lost their jobs or couldn't find work. Traditionally, people flock to the food industry during times of economic hardship. They want to find a career they're passionate about, need part-time work, or want to become their own bosses. A restaurant costs a minimum of a few hundred thousand dollars to open, but a food truck can cost significantly less than $100,000. Which do you think is a better place to start? A food truck is the perfect entry-level project for an entrepreneur looking to test the waters with a new idea.

Second, Americans love to eat out. But what happens when you want to eat out and your income has declined? You look for cheaper options, such as food trucks. Food trucks aren't just less expensive, however. Food trucks tend to focus on specialty items, often from the youth or ethnic background of the truck creator. This is exactly the type of comfort food people are looking for when the rest of their life feels uncertain.

So, why don't Americans just go to McDonald's or Burger King for a cheap meal? Modern young professionals are very conscious about what they put into their bodies. Gourmet food trucks are clearly more appealing to this demographic than calorie-laden, over-processed fast food. Food trucks make most of their food from scratch with high-quality, fresh ingredients. Therefore, customers are getting something that is better quality and healthier at a similar price.

Technology

The next element in the perfect food truck storm was technology. The advent of social media (Instagram, Facebook, Twitter, Snapchat, and Foursquare) and the ubiquitous nature of the internet made for the perfect platform for marketing food trucks.

Using social media was like adding gasoline to the food truck fire, allowing trucks to communicate with their followers hourly, announce their location in real time, and build an online community with a delectable selection of food photos. For customers, the game of finding the trucks and having the latest information about them became almost as important as the meal itself. Social media, combined with the spread of information through food blogs and other websites, made gourmet food trucks an overnight trend.

Foodie Culture and Social Media

Long gone are the days of Julia Child demonstrating classic French food to housewives. Over the past 25 years, food has become theater and chefs have become celebrities. We're more conscious then ever of what we're consuming, and we love to talk about it. Regardless of whether it's cheeses, cured meats, wines, burgers, meatballs, cupcakes, exotic olive oils, or even the grossest foods in the world, I promise you there's a magazine, television show, or blog dedicated to discussing its taste, aroma, and the best place in the world to eat it.

Food trucks are no exception. Celebrity chef Tyler Florence hosts the Food Network show *The Great Food Truck Race,* in which food trucks compete against one another. A search for the term "food truck" on the food blog Eater.com generates tens of thousands of results. Our culture has embraced the food truck as a testing ground for the future of the food industry and, more importantly, a regular stop for gourmet goodness.

Combine all these factors and you have all the ingredients necessary to create a mouthwateringly profitable revolution. The question is how do you get your piece of the pie?

The World of Food Trucks

The following sections explore the many types of food trucks dominating the scene.

Taco Trucks: The Original

Taco trucks were one of the original food trucks on the scene. With thousands of taco trucks in existence, you could stop at a new one every day for years and never repeat. The mighty taco truck has spread far beyond its Los Angeles origins with trucks throughout the United States and abroad. The two dominant forms are the classic Southern California style and fusion, the Kogi style.

Classic taco trucks offer some of the best Mexican food available with specialties ranging from pescuezos (chicken necks) to onboard suadero (rotisserie pork and pork fat seasoned with onion, lime juice, salt, and adobo). Taco trucks represent all aspects of classic Mexican cuisine. Some restaurants, like the El Gallito chain, park their own food truck in front of their bricks-and-mortar business to showcase specialty items. The Gallito truck specializes in Birria de Chivo, a traditional Jaliscan goat stew made of shredded goat mixed with roasted chiles, toasted cloves, and fresh oregano. Wrap it up in a tortilla, wash it down with a cold Modelo, and go back for more.

Fusion trucks tend to combine another cuisine such as Asian with the standards of tacos, protein, veggies, and sauce wrapped in a hard or soft tortilla. I've already discussed the importance of the Kogi truck to the food truck revolution, but there are countless similar trucks throughout the country. In New York City, you find the Korilla and Kimchi BBQ trucks; in Dallas, the Ssahm BBQ truck takes to the road; and in Portland, Oregon, the fleet of Koi Fusion trucks are customer favorites. The fusion tacquerias seem here to stay and are crossing over into bricks-and-mortar restaurants, essentially defining a new cuisine.

Pizza Trucks: It's All About the Ovens

Pizza is one of the most popular foods in America, and pizza trucks are one of the fastest-growing segments of the food truck industry. Strolling out of my door at lunchtime in Manhattan's Financial District, I bump into the Eddie's, Jianetto's, and Vinny Vincenz pizza trucks. Eddie's Pizza's bricks-and-mortar operation has operated in a New York suburb for decades, and its fan base expanded when HBO's *Entourage* featured it. Its New York City truck specializes in the thin crust variety and has average waits of more than an hour during the busy part of the day. Jianetto's has a more diverse menu of Grandma slices, which are Sicilian-style slices served with dots of plum tomato sauce above the cheese. And Vinny Vincenz serves classic New York–style slices for $1 each. Who needs to go to the pizza parlor when the pizza parlor can come to you?

The main concern when starting a pizza truck is product differentiation and quality. Look for inspiration from someone like Casey's Pizza in San Francisco, which focuses on a well-prepared pie using only the best ingredients, or California Pizza Kitchen, which has built a chain through the use of unusual toppings and combinations.

Dessert Trucks: Nighttime Sweet Spots

It was only a matter of time until deliciously decadent sweets made their way into the food truck game. On the night before Halloween 2007, direct from some underfed college student's dreams, came DessertTruck. The vehicle, which parked outside New York City college dormitories, served pastries you would have to go to cooking school to learn how to concoct. Jerome Chang, the creator of DessertTruck, went to the French Culinary Institute and left a job at the world-famous restaurant Le Cirque to establish his own brand selling Warm Chocolate Cake and Espresso Panna Cotta. He has since moved to a permanent location on the fashionable lower East Side.

The idea for DessertTruck came from a chance snack that Chang and his roommate, Columbia Business School student Chris Chen, came up with in their apartment. A combination of toast, Nutella, caramelized bananas, and sea salt ignited their passion for sweets on the street. Chen and Chang chose a truck because it had more space than a cart and lower overhead than a storefront. They invested about $60,000 to purchase and design their truck. They prepard their items in a kitchen during the day and sold their desserts at night.

Another dessert truck includes Cupcake Stop, specializing in nostalgic cupcakes including Betty Crocker–style cake with buttercream icings or exotic flavors like chocolate caramel pretzel. Flip Happy Crepes, an old-fashioned trailer in Austin, Texas, serves French crepes. Wafels & Dinges, doles out Brussels wafel, the "mother of all wafels" with sweet and savory artisanal toppings.

While dessert trucks can be great, they also have more limited sales options. Not that many people are looking for cupcakes at lunchtime. Dessert trucks flourish where students are looking for a quick sugar fix or couples are strolling after a nice dinner. To maximize revenue, many successful dessert trucks focus on delivery, catering, and providing sweets to savory truck operators.

Ice Cream Trucks: Good-Bye, Good Humor

Oh, how the ice cream truck has changed! Generally the lines in front of the Van Leeuwen Ice Cream trucks are so long that you'd think they were giving it away, but that's only until you get a taste. Ben Van Leeuwen's off-white postal truck, and now his similarly designed stores, are decorated like shabby chic Italian farmhouses, and have a loyal following of folks looking to satisfy their sweet tooths.

Ben is a youthful former Good Humor truck driver who makes his ice cream from local, hormone- and antibiotic-free milk and cream. He combines his 18 percent butterfat ice cream with special ingredients, such as Michel Cluizel chocolate and Tahitian vanilla beans. A farm in Sicily harvests the nuts used in the pistachio ice cream, and all the toppings are organic. In addition, Van Leeuwen uses biodegradable cups, napkins, spoons, and straws. Van Leeuwen is the haute cuisine answer to ice cream trucks and a product of the Whole Foods generation.

Van Leeuwen is joined by many other gastronomists in his attempt to put his old employer out of business. Two standouts are the Coolhaus trucks, which now has 10 trucks in 3 states and distributes nationwide, and specializing in creations like coffee toffee ice cream covered in red velvet cookies, and the King Kone, which delivers soft-serve and flavored shaved ices to your doorstep.

But don't forget, The ice cream business is great in the summertime, but business chills when the weather turns cold. If you're planning an ice cream truck, assume your business will be seasonal or find a warm-weather climate.

Dumpling Trucks: Simply Delicious

What do you get when you combine high-quality ingredients and tasty dipping sauces with a childhood craving? Chirba Chirba Dumpling truck, of course. Chirba Chirba was created by owner Nate Adams after he moved to the United States from overseas and couldn't satisfy his childhood craving for delicious dumplings. Since this truck's inception, it has expanded it's fleet to two trucks and Nate is working on a brick-and-mortar restaurant. When you have a restaurant as well as a truck, you can share overhead and have fewer start-up costs, which means more profit for you. During slow months, you don't have to take your truck out. Having a bricks-and-mortar establishment, even if it's small, is a massive advantage in creating a successful food truck business.

Dumplings are the perfect food truck item. Most of the prep is done off the truck, with the dumplings just steamed or fried on board. They lose none of their freshness, cook quickly, and are easily served and eaten alongside a salad and a dipping sauce. Done right, dumplings are simple, fresh, clean, and, most importantly, authentic.

"Chirba Chirba" means "Eat eat!" in Mandarin Chinese. Nate chose this name because he felt it "embodies a very warm and hospitable feeling, especially to a friend or guest." When the big yellow Chirba Chirba trucks drive up, they want their guests to feel "This is so delicious and it makes me extremely happy to see you enjoy it, so please, eat!" And since 2011, they have been growing their business and scoring awards all over North Carolina.

Burger Trucks: Look Out Mickey Ds, We're the Burger Kings!

The Latin Burger and Taco Truck was launched in early 2010 by Ingrid Hoffman of the Food Network, along with her boyfriend, Jim Heins. It was one of the first gourmet trucks in Miami and is best known for the Latin Macho Burger, with a patty made of blended chorizo, chuck, and sirloin topped with Oaxaca cheese, caramelized onions, avocado sauce, and red pepper mayo. The result is an over-the-top, melt-in-your-mouth creation that proves burgers have a home in the food truck game.

Burger trucks have taken hold throughout the country. In Baltimore, Kooper's Chowhound Burger Wagon is widely known as the city's best burger. It's perfectly situated next to Kooper's Tavern for that perfect late night snack. La Cense Beef, a grass-fed beef company, has created a truck to promote their brand of beef. And, in Los Angeles, Baby's Badass Burgers are being featured on the Travel Channel and CBS. The ladies of Baby's

Badass sell burgers such as the Au Natural and the Covergirl, referring to the owners' feminine charms.

But don't forget, propane is the key to the burger business on a truck. Grills (burgers) and fryers (fries) use a lot of propane, so you'll need to work the cost of extra tanks into your numbers.

Mediterranean Trucks: New York's Taco Truck

Souvlaki, gyros, and falafel have always been favorites in the world of street food. Nowadays, a new breed of Mediterranean trucks are taking hold, such as the Vendy Award–winning, Souvlaki GR. For those of you that don't know, the Vendy Awards is an annual award ceremony organized by the nonprofit street vendor project. The event celebrates New York's street vendors and awards prizes in categories such as "Rookie of the Year" to top street vendors.

Souvlaki GR specializes in the signature street food of the founders' beloved homeland, Greece. With a commitment to only the freshest handmade ingredients, the company has created the ultimate Greek food truck. Their signature souvlakis are available on sticks or wrapped in hand-rolled pitas, and they are served alongside signature salads, such as the Prassini, which features chopped greens, dill, and feta cheese in a lemon–olive oil dressing.

Mediterranean trucks are Manhattan's answer to the taco trucks of Los Angeles. Moshe's Falafel and Taim Mobile are engaged in truck-to-truck combat for New York's best falafel truck, both serving some of the crispiest falafel, smoothest hummus, and freshest salads in Manhattan.

The types of trucks mentioned here are mere samplings of the many possibilities for food on wheels. Just because you don't see your favorite cuisine on the list, don't be discouraged. Part of what makes the food truck industry so successful is that people aren't afraid to experiment and take a risk. Whatever you choose, make it yours by letting your personality show.

Secrets of Food Truck Success

I have spent a lot of time in London taking in the local food scene. One of my favorite places to visit is the incredible Borough Market. For those of you who don't know, this outdoor food bazaar offers a spectacular mélange of the best food in Europe. Local farmers and artisanal producers sell their products; it's like Manhattan's Union Square Greenmarket on steroids. When I visit these kinds of food markets, I feel like Augustus Gloop upon his arrival at Willy Wonka's chocolate factory—I want it all.

When I walked through the Borough, my senses were inundated by smells and tastes. Everywhere I looked, something was tastier and more exotic: salted beef, apple pie ice cream, barbecue, cured meats, fresh focaccia, duck burritos, homemade raviolis, and extra creamy English cheeses and butters. I became so overwhelmed by the largess of the offering that I ended up trying everything. My boyish glee was replaced by bloat, dissatisfaction, and regret. It was better than falling into a chocolate river but still not the desired outcome.

A similar scene is playing out repeatedly in American restaurants, food halls, and food truck parks. Let's look at Taco Bell, for example. The menu offers tacos, burritos, gorditas, salads, nachos, chalupas, specialties, desserts, sides, and beverages. Not only does it offer dozens upon dozens of menu items, but it also has multiple menus, such as the Value menu, Power menu, and Vegetarian menu.

The antithesis to this traditional approach comes from the trendier, more guerrilla segments, like pop-up restaurants, food trucks, and small independent operators. Unable to afford the overhead required for a large offering and needing to differentiate their positioning, operators in these segments are trending toward concepts that are ultraspecialized. They're serving things like mini cupcakes, Asian-style hotdogs, Italian porchetta sandwiches, and Korean tacos. In an extreme example, I was recently at a food festival and drawn to a very busy booth serving only *poffertjes,* a mini Dutch pancake. This isn't necessarily a sustainable business, but it is very tasty.

One of my personal favorites is the ultrahip and always-crowded Meatball Shop in New York, Washington, D.C., and Connecticut. Founded by Daniel Holzman and Michael Chernow, the concept focuses on meatballs served with "simplicity and deliciousness." Once you pick the type of meatballs you want—there are six varieties daily—the only other choice is how you want them prepared: naked (just sauce), on top of pasta, with vegetables, or in a sandwich. These guys don't skimp on ingredient quality or the other critical areas of their business, but they chose to focus on something they could be "best in the world at", and it paid off in a big way.

Barry Schwartz's book, *The Paradox of Choice,* explains the success of specialized restaurants and products. Schwartz says many businesspeople think offering consumers more choice will satisfy their needs, but this conclusion, though logical, is not accurate. A paradox exists. Excess choice makes the consumer-buying process much more difficult and less satisfying. When consumers see a menu with a breadth of choice, they overthink, change their minds, give up on their purchases, or even worse, regret the whole experience. Nothing is less conducive to repeat business than a dissatisfying spend. The more complex your offering is, the less likely your guests will become customers for life.

Successful food truck operators reduce the effort behind making a choice, without reducing the appearance of choice. For example, if you specialize in salads, you could offer two base options—such as a salad and a salad sandwich—alongside an array of toppings and dressings. This is a perfect way to give your customers a choice without confusing them with your offerings. You are combining a simple base idea with a choice that is easy to execute and explain. Creating a guided decision-making process will lead to a happier and more satisfied customer.

Jim Collins, the world-renowned business writer and author of *Good to Great,* said, "If you cannot be the best in the world at your core business, then your core business absolutely cannot form the basis of a great company." As the food and drink business continues to grow globally, specialization is critical to differentiating new concepts and protecting established brands.

Don't be like Augustus Gloop in *Charlie and the Chocolate Factory,* flailing down the river, helpless and bloated. When you are planning your next move, be like Charlie, simple and good.

Success

Success in the food truck business is, in large part, determined by the decisions you make at the beginning of the process. As you develop your business, you will make hundreds of small decisions, but the early ones affect all the others that follow. Early decisions about your concept and how you execute food production will determine whether you succeed or go bust.

For example, you might make the best burritos in the world and are certain your burrito recipe is the perfect food truck concept. But when you really start to apply your product to the food truck business, things don't look so rosy. Here's why: when you make your burritos at home, it takes you about 10 minutes to make each burrito, with a total cost of $8 apiece because you use special meats and cheeses. You may have a great product, but it costs a lot to make and takes a long time, which is a recipe for disaster in the food truck business. (Ten minutes is a long time in the food truck business.) In this chapter, I discuss the importance of thinking with your head, not your heart, when developing your food truck concept. Remember, you're a businessperson now.

Embracing Uncertainty and Fear

All of us should conquer something in life, and it needs a lot of work and it needs a lot of risk. In order to grow and to improve, you have to be there at the edge of uncertainty.
—Francis Mallmann, chef, restaurateur, author

Uncertainty is defined as a situation with unknown or imperfect information. Being uncertain of your goals or direction is frowned upon in our society and has negative connotations.

Possibility is defined as something that's able to be done or within your power or capacity to do. Possibilities are exciting and have positive connotations.

Uncertainty is the glass half empty. Possibility is the glass half full. They mean the same thing, just from different perspectives. Whatever your perspective, avoiding uncertainty limits what's possible, while embracing uncertainty makes everything possible.

Embracing uncertainty is precisely what enables some successful food truck owners to realize their potential. They achieve a distinct balance: they're absolutely certain in their overarching purpose and confident in their abilities, while also knowing they must deal with the unexpected. You must shut down the fear that comes from that knowledge, as it can lead to making short-term decisions that limit long-term prospects. Know in your heart that you will succeed, but also accept that your path will be unclear, and at times, invisible.

While this way of thinking is illogical, it's important to note that by definition, unbelievable achievement is illogical. It isn't logical to think you'll create a multibillion-dollar food truck company where nothing previously existed. Yet, it can happen, and it's when things are the most uncertain that the most possibility exists. Think of it like risk and reward. As RZA of the Wu-Tang Clan explains, "Confusion is a gift from God. Those times when you feel most desperate for a solution, sit. Wait. The information will become clear. The confusion is there to guide you." I cannot tell you how many times I have reminded myself of this concept and benefited from not acting until I reached a deeper level of clarity.

Uncertainty and fear go hand in hand, and they try to distract you from your ultimate goals. But manifesting your food truck dream is the fun part; it's the point in the process when you finally get into your flow and begin to see your dreams come to life. In addition, it's the part of the process when you're exposing the most intimate parts of yourself and your natural emotional fear kicks in. You must embrace your fear instead of running from it. You can't allow it to stop you from achieving your food truck dream.

While it may be easier said than done, the most effective method I know for embracing fear is understanding its nature. Fear is our most instinctive method of protection. When you find yourself in the type of situation where you've been hurt in the past, you are fearful. While that may sometimes be irrational, just think what would happen if that instinct didn't exist: You would burn your hand on a hot pot, then go back and burn your hand again. In order to attain a level of consciousness where we can manifest unbelievable success, we must confront and overcome our fear.

Let's explore fear further through the lens of "emotional labor". For most of us, the journey to manifesting our potential as a food truck owner will be a journey of emotional labor, engaging with and managing our emotions throughout a long process of creation, rejection, and improvement. For example, when you first try to shoot a basketball, inevitably, you experience the challenge of missing more shots than you make. However, Steph Curry didn't become the greatest shooter of all time by quitting when he missed; instead, he shot the ball thousands of more times until he reached his goal, paying close attention to *why* he failed and moving through it and refining his process. That is how you and your food truck will become great, by confronting your fears daily and overcoming the pain, embarrassment, or frustration until you reach your goal.

Apply this same dedicated approach to your emotional labor. You will experience fear of rejection, fear of failure, or fear of standing out. As Seth Godin said, "The difficult task [with emotional labor] is confronting the fear of failure. That is what we are paid to do, that is what we are rewarded for." Throughout the process of bringing your food truck dream to life, you must accept your fear and not let it distract you from what you must do to achieve true and lasting fulfillment. Or as our friend Seth puts it, you must "dance with the fear."

Understanding the Business Model

Once you overcome your fear and uncertainty, you must decide on your business model. The business model of food trucks is fairly simple: choose a simple concept and sell as much food as you can in as little time as possible. Sounds easy, doesn't it? But what happens when it rains and nobody comes by the truck, or you get a flat tire, or an employee doesn't show up and you have to fill in yourself despite other commitments? All these variables make seemingly simple ideas complicated, and that's why you need systems in place to take all these variables into account.

Projecting Food and Labor Costs

Controlling your food and labor costs are key to profitability. Your food cost is determined by how much it costs you to purchase the food for your menu over a set time period. This includes food that you don't sell, which is known as *waste*. Your food cost should be targeted at or below 30 percent of *gross sales*. Gross sales—also called *gross revenues*—are your sales minus taxes and gratuities. Your *percentage of waste,* which is the wholesale value of food purchased divided by total food sales, should be no more than 5 percent of your gross sales.

I recommend serving fresh food every day, so it's very important that you closely control your purchasing and keep a record of sales. Good sales records will help you make accurate forecasts. Labor cost should average around 30 percent of gross sales as well. This means to prepare, cook, drive, and serve the food for your concept, your costs should be no more than 30 percent of your gross revenues.

To determine your food cost—without taking into account any secondary factors such as waste—you need to figure out what you believe is an acceptable price to charge. Let's say for this exercise that you plan to charge $10 for a burrito. You need to get pricing from your suppliers to determine the cost of all your ingredients. If your cost is below $3 for the ingredients, or 30 percent of the cost of food, you're off to a good start.

However, you probably won't be selling only one kind of burrito. You might serve a lobster burrito, where the ingredients cost $3.50, or 35 percent, and a chicken burrito that costs only $2.50, or 25 percent, to make. You're okay as long as the average of all the burritos you sell is no greater than 30 percent of the price you charge for it.

You must also consider secondary factors, such as waste and menu mix, when determining your "true" food cost. For now, however, let's stick with the "simple food cost."

After you've determined whether the concept you've chosen is practical from a food cost perspective, you must look into labor. Average trucks have anywhere from two to six workers. For this exercise, let's assume that you aren't working in the truck yourself (though if you are, you should pay yourself as an employee). A food truck employee will make an estimated $20 per hour—depending on your location and the level of skill required for your concept—with a minimum of six-hour shifts.

Estimating Average Sales

To calculate your labor cost, you need to generate a simple forecast of how much you expect to sell in an average week. Follow these steps:

1. Estimate how many items you expect to sell each a week.

2. Multiply the number of items sold from Step 1 by the amount you plan to charge for that item.

3. Multiply the result from Step 2 by 80 percent. This deducts 20 percent from your total to account for things like slow seasons, rainy days, and overly optimistic estimates.

You now have your estimated gross weekly sales.

If you estimate that you will sell 2,000 burritos a week and plan to charge $10 per burrito, you multiply 2,000 by 10 to get 20,000. Next, you multiply that by .80 to get an estimated gross weekly sales amount of $16,000.

For the sake of simplicity, the preceding instructions assume that you sell a single item at a single price. In reality, you will probably sell multiple items at different prices. To account for that, repeat Steps 1 through 3 to calculate the estimated gross weekly sales for each item, and then add these totals to generate your total estimated gross weekly sales.

Estimating Labor Costs

You need to pay staff to prep, cook, and serve your food, and you need to calculate the costs.

1. **Determine the number of staff hours for prep time per week.**

   It's fairly common for most food trucks to require three hours of prep daily, by a minimum of three people, for a total of nine staff hours per day (three hours × three people). If your truck operates seven days a week, your weekly prep time is 63 hours.

2. **Determine the number of staff hours on the truck per week.**

   If you have two shifts—11 A.M. to 3 P.M. and 5 P.M. to 9 P.M.—that's a total of eight hours. If you have three people on the truck for each shift, your total number of staff hours on the truck per day is 24. Multiply this number by 7 to get your weekly total, which is 168 hours.

3. **Add your weekly staff prep hours from Step 1 and your weekly staff truck hours from Step 2 to get your total weekly staff hours.**

   In this example, you add 63 and 168 to get a total of 231 hours.

4. **Multiply the total staff hours by the hourly pay rate.**

   If you pay each staff member $20 an hour, your total weekly labor costs, excluding payroll taxes, are $4,620.

Determining Whether You Pass the Test

Your labor costs shouldn't exceed 30 percent of your gross total sales. To calculate whether your estimates are in line with this guideline, follow these steps:

1. **Divide your total weekly labor costs by your gross weekly sales and round up to the nearest hundredth.**

   In this example, total weekly labor costs are $4,620 and gross sales are $16,000. If you divide 4,620 by 16,000 and round up to the nearest hundredth, you get .29, or 29 percent.

2. **Pat yourself on the back if your estimated labor costs are less than 30 percent—so far, your estimates are in line with running a successful food truck business. If your labor costs exceed 30 percent, you need to rethink your business plan.**

   If your labor costs are above the accepted range, it's important you look into the number of steps involved in preparing and serving your food items. Other than the preparation of food, the labor on a truck is standard. In order to cut labor costs, you may want to look into simplifying your menu by cutting items or ingredients. Also make sure that you're using foods multiple times on your menu. For instance, if you're using chicken in a burrito, use the same chicken in your taco. Another way to cut labor costs is purchasing pre-prepared items, such as premade tortillas, rather than using homemade items. Just make sure you are not sacrificing the quality of the final product. Balance is the key to making this work.

Testing Your Production Time

Later in the book, I show you how to streamline your production process (see Chapter 14), but for now, let's do a test. Go to your home kitchen and *prep* your item. To prep a menu item means to do everything necessary to a menu item prior to a customer placing an order for it, such as seasoning the chicken in preparation for grilling it.

After you've prepped the item, make 20 orders of it in a row. If you can make 20 plates in a row, at the same quality level, and in less than 5 minutes per plate using minimal equipment, you've got a shot of doing the same on a food truck.

Hitching Your Truck to Three Revenue Streams

Food trucks can be a source of three streams of revenue. In a business that has such razor-thin margins, you must have a concept that utilizes all three of them, as follows:

* **On-truck sales:** The primary source of revenue. Sales from customers coming up to the truck and purchasing food should account for 60 percent of your revenue. The expected profit margin from these sales is 15 to 20 percent.

* **Catering:** The second and most profitable revenue center involves selling packages or orders of food for 10 or more people per head or per tray. The profits for catering can be up to 50 percent of the total revenue. Thus, the catering component is crucial to your truck's success and should account for 30 percent of your business.

* **Delivery:** Depending on where you're parked, you should be able to make deliveries to local businesses and individuals. Delivery should represent 10 percent of your business and will have the same profit margin as on-truck sales (15 to 20 percent).

Estimating Commissary Costs

Your commissary is where you park, clean, and stock your truck. It's also where you do all your prep work and—for some concepts—the majority of your cooking. You also store your food and dry goods at your commissary.

Some food truck operators use their homes as their commissaries, while others rent commercial space. You must have access to a commercial kitchen outside of your truck. Health departments inspect commissaries regularly. It's of the utmost importance for food safety purposes as well as the quality of your product that you use a high-quality commissary.

A New York City commissary costs about $650 per month just to park your truck. To park and have basic access to a kitchen runs a minimum of $1,200 a month and goes all the way up to $2,500 for one truck. In California, a commissary runs from $500 to $1,200 for basic water, electricity, and parking. No matter where you open your truck, your commissary's quality and related costs will be integral to the success of your truck. More information about commissaries can be found in Chapter 4.

Choosing an Authentic Concept

You are your concept. If you spent your entire life cooking Italian food, don't tell me you want to open a Chinese food truck. Unless you have an incredible competitive advantage or a Chinese chef partner, the percentages say you won't succeed.

A food truck takes on the personality of its owner. As one food truck owner told me, "This is not like a restaurant where the chef can hide in the kitchen." As a food truck owner, chef, or server, you're front and center with your customers, and they want it that way.

You need to be open, interactive, and authentic in every aspect of your truck business. If you aren't, your customers will know, and not only will they not come back, they'll blog about it!

No one wants to eat at a corporate food truck. When the guy who writes a food blog and reviews four trucks a week on Yelp shows up, he wants to see you or at least your brother. He wants to know that you're making the same meatball recipe your grandmother made 50 years ago. Not only that, he wants to know that you're going to the same butcher in Brooklyn and that you make the sauce every morning using Grandma Lally's ladle. As a truck operator, you need to create an authentic connection with your customers, and then maintain that connection with hard work and honesty.

Your truck must be true to your beliefs. Choose a concept that represents who you are and not what you think you should be or want to be. Look to your roots as an individual or a family, and then apply that to your choice of concept.

Making Sure You Have Sufficient Start-Up Capital

I devote two chapters to the financials of the food truck business (see Chapters 6 and 7). However, looking at the basics, you need to consider the minimum capital requirements to get your business started. It's going to cost you at least $50,000 to start a food truck business, but I recommended that you budget at least $100,000.

Where will all that money go? Here are some of the big-ticket items:

* **A high-quality truck and mobile kitchen.** You could spend less, but what's the point if it's going to cost you the same amount in repairs and lost sales later on?

* **Enough operating capital to help you get through the start-up period.** It's going to take a while for you to build your business to the point where it turns a profit; until that time, you need to have reserve funds available to cover all your expenses.

* **Your weekly paycheck.** If you don't pay yourself anything while you're getting your business off the ground, you might create your own personal financial problems, which will hurt the business.

After you come up with a budget for your project, add 20 percent to that total. It gives you some financial breathing room and is probably a more realistic figure anyway.

Don't go overboard and spend too much money creating your food truck business. Some people spend $250,000 or more on their truck, which doesn't make sense for two reasons. The first is that the return on investment isn't high enough to justify the cost. Why spend $250,000 to make $1,000 dollars a week in profit? The second is that people don't like expensive food trucks. The truck business is a countercultural movement, and anything that yells big and expensive is against everything the industry stands for. Most people will take an authentic truck over an expensive one any day of the week.

Generating Volume, Volume, Volume

The key to the food truck game is volume—in other words, selling as much as you can. The check at most food trucks is no more than $20 per person. At 10 percent profit, you're making around $2 per person on every item sold. In order to make $100 dollars, you must sell 50 of whatever it is you're slinging. You aren't spending $100,000 on a truck business to make $100 dollars a day, so you need to be able to attract and serve large volumes of customers.

Identifying Your Spots

The key to selling large volumes of food is identifying and building your spots. Within each neighborhood are areas where food trucks are known to park or people are known to eat a particular meal, such as lunch. You need to identify a location that has good business but isn't oversaturated. You also need to establish positive relationships with the businesses on the street, so they don't become hostile to your presence.

Once you identify a few potential spots, you must begin to establish a presence there. This might involve being there every day—or certain days of the week—at a particular time. Additionally, you must advertise it to the local community and businesses. Let them know through social media and flyers that you plan to be around the neighborhood. Offer complimentary samples during your first couple of weeks to establish that you have a good product. Deliver complimentary food baskets to businesses in the neighborhood. See Chapter 5 for an in-depth look at finding the best parking spots for your food truck business.

Creating an Assembly Line

To service the volume required to sustain your business, you must create an assembly line system. An assembly line is the process in which parts—or in our case, food—is added to a product in sequence.

The assembly line, developed by Ford Motor Company between 1908 and 1915, enabled mass production at reasonable prices. The McDonald brothers, Maurice and Richard, are rumored to have been the first to apply it to a restaurant in the early 1940s. It was called the Speedee Service System, and restaurateurs from all over the United States tried to duplicate it. The key was to become less dependent on skilled cooks by making unskilled labor responsible for just one part of the cooking process. Unskilled labor is paid less and takes less money to train. Using the system got food out quicker while tasting just as good.

Your assembly line involves cooks and servers working in unison to place, prepare, and deliver orders in a timely fashion. For a food truck, that means under five minutes from order to delivery.

If you have four people on your burrito truck, here's how your assembly line might look:

1. The server takes the customer's order at the truck window, hands the order off to the cooks, and accepts payment from the customer.

2. One cook heats the tortilla, cooks the meat, and hands the order off to the next cook.

3. The second cook fills the tortilla with the vegetables, beans, sauce, and cheese, and hands it off to the third cook.

4. The third cook wraps the tortilla, puts it in the serving container, and hands it to the server.

5. The server calls out the name of the order and hands it off to the customer.

If one member of the team isn't doing his or her job well or fast enough, the entire system will break down, and you'll lose a customer. Lose enough customers and you'll be out of business. If you deliver enough high-quality meals quickly, you just might turn a profit. Chapter 14 delves into these issues in more detail.

Getting from Place to Place Efficiently

Spending as little time as possible in each place is critical to the success of your truck. The less time you spend during each part of your operation, from prep to travel to sales, the more money you make. The more time you spend, the more labor cost, fuel cost, propane cost, and food waste you'll have. Spending 30 extra minutes during each stage of your day could cost you an extra $300 to $400. Failing to be prepared can easily cut daily profits by 30 to 50 percent.

To maximize efficiency and profitability, you must have a plan. You need to think of every detail *before* you start moving forward, not after.

* How long will it take you to prep?

* How long will it take you to travel?

* Once you park the truck, how long will it take you to get set up?

* Will you have to send someone ahead with the truck to get the parking spot early and then deliver the food?

* How long will it take you to break down the truck and move to the next shift?

I recommend creating a timeline for your day. Take a piece of paper or use a spreadsheet program and literally break down the entire process into 15-minute increments; assign very specific tasks to each quarter hour.

* What needs to be happening at the commissary from 6 to 6:15 A.M.?

* What about from 7:16 to 7:30 A.M.?

* What needs to be happening on the truck from 5 to 6:30 at night?

Next, assign every task to a particular person. After you've made the assignments, you need to provide each worker with a clear schedule, breaking down his or her specific daily duties.

The hardest part of this process is proactively and positively managing and motivating your workers to stay on schedule, a skill I'll talk about in Chapter 12.

Achieving Consistency

Market research indicates that the primary reason people choose where they're going to eat is the location of the establishment. The second most important factor is the consistency of the food. Consistency—repeatedly making the food item the exactly the same way—is the key to restaurant success. For example, McDonald's Big Macs are the same at every location.

Customers like to know what they're getting, how much of it they're getting, what they're paying for it, and that it's going to be served exactly the way they want it. That's the key to repeat business, and the more repeat business you have, the more successful you'll be.

You can ensure consistency of your product through recipes, sampling, training, hands-on management, and great employees.

Perfecting Your Recipes

You need to handle every aspect of every menu item you sell precisely the same way each and every time you make it. If you're cooking burritos at home for friends or family, it's okay to switch brands of salsa or try a different cheese. It's also okay to change the quantity of beans you add to the tortilla. But when you're serving food from your food truck, all these things—from the brand of salsa and type of cheese to the amount of each ingredient you use and how long you grill the meat—must be handled exactly the same way for each burrito you serve. If you served your burrito with a slice of orange as a garnish the last time a customer ordered it, he's going to expect an orange garnish the next time he orders it, too.

You need exact specifications for everything from the look of the plate to how much lettuce goes on your burger. Your recipes are your lifeblood and your trade secrets. Anyone who prepares your food must know exactly what to do to prepare all your menu items.

Sampling Your Food

You, and only you (because this is your dream), must constantly sample your products. You need to test at least two items daily to make sure the taste, texture, and presentation are perfect. You should also do this randomly during different points in the process. This will give you a true sense of the customer's experience, as well as enable you to pinpoint any possible issues within the process.

You can also test your product using secret shoppers. These can be friends, or you can even use a paid service that dines undercover at your truck a couple of times and provides you with feedback on the products and service. Secret shoppers provide an unbiased view of your business and products from the consumer's point of view.

Training Your Staff

You need to actively train all employees prior to them taking a role in your business. You need to teach them the exact methods you use to prepare your product. To ensure uniform training of your staff, create an employee manual that outlines all the processes of your business. It should include photos of the physical item and step-by-step instructions for preparing the item. Additionally, it should provide standard language for answering customer questions and referring to menu items.

Finally, employees should be empowered in the art of *service recovery*. Service recovery describes the paradox in which a service or product failure can offer the chance for a business to receive higher customer satisfaction than if the problem had never occurred. People make mistakes and fixing the situation with a customer through a complimentary check, drink, or discount is the fast track to making a customer for life.

For details on the training process, refer to Chapter 12.

Taking Charge

All ships need a captain, and either you or your manager is the captain of your food truck. You're accountable for all the decisions made by everyone involved in your business, so you must be there, leading by example. If you aren't on hand and included in all aspects of your creation, you won't realize your dream of creating a successful food truck. You need to be knowledgeable about all aspects of the business, and you must be able to fill in for any of your employees at a moment's notice. Your presence will make everyone work a little bit harder and ensure that your customers receive the best product every time.

Hiring Great People

The people you choose to represent and execute your business are critical to it becoming a success. You're looking for "51 percenters," a term I'm borrowing from restaurateur Danny Meyer. He doesn't believe in pursuing the so-called 110-percent employee; that's about as realistic as working to achieve the 26-hour day. You're looking for employees who will go that extra step every time to get the job done, with skills divided 51/49 percent between emotional hospitality and technical excellence.

Meyer says a 51-percenter has these five core skills:

* **Optimistic warmth:** Genuine kindness, thoughtfulness, and a sense that the glass is always at least half full.

* **Intelligence:** Not just "smarts" but rather an insatiable curiosity to learn for the sake of learning.

* **Work ethic:** A natural tendency to do something as well as it can possibly be done.

* **Empathy:** An awareness of, care for, and connection to how others feel and how one's actions make others feel.

* **Self-awareness and integrity**: An understanding of what makes someone tick and a natural inclination to be accountable for doing the right thing with honesty and superb judgment.

My recommendation when hiring is to choose people you like. The first minute you meet someone, you get an initial feeling in your gut about that individual. That feeling says either "I like this person" or "I don't like this person". Trust that instinct. You're going to spend a tremendous amount of time with these people, and if you don't like them, the truck will become unbearable. More importantly, good people who like each other combine to form a great team that makes an awesome product every time!

Adding Value

Magnificent food and fabulous service are sometimes enough, but in today's hypercompetitive hospitality environment, you need something else—something intangible that differentiates you from the crowd. I call these intangibles "emotional attachment" and "personality".

Creating an Emotional Attachment

There are tons of fast-food restaurants in the world. Two of my favorites are Roy Rogers and White Castle. Why do I love them? It definitely isn't because they're the most popular. It probably isn't because they have the best food, although I do enjoy them on occasion. It's because my grandmother used to bring me White Castle hamburgers and my mother used to bring me Roy Rogers fried chicken. I have an emotional attachment to these brands.

Turning on the Personality

Now that you have a great product and a great brand, do you need anything else? Yes, you need an associated personality. People don't want to talk to your brand; they want to talk to a person. The person makes it real; the person has emotions, struggles, and a story. You are that person. You are your truck. Would you prefer to go to a great restaurant or a good one where the owner knows you and takes care of you? Most people would choose the latter. There's no substitute for a personal touch.

How do you translate that to a food truck? There are two ways: you are present, and you pleasantly surprise your guests.

You are present. You should be on or around your food truck 80 percent of the time it's open. If you can't be, you need to find a strong manager who's outgoing and can take on this role for you. (Although I strongly advise against the latter.) Just keep in mind that no one will care more about your truck or your customers than you. When your customers see you daily, they'll associate your smiling face with the food truck and miss you when you're gone.

You pleasantly surprise your guests. The pleasant surprise is an art form that has been perfected by great hosts since the beginning of time. Here's an idea of how it works. You have a great business going with your pizza truck. One guy shows up at your truck every day of the week. He buys the same lunch every day, pays, doesn't say much, and goes back to work. One day he shows up and places his order. He puts his hand into his pocket to pay for the food and *bam*—you tell him lunch is on you today. Instantly a huge smile comes over his face, and he thanks you. You've made him feel special, and that means more than you can possibly imagine.

The business of hospitality is all about servicing your guests and making them feel exceptional. You've just made a customer for life. Not only that, he's now a walking advertisement. He goes back to his coworkers, friends, and family to tell everyone how incredible your pizza is and that he'll "hook them up" if they go there. It's a win-win!

You're on your way to food truck success!

The Right Concept and Food

It was the summer of 1947 when Harry Snyder, a World War II veteran, wandered into a Seattle restaurant and fell in love with his waitress, Esther. She'd recently graduated college with a degree in zoology, but she also had a strong affinity for the culinary arts. On Esther's break, they sat together in a diner booth, shared a hamburger, and discovered they both wanted to move to California. Ten months later, married, they pooled their resources, relocated to L.A., and opened a little burger joint across the street from Harry's childhood home. The fast-food business concept was just taking off at the time. McDonald's had arrived locally just a few years earlier, but the Snyders' establishment stood out. By utilizing a two-way intercom, it was the first drive-thru burger experience in California, aptly named In-N-Out Burger.

Fast-forward 70 years. In-N-Out Burger has grown to 300+ locations employing more than 18,000 people. While that's significant growth, it's paltry compared to the 37,855 McDonald's locations with 420,000 employees, or Starbucks' estimated 29,000 locations with 291,000 employees. The reason behind In-N-Out's measured growth is that the company has consciously resisted franchising its operations or going public.

All In-N-Out Burger restaurants are west of the Mississippi River. Being no more than a day's drive from their regional distribution centers makes it possible for the company to control the quality of their product by serving only fresh, unfrozen burgers and buns. It also enables them to control the quality of the experience with rigorous training and employee standards. Furthermore, the selective nature of their locations has led people to put an even greater emotional value on their delicious burgers. For years, customers have been begging In-N-Out Burger to expand beyond its comfort zone—to cash in and follow society's belief that bigger is always better. Instead, the company's founding family has exhibited uncompromising discipline, remaining true to their core values and focusing on quality over quantity. Their commitment to staying within their flow—concentrating their energy on a singular pursuit—has created a business that feeds itself through fierce customer loyalty and word-of-mouth marketing. In-N-Out Burger is a great company that sells itself.

You'll receive a daily barrage of messages trying to influence your actions and distract you from what's most important—your food truck's potential. If you hope to manifest your creative potential, it's critical that you tune out these messages. Anything that distracts you from getting closer to your true purpose diminishes the likelihood that you'll reach the pinnacle of achievement you seek. To quote Harry Snyder, "Keep it real simple. Do one thing and do it the best you can."

Staying True to Who You Are

In the food truck business, the right concept and food doesn't exist; there's just the right concept and food *for you and your clientele*. Our mantra for defining what's right for your truck is *Do You*. In other words, stay true to who *you* are. Over the years, I've spoken with many ultrasuccessful people, and that's the one concept that connects all of their stories. In this chapter, I help you decide how to select the best menu for *your* food truck concept.

Successful people stay true to who they are, their roots, and their values. They choose a path and product they believe in with every inch of their humanity. To be successful, you need to follow their lead. If you try to create a truck that's not representative of you and your skills, the customer will know, and I can guarantee you that it won't lead to success.

Here are a few examples of food truck entrepreneurs who stayed true to themselves and succeeded:

* **Souvlaki GR** is run by a Greek immigrant who serves authentic and fresh Greek food.

* **Van Leeuwen Ice Cream trucks**, run by a former Good Humor ice cream man, use locally sourced gourmet ingredients.

* **GastroPod** is owned by a gourmet chef with experience in Europe's and America's most avant-garde kitchens. He serves experimental and seasonal comfort food from a 1962 Airstream trailer.

Can you see that all these trucks somehow make sense? The proprietors' beliefs, passions, and personalities are inseparable from their products. If they're hip, their truck is hip; if they love dumplings, they sell dumplings. It isn't rocket science. It's actually the exact opposite; it's the science of simplicity.

Picking Your Niche

Great food truck brands have a clearly defined niche. Successful food trucks do one thing and do it really well. Whatever you've chosen to sell, your brand should be centered on showcasing and promoting it. The simpler, the better; not only does this keep your operational costs down, it enables you to focus your marketing and branding messages.

To start, let's break down the truck categories:

* **Cuisine trucks:** Focus on a particular cuisine like Greek or Mexican.

* **Item trucks:** Focus on an item like pizza, tacos, cupcakes, or burgers. They're the most common truck type and, I believe, the most effective. By focusing on being the "best in your world" at one specific item, it's easier to control costs, target your marketing efforts, and establish a following.

* **Meal trucks:** Serve menu items consisting of a particular meal, such as breakfast, lunch, or dessert.

You can achieve success with any of these types of trucks as long as you execute the truck category correctly. Whichever truck type you choose, you must seek to be the best. It means looking at your target area and ensuring you're able to make the best version of the food you're selling. There's no point in setting out to be the second-best taco truck in downtown Cleveland. Nobody wants to eat at the second-best taco truck; they want the best.

Now that you know the importance of determining your niche, how are you going to figure it out? Try not to complicate that idea. Instead, focus on the simplest aspects of your idea as you develop it. Whenever you're making decisions about your truck and you don't know what to do, sit down, and take a deep breath. Try to simplify your problem. Then choose the simplest solution and begin. Overcomplicating your business likely will lead to failure.

For example, if you grew up in an Italian family and love cooking Italian food, particularly your infamous meatballs, one option is to consider opening an Italian food truck. You could sell chicken parmigiana, pizza, meatballs, spaghetti, salad, garlic rolls, tiramisu, etc. However, keep in mind that your specialty is meatballs, not the best chicken parmigiana, pizza, and tiramisu. So, why complicate your life by making all that other stuff?

Your diamond is your meatball, and you should focus solely on it. In other words, you should focus on creating a meatball truck, not an Italian food truck. By simplifying your concept, your food and labor costs will be lower, your marketing message and target market will be more defined, and you'll be able to focus on being the "best in your world" at meatballs.

But what if there's already an Italian restaurant famous for its meatballs where you're planning to park your truck? Can you be better than them? And, even if you can, is it worth the time and energy making it known that you are?

Because you have a truck, you can simply put your key in the ignition and find a place to park where there's less competition. So, you hit the streets, do some research, and guess what? A better location exists—a parking lot between three office buildings with one shopping center within walking distance and no Italian restaurants nearby. Now you have the best product in a location with a need. And, you've further defined your niche.

The point isn't simply defining *a* niche, it's defining *your* niche. You don't have to be the best in the entire world; you just have to be the best in *your* world.

While you've determined your product niche, you're only halfway done deciding on your concept.

Determining Your Cultural Perspective

At one time, it would have been okay to define your niche and go to work; however, food trucks are now a microcosm of modern business. They showcase many aspects of the future of the business world, including social media, mobility, and micro markets, which brings us to the second layer in defining your concept: determining your cultural perspective.

In today's hypercompetitive business landscape, having a good product is definitely the most important factor, but how you communicate about that product—and how the product itself looks and feels—is becoming almost as significant.

The Mud Truck, a coffee brick-and-mortar shop in Manhattan with multiple locations, sells coffee, but it's also selling a lifestyle. It's the anti-establishment coffee retailer, which is perfect considering their target market in downtown Manhattan. Since its inception, the Mud Truck has spun off into bricks-and-mortar locations, apparel, and wholesale coffee.

Another example is Ben & Jerry's Ice Cream. Do they just sell ice cream? Nope. Ben & Jerry's sells a cultural perspective. They're socially responsible, and that stems from the associated personalities of Ben and Jerry. When a truck owner tweets or the truck is written about on food blogs, the business needs to have a point of view and a voice.

What you say is as important as *how* you say it. If you're located downtown and most of your customers are going to be under the age of 30, you need to talk like they do. You should even be referencing their favorite music, TV shows, and movies. You might even create a menu item that's the favorite of a local indie rock band or food writer. Our pals Ben and Jerry did exactly that with the bands Phish and the Grateful Dead. They knew their target market really loved the bands' music, and the bands shared their cultural perspective. It led Ben and Jerry to develop the flavors Phish Food and Cherry Garcia.

Think back to your world—the people, places, and things you and your soon-to-be customers interact with every day. Once you find your cultural perspective, identify the cultural elements you can use to integrate this perspective into your customer experience. It will add a second layer to your food truck brand that speaks to your core clientele. That core must identify themselves with your brand over your competitors. It's the same reason people drink Starbucks or Dunkin' Donuts coffee. Either you're a Starbucks person or a Dunkin' person; rarely is someone both.

In order to choose your cultural perspective, you need to study your target market to see what makes it tick. Next, you must look at yourself and see what defines you. List the 10 lifestyle characteristics of your target market and the same list about yourself. Compare the lists and analyze the areas in which there are similarities. Once you identify the similarities, narrow them down to two or three and then choose the one characteristic you believe applies most accurately to the food business.

Let's say you're planning a burger truck and you've determined that you and your target market both love rock music and computer games. Common sense tells you computer games wouldn't be the ideal marketing partner for hamburgers, but rock music just might work. Maybe your burger truck could be called Rock Burger or Zeppelin Burger, and the logo and menu could reflect rock culture and icons. You could also play rock music in your truck and be known for parking outside all the major rock concerts.

Identifying a nonfood connection with your customer is vital to your truck's success and is critical in defining your branding and marketing efforts.

Knowing Who You're Feeding

Would you open a lobster roll truck in a college town? I know of a lobster roll truck that does $13,000+ in revenues every single day. That's a lot of money for a truck; sounds like a good business to me. Their *average cover,* which is what one person purchases when dining at your truck, is around $20 per head. When parked at the right location, these rolls can sell like wildfire. If you did 60 covers, you served 60 people. You can figure the average cover by taking the total revenue for a time period and dividing it by the number of people you served during that time.

I attended Cornell University in Ithaca, New York. Ithaca is frigid eight months of the year, and it's mostly inhabited by college kids with very little disposable income. They spend what money they do have on chips, pizza, sandwiches, soda, and beer. A lobster truck selling an expensive item that's in high demand primarily during the summer months doesn't seem like it would work there. So, even though a lobster roll truck can make a lot of money, the demand probably doesn't exist among poor students in freezing cold Ithaca, New York.

A better location for a lobster roll truck would be a high-end beach resort or affluent urban neighborhood during the summer months. Both locations have heavy foot traffic and clientele with disposable income. In this example, you're enabling macro trends, such as weather and income levels, to build your business. You never want to be fighting the current. Instead, you want to ride the wave to success.

Profiling Your Food Truck Clientele

The lobster roll example makes it clear that you need to define your *target market* and match your concept to that market. A target market is a group of customers to whom you aim your marketing efforts and product. They are your ideal customers.

The target market combined with your product, place, promotion, and price—collectively called the four Ps—are the main elements that determine whether you'll succeed or fail in the coming months. Determining your target clientele and their demand for your product is crucial to your success.

It actually took the people who run the Kogi Korean BBQ taco food truck months before they were able to create awareness within their target market. They used traditional media to advertise their business. However, it turned out their clientele was on the internet, using blogs and social media, which is actually where most of the food truck clientele hang out.

Based on my research, here are some estimates about the typical food truck customer:

* Approximately 90 percent of food truck customers are below the age of 45, with the core group landing between the ages of 25 and 45.

* The core group is highly active on the internet and social media.

* Approximately 60 percent of customers are male; due to the nature of the food. (Although the food is made with high-quality ingredients, it tends to be heavier and greasier, which seems to appeal more to men.)

The core group of food truck customers spend hours online each day. They actively seek out the newest and most interesting experiences through websites like Eater.com, UrbanDaddy, and Thrillist.

Most food truck customers are looking for an exotic and rewarding food experience that will both satisfy their craving and provide a story that they can tell their friends. Many people may even write their own blogs about their experiences at food trucks and will probably post pictures and reviews on social media pages like Facebook, Twitter, and Yelp. They aren't highly price sensitive, but they're definitely value oriented. If they feel like a truck is ripping them off or taking advantage of them in any way, they'll be extremely vocal about it.

It's very important to develop a focused group of customers who will tout your truck's virtues to their peers. The more regular customers you have, the quicker you'll reach your tipping point—the point when something reaches critical mass. How will you know when you reach your tipping point? You'll know when you show up to your spot and the customers are already waiting for you.

Your food truck clientele is part of the general pool of people who eat at food trucks. Let's say 100 people eat out in a neighborhood. Fifty of those people are open to eating at food trucks. These people will be your easiest targets. The key is to serve a type of cuisine or item that appeals to as many of these people as possible.

Your choice of concept and food has a massive effect on your business at the seed level. If you can determine that you'll be able to appeal to a significant portion of this base level, you know you'll be able to survive.

Italian food is the most popular dining-out cuisine in America. Think about popular food and study your local market when deciding what you want to sell. It's always easier to go with the trends and tastes of the public than to go against them.

But really, who just wants to survive? You're in this to make the big bucks. To reach those heights of success, you need to pass the second test: can you be the best in your niche, not just against other food trucks, but as part of the general market?

You shouldn't just want to have the best burrito truck in the neighborhood. You should want to have the best burritos in the neighborhood, period. If you're able to achieve this type of critical acclaim or word of mouth, the number of customers you can draw vastly increases, as do your future opportunities. Seek to make your product and brand appealing to the point that you break out of the smaller pool of just "food truck customers" and into the ocean of everyone in your neighborhood who eats out.

Meeting a Demand

When deciding on a concept for your food truck, choose something that the market demands. Spend some time in the neighborhoods you plan to target and see which restaurants are busy. If you don't have time, just drive around after everyone is closed to see who has the most garbage outside. The restaurant doing the most business has the most to throw out.

If the pizza guy is doing well, but the Japanese guy isn't so busy, what can you infer from your observation? Go into the restaurants and try the food. As long as both products are of similar quality, it probably means there's a high demand for pizza but not so many customers for Japanese in the neighborhood. Many factors can determine this, but all that matters for your purposes is determining the underlying demand within a particular location.

Try looking for a food type that's missing in the neighborhood. Maybe there are excellent Chinese and Italian restaurants but no burger joints. If you assume that neighborhood people like burgers, which is a pretty fair assumption, then this area would be ripe for a burger truck.

The questions you're asking yourself may seem simple, but you'd be surprised by how many people don't ask them. As a food truck operator, it's vitally importance that you do this for multiple locations. You'll need to have three or four parking spots that you hit regularly, so scoping out several neighborhoods is crucial.

Matching Your Menu to Your Concept

Your menu is everything. You'll live and die by making the proper selections so you're able to produce the food quickly with low costs and high-quality levels. Yet, that's only half the battle.

Your menu is the main sales weapon in your arsenal, so you must present it in an appealing manner. It must be attractive enough to lure customers into making a purchase, and then it must maximize the amount of money they spend on that purchase.

Making the Proper Selections

As I pointed out in Chapter 2, you can only make money with your truck if you keep food and labor costs below 30 percent of the gross revenues (after taxes and gratuities). To achieve this goal, you must choose menu items that you can produce and sell for less than that amount.

The more menu items you have, the more food you need to purchase. It also means your inventory is higher, and you either have to store it or sell it. If you don't sell it, the food goes bad and you lose money. You could sell every chicken you have, but if you also have beef on the menu and it doesn't sell, then your lose all your profit.

The more menu items you have, the more prep work you also have to do. The more prep work, the higher your labor costs are. If your labor costs are over 30 percent, you won't make money.

Any way you slice it, you need to keep your menu items to a minimum. Especially on a truck where your margins are so critical, there's no room on the menu for items that don't sell or take too long to prep or cook. Choose a maximum of three signature items and stick to them. You can have variations, like toppings or different meats, but you should keep those to a minimum as well. With three signature items and three variations for each, you already have nine potential preparations, and that's not even counting sides, desserts, or drinks. See how things can go from simple to complicated very quickly?

I highly recommend no more than 10 total items on your truck menu, breaking it down as follows:

* Six main items, such as sandwiches, salads, or plates

* Two sides, such as fries and/or vegetables

* Two desserts

The main items and sides should share common ingredients to keep the total number of ingredients you're dealing with to a minimum, as well.

For instance, if you're using cheese on your burgers, use the same cheese on your side of cheese fries. Or if you're selling a side of chili, you could add a chili dog to your menu. By minimizing your menu items and ingredients and utilizing ingredients in multiple items, you vastly increase your chance for long-term success.

My final recommendation for making proper menu selections is matching your food concept to your truck. In the next chapter, I talk about finding the right truck. Your menu should drive your truck's internal design. You should design your entire kitchen around the cost of producing these items. To keep costs low, don't pick items that require complex equipment to execute; complex equipment will completely throw off your start-up costs and cost way more to maintain and power.

Presenting Your Menu

Menu presentation is critical to getting your customers to make a purchase and maximize the revenues from that purchase. Menu psychology is real, and it works. Place a dollar sign or an item in the wrong corner, and you could cost yourself hundreds of dollars in sales and/or reprinting. So, let's get to the details.

Grandma's is always better. When naming items on your menu, personalize them—for example, Aunt Gertie's Pot Roast Sandwich or Jimmy's Homemade Hot Sauce. Customers will want to get a taste of Aunt Gertie's sandwich more than just a simple pot roast sandwich. Personalize one or two items or variations that you want to push.

Romance the description. What's the point of putting your heart and soul into making the best hamburger in the world and just calling it a hamburger on your menu? You need to use descriptions like "handcrafted", "triple-basted", or "home cooked" to describe the item and the ingredients. "Alan's Signature Burger, a special blend of brisket and Angus beef grilled on an open flame with Tillamook cheddar cheese, applewood-smoked bacon, and spicy chipotle pepper sauce" seems a lot more delicious to me than "hamburger with cheese, bacon, and pepper sauce."

The top-right. Customers read menus the same way they read newspapers. The information on the top-right of the page is where their eyes head first. Use this menu area to feature your signature item, and magnify its presence by framing it and adding some extra white space around it.

Review, review, review. Nothing will make you look more foolish and cost you more money than mistakes on your menu. Make sure it's proofread for spelling and grammatical errors at least three times prior to printing. If you can't put enough time into ensuring your menu is perfect, what does that tell customers about your food?

Pricing to Your Market

Pricing is a tricky business. You must consider three areas of concern when deciding on your pricing strategy.

Calculating the Price-Value Relationship

You want your items priced high enough that the customer believes your product is high quality, but low enough that they think they're getting good value for their money. In other words, you need to achieve a balanced price-value relationship.

You can determine your price-value relationship by analyzing your competition. Take a look at other trucks in your area. Create a spreadsheet listing the pricing for main items, sides, and drinks. You can also guess what an average cover would be by determining what you believe a person would generally order. Take a sample set of at least 10 of your competitors. Your pricing should fall in line with the third or fourth most expensive. It puts you a little above the middle of the pack, which is acceptable for a high-quality truck, and it provides enough value to not alienate customers.

Ensuring Profitability

To make money, the average cost of all your items can't be more than 30 percent of your retail menu price. When you calculate the cost of producing your item, you should multiply it by 3.33. The result is the minimum price for which you should be selling the item. With that said, you can get away with charging more for some items, and for others, you'll have to charge less. The most important factor is based on your *menu mix,* or how much of your gross sales each item on your truck accounts for. If you sell $10,000 worth of food, and burritos account for $2,000 of those sales, then burritos make up 20 percent of your menu mix.

Downplaying the Price for Customers

Unless you're offering the deal of the century, which doesn't send the right quality message, you should always downplay pricing on your menus. Menu psychologists tell us that dollar signs and the word *dollar* trigger the "pain of paying". You're not in the pain business; you're in the pleasure business.

Eliminate all dollar signs and use a font that downplays pricing. Never use a bold or large font; the idea is to make the price an afterthought. When it comes to cents, .95 is always better than .99, but I recommend no cents at all. And, if you want to sell one item more than any of your other items, place it next to something more expensive or less desirable. Customers tend to purchase items whose prices fall in the middle.

Defining Your Purpose

The secret to a successful business—in our case, a food truck—is to discover what excites you, what you love to do, and then focus your energy passionately pursuing, sharing, and manifesting that purpose. Purpose is "the reason for which something exists." It's the *why* behind everything you do. Yet, despite the fundamental importance of purpose, most entrepreneurs are not fully in touch with it, and worse, they have no conscious desire to figure it out.

This lack of purpose is due to most organizations being focused on practical elements— what they do ("we sell gym equipment") and how they do it ("through our website and retail stores"). What really unlocks your creative potential is getting in touch with the purpose behind what you're doing.

In today's market, the only way to sustainably incite your audience to act is to inspire them with meaningful purpose. Purpose is extremely important when creating an awesome food truck. Once you discover your purpose, your goal will be to apply it to the creation and operation of your food truck business.

For an example of a food business manifesting through purpose, let's look at the restaurant group Sweetgreen. Founded in Washington, D.C., in 2007 by three college students, Sweetgreen is a fast-casual restaurant chain that describes itself as "a destination for delicious food that's both healthy for you and aligned with your values". The Sweetgreen statement continues, "We source local and organic ingredients from farmers we know and partners we trust, supporting our communities and creating meaningful relationships with those around us. We exist to create experiences where passion and purpose come together."

Notice how the messaging combines what Sweetgreen does practically with what it does emotionally? While Sweetgreen specializes in serving healthy salads and grain bowls, there are dozens of salad and health food restaurant groups that do the exact same. It's Sweetgreen's commitment to their higher purpose that sets them apart.

Through this purpose, Sweetgreen has become more than a restaurant—it's become a movement and a community. People are so proud to be a part of it that they share Sweetgreen content on their social feeds and wear T-shirts emblazoned with its logo. Sweetgreen's founders remain committed to their differentiating core values, such as "creating solutions where the company wins, the customer wins, and the community wins", and have used those values, rooted in their purpose, to drive the company forward. It led them to make choices that weren't always necessarily best on a short-term financial basis, but that aided the business and its stakeholders in the long term.

For example, when their second store wasn't performing well, they purchased a giant speaker, placed it outside facing a park, and threw a block party. They played great music while handing out menus and building individual relationships with community members. This approach, driven by sharing their love of food and music with their community through combined their passion and purpose eventually led to an annual multiday concert series known as the Sweetlife Festival. The 2017 festival was attended by 20,000 Sweetgreen devotees. Even better, all the proceeds went to benefit their "Sweetgreen in Schools program," which teaches local kids about health, fitness, and sustainability.

The crowds aren't coming to Sweetgreen stores and the festival simply for great salads or cool music acts. They're coming because they buy into what Sweetgreen represents, and because, on a deeper level, they feel a reflection of themselves in Sweetgreen's purpose, which is itself an honest manifestation of what the people behind the business believe and represent.

Purpose Exercise #1: The Ultimate Question

Now, let's do a quick exercise to begin discovering your purpose.

First, close your eyes and take a couple of deep breaths; try for 10, however, 5 will suffice.

Imagine your time on this Earth is ending. A doctor is sitting in front of you telling you it's all over in two weeks, and there's nothing she can do. Sit with this realization for a moment.

What would matter to you? What would you want people to know about you? Take a few minutes to reflect on this question.

Then take five more deep breaths and open your eyes. Write down the five things that matter to you most.

Death has a powerful way of cutting to the core of things, doesn't it? I'm pretty sure that most of you didn't think of your car, clothes, hair, or bank account? For most people, your thoughts settle on the people you love and the things you've done or do that make you really proud. Those five things are the first clue in the mystery of discovering your purpose.

Now, let's revisit our definition of purpose: the reason for which something exists. It's the *why* behind everything you do, what drives you, and what makes you different. It's your essence, and figuring that out isn't as easy as performing one quick exercise. According to Nick Craig and Scott A. Snook, who wrote "From Purpose to Impact" for the *Harvard Business Review,* "when you have a clear sense of who you are, everything else follows naturally."

Purpose Exercise #2: Self-Discovery Q&A

When I introduced purpose earlier the chapter, I mentioned some questions—it's finally time to get back to them. These questions are the next step in the process of discovering your purpose and eventually refining it into a simple statement.

* How would you describe yourself? How would your closest friends and/or family describe you?

* How are you different from your peers? What are your defining characteristics?

* What motivates you to get out of bed every morning? What do you think about before you go to sleep at night?

* When you have nothing else going on, what do you think about?

* What would you do if money or resources weren't an issue?

* What's unique about the way you perceive the world?

* What did you naturally enjoy doing when you were very young, before the world began telling you what you should be doing?

* What have been your most challenging life experiences? What did you learn from those experiences? List at least three.

* In your life right now, when do you feel most naturally fulfilled? When do you feel the most harmony with the surrounding world?

* What do you find easy that many of your friends or colleagues find hard?

After you've written down your answers to these questions, ask at least two people you trust and respect to answer them for you as well. It's difficult to see who you are fully and completely, and insight from those you trust will help you create a more complete picture of yourself.

The Result: Your Defined Purpose Statement

Once you've compiled your feedback, you can begin to construct a brief but meaningful statement of purpose: a simple sentence—two sentences max—that distills what makes you different and what's important to you. This declaration should begin with

"My purpose is _____" and should be written in your own words, encapsulating your essence and summoning action. Here's mine as an example:

> My purpose is to guide and inspire individuals and organizations in manifesting and sharing their creative potential.

Hence, the reason I've written this book!

Your statement is extremely important, as it will be your North Star. Every decision you make will be primarily measured by whether it brings you closer to living the purest manifestation of your purpose that is captured in this statement. As a business owner, you can look at your purpose statement when analyzing strategic plans to see if you're remaining focused on your unifying thread. Even better, it should be a rallying cry for your truck employees—an idea to inspire them and help them make the best decisions when you're not around.

Creating Your Brand

The first step when manifesting your brand is to marry the emotional and practical elements of your idea into a defined concept. If you've worked through the purpose exercises earlier, you know your purpose and have a clear, concise statement of that purpose—one that should be entirely emotional. Now you need to connect that emotional purpose with a practical application.

Step #1: Define Your Concept

As an example, let's look at Ikea. Their purpose is to "create a better everyday life" for many, but their concept is to "support this vision by offering a wide range of well-designed, functional home furnishing products at prices so low that as many people as possible will be able to afford them." While the two are related, they are quite different. One is a feeling; the other an offering.

> Purpose Statement = Emotional
>
> Concept Description = Practical

To define your concept, write down two to three simple clear sentences describing what you're trying to create. The best way to do that is to write down everything in your mind without overthinking or letting it limit or confuse you. You know your purpose; just let the concept that comes from that purpose flow.

Write your concept description here:

_____

_____

_____

_____

Once you have done this, refine your concept description by considering the following questions:

* Is this description aligned with my purpose statement?

* If not, how can I align it with my purpose?

* Is this my highest and best challenge right now?

* How can I set this up in a way where I can meet my short- and long-term needs while making it a reality?

Let's look at an example. Say you wanted to open a fried-chicken restaurant. Well, the first question would be: What makes your fried-chicken shop different from other such shops? This is your *unique value proposition*, or UVP. For our purposes, let's use the following features as the ones making up your chicken shop's UVP:

* We only serve chicken fingers.

* We have 20 homemade sauces.

* We use organic farm-raised chickens.

* We only do takeout and delivery; no in-store dining.

* We employ former foster children for all nonmanagerial positions.

With this in mind, your concept description would be as follows:

> We are opening a casual, quick-service chicken restaurant specializing in organic chicken fingers served with our one-of-a-kind homemade sauces. The restaurant will focus on takeout/pick-up and delivery business. Our service staff will consist of former foster children, 18-24 years of age, in order to provide them the necessary skills to succeed both personally and professionally and give back to the community.

Most people never even get to the point of defining their concept. They get so excited about an idea that they start the process of creating without ever truly defining their UVP, and without seeing if it aligns with their purpose and understanding if a market demand exists. Your road to successfully manifesting your idea starts at the seed level: thought must precede action, and understanding what makes you different from everyone and everything else in your world is critical to creating something truly special.

Note: By referring to *your* world instead of *the* world, I'm making a critical distinction. You don't need to be the best in the world at what you do. You need to be the best in the world *in which* you are doing business. For example, let's say you opened a North Carolina brewery; you don't need to be the best brewery in America or the world to succeed. You only need to be the best in your competitive zone—the state of North Carolina or the southeast United States. You must set up your business plan to maximize your likelihood of success in that specific region. Defining your competitive zone is crucial, and when you are the best in *your* world, the likelihood of greatness in *the* world goes up exponentially.

Concept Exercise

Have an idea? Take a moment to refine your concept description. Ensure you ask all the right questions, and share your description with some people you trust.

_____

_____

_____

_____

Step #2: Define Your Brand

The next step in the manifesting process is to create your brand. What that means is taking your practical concept statement and turning it into a combination of...

* Visuals—The way it looks.

* Values—The way it feels and acts.

* Vocals—The way it speaks.

More specifically, it means items like a logo, tagline, core values, and any other creative outputs (such as videos) capture the essence of the message, feelings, and user experience you are trying to create. Together these visuals, values, and words can create a brand that you'll eventually turn into an actual product.

An easy way to understand visuals, values, and vocals is to compare yourself to friends or family. What makes you different? Is it how you dress, your hair, your glasses, or how you sign your name? These are your visuals. What's important to you that isn't as important to everyone else? These are your values. How you speak—these are your vocals. Together, they make up who you are. For a company, it's the brand. For instance, Richard Branson and Virgin are rebellious change-makers. Timberland and Patagonia are adventurous explorers. Mercedes and Ritz-Carlton are stable, old-guard rulers. Campbell's is a comforting caregiver. Nike is the hero, the victor.

These brands didn't always represent these archetypes—they didn't always make people feel. They acquired that power over time by consistently delivering on their point of difference—their UVP. That consistent difference resulted in a distinct feeling among their audience. That feeling will eventually be the emotional part of your brand, which exists right now only in your mind. When enough people feel one way about you, they become your community or tribe. Your tribe validates your brand. As Amazon founder Jeff Bezos put it, "A brand for a company is like a reputation for a person. You earn reputation by trying to do hard things well."

Few companies execute that better than Starbucks. Originally, only a few places existed to get coffee, a basic commodity. However, consistently over time, Starbucks made people feel their point of difference. Eventually, we all knew what to expect from them, and they gained our trust. Now, we can get an Iced Green Tea anywhere in the world and feel that combination of familiarity, aspiration, and caffeine that so many of us crave. And, we're willing to pay a premium for the trust that comes with such consistency.

Brand Exercise #1:

To determine your brand, as an individual or an organization, try answering the following questions. We'll use Starbucks as our example:

Who are you?

We're Starbucks, a multinational coffeehouse experience.

What do you do?

We're not just passionate purveyors of coffee. We supply everything else that goes with a full and rewarding coffee-house experience. We also offer a selection of premium teas, fine pastries, and other delectable treats to please the taste buds.

Why does it matter? (Values)

Every day, we go to work hoping to do two things: share great coffee with our friends and help make the world a little better. Ours is a place for conversation and a sense of community. We inspire and nurture the human spirit—one person, one cup, and one neighborhood at a time.

What does it look like? (Visuals)

Brand Exercise #2:

To express and share your brand, I recommend you make a *concept deck*. A concept deck is a simple document that's one- to two-pages long or an 8- to 10-slide PowerPoint presentation that you can share with others and can consistently refine to describe your idea. (Presentations are bigger, but please don't be intimidated.)

In a Word, PowerPoint, or a Keynote document, fill out the following outline, either as bullet points or slides. Here we've used our chicken restaurant for our example:

* **Title:** Write your brand name or insert your logo here.

* **Purpose Statement:** Add your purpose statement here.

  Create a better everyday life for many.

* **Concept Description:** Write out a small paragraph detailing your restaurant's concept here.

  We are opening a quick-service chicken restaurant specializing in organic chicken fingers served with our one-of-a-kind homemade sauces. The restaurant will focus on takeout/pick-up and delivery business. Our staff will be made up of former foster children, 18-24 years of age, in order to give back to the community and provide them the necessary skills to succeed both personally and professionally.

* **Unique Value Proposition (UVP):** List the key differentiating points about what you are trying to create here.

    * *We only serve chicken fingers.*

    * *We have 20 homemade sauces.*

    * *We only use organic farm-raised chickens.*

    * *We only do takeout and delivery.*

    * *We employ former foster children.*

* **Core Values:** Note the key attributes you'd like people to feel about your business. For example, "always fresh and friendly".

* **Visuals:** Go on Instagram, Pinterest, Google images, Behance, or other platforms and find pictures, logos, and sayings that you believe capture the essence of what you are trying to create. Save these images, select the best ones, then add them to your deck to provide an idea of the "look and feel" of your brand.

* **Target Audience:** This audience is the demographic or psychographic that you're trying to reach. For example, your target audience is comprised of young adults interested in street style and entrepreneurship between the ages of 25-40 years old. Or, perhaps it is people who believe that the government should be smaller and they should pay less in taxes, such as Republicans (a psychographic).

Once this document is complete, engage a graphic designer. They can be found through a friend; on Behance, Fiverr, Craigslist; or at a local university or coworking space. Ask the designer to help you refine your presentation into a simple, visually compelling explanation of your product or service. We've referred to this as your concept deck. Ideally, your designer could also help you with the creation of a logo. While it may cost a few extra dollars, a logo will be valuable when interacting with potential customers, partners, or investors. Remember, perception is reality.

Congrats! You are on your way.

Testing Your Concept with a Focus Group

There's no exact formula for creating your brand's name, so once you've brainstormed for a few days, take your best idea and test it out with a focus group.

Your first step is to create a one-page description of your concept. It should include…

* A mission statement.

* A one-paragraph concept description.

* A one-paragraph menu description.

The mission statement should say in one sentence what you plan to create or establish. For instance, "Establish the Meatball Factory as the premier meatball food truck in Miami Beach."

The concept description is more detailed and speaks specifically to what makes your concept unique. For example, your concept description might read as follows:

> The Meatball Factory will target young people during their day at the beach and after they visit nightclubs. We'll serve one type of meatball, in a bowl, as a slider, or as a hero, and three types of sauce to go along with it. I plan to do this because my grandmother made the best meatballs and they're a high-profit item. We'll attract customers by having a young rock 'n' roll image because I've spent the last five years following rock 'n' roll bands; they're what I love and I think my customers will relate to them.

Finally, describe your menu:

> I'll serve only organic beef meatballs made with my grandmother's recipe. The sauces will be spicy tomato, creamy Alfredo, and pesto. The bread will be from a local bakery and will be picked up fresh every morning.

You should have samples of the menu items prepared for the group. Invite at least six people to be in your group. Do your best to have people who don't have a vested interest in your success and won't be afraid to tell you the truth—even if it might hurt your feelings. You can offer them some sort of compensation if you'd like, but I find that a free meal usually does the trick.

Have a list of questions for the group members to answer anonymously. You want them to give you honest feedback on your idea and food. Sugarcoated answers won't help you, so it's important you tell them to be honest with their opinions. Your questions should have numbered answers, along with options for additional comments.

Here's a sample of the types of questions you should ask your focus group:

* How would you rate each food item on a scale of 1 to 10? (With 10 being "perfectly awesome" and 1 meaning "I would never pay for this food.")

* How would you suggest I improve these items?

* How would you rate my concept on a scale from 1 to 10?

* How would you suggest I improve my concept?

* Does this concept feel authentic? Does it match my personality?

* Would you pay X [insert average expected price per person] to eat at this truck?

* If not, what do you think is a fair price for the product?

* Where do you think a truck like this should park?

* How do you think we should package our food so that it's easiest to eat on the street?

You'll garner loads of information by listening to the answers to these questions. Most importantly, you'll find out how people react to your concept. As much as I can teach you about food trucks, the feedback you receive from unbiased people will show you the true potential of your idea. If the group doesn't like your idea, it's important that you understand why. Maybe they love the taste of the food but not the branding? Maybe they like the branding but don't like the pricing? Maybe they love it all and you'll be the next Kogi? Nobody knows ahead of time, but I can't wait to find out.

Focus. Focus. Focus. I cannot say it enough. Remember to stay focused with your concept and your food. In the modern market, there's tremendous value in being the best in your world. For example, the best hamburger truck in downtown Manhattan always has a line of customers. The others, sometimes they are busy and sometimes they aren't. Don't make the mistake of trying to be everything to everyone. Instead, do what you know how to do best, better than everyone else.

The Right Truck

There's one solid rule when you search for your truck, and you must promise to keep repeating it to yourself during the process:

You get what you pay for.

If you try to take shortcuts, you'll pay for them later. Gas lines, generators, fryers, ovens, miles per gallon—if you skimp on any of them, you'll lose big time. When it comes to buying a quality food truck, you literally have to put your money where your mouth is.

The "right" truck doesn't exist yet; it's the one you're going to build to perfectly match your concept. If you're selling empanadas and plan to do most of the cooking off the truck, your truck is going to need more storage and heating equipment than actual cooking equipment. If you're selling burgers and fries, your truck must be equipped with grills and fryers. Maybe you're selling slushies? If so, you'll need multiple high-capacity slushie machines to pump out loads of icy goodness.

Your marching orders are to locate a truck in the best condition possible, and then customize it specifically for your needs. Used or prefabricated trucks won't exist for the your business's specific needs. Trucks are usually built for general use or past owners' uses, often including old equipment you won't need. Even if you buy an inexpensive used truck, it's highly likely you'll need to spend money customizing it to your needs.

In this chapter, I start from the beginning and break down the most common types of trucks employed in the food truck industry.

Types of Trucks

You can choose from three main types of food trucks:

* Chevy Step-Vans

* Grumman Olsen step vans

* Mercedes-Freightliner Sprinter vans

Of course, people adapt other vehicle types for use as food trucks, too, such as Airstream trailers or other highly customized vehicles. But because we're talking about creating the most viable business, and these vehicles require extensive custom renovations, so I don't recommend them.

Many trucks come with propane tanks and generators located inside the truck. Propane is dangerous, and having it inside your truck is a recipe for disaster. The Frites & Meats truck had their propane located in or under the truck, and it exploded, sending two people to the emergency room. Also, your generator must be housed securely outside your truck, so you can easily replace or repair it. Picture yourself in the middle of service when your generator goes. If you don't have easy access to it, you won't be able to fix or replace it. You'll lose a whole day's revenue, as well as your hard-earned reputation.

The following sections consider each of the three primary vehicle types people adapt for food truck businesses.

Chevy Step-Vans

Step-Vans are the most economical and effective base on which to build your food truck. Also known as multistop trucks and walk-in delivery vans, Step-Vans are light- or medium-duty vans created for local deliveries. The following features make these vans ideal food trucks:

* They're usually designed to be driven either sitting down or standing up.

* They provide easy access between the driving area and the back.

* They usually have enough headroom to allow for an average-size adult to stand up in the cargo areas.

* They have enough space in the back to comfortably accommodate food truck equipment.

Step-Van trucks are durable, have strong chassis, and tend to be less pricey than other options.

Step-Vans have drawbacks, as well. They aren't easy to drive or park, so only trained members of your team will be able to operate them. Also, it can be difficult to find newer vans, as opposed to Sprinter vans, which are readily available at dealerships.

Step-Vans are available in many different sizes and models. Unless you're running a "cold" truck, selling ice cream or slushies, which requires less space for food preparation, the ideal truck is 14 feet long by 9 feet wide. A length of 14 feet gives you plenty of space for selling and for prep and cooking areas, but anything longer than that will be nearly unmanageable to drive and especially difficult to park. In terms of width, you need at least 8 feet of space to create an efficient internal layout. Generally, you can park in most spots with a width of up to 9 feet. If you choose a van that's smaller than 14 × 9, you'll make your working life more difficult because your interior working space will be limited.

I suggest that you buy a Step-van that runs on gasoline, not diesel. Although diesel models are typically cheaper, gas vans are more reliable and easier to fix. Also, buy the newest van you can afford. Ideally, it should be no more than seven years old and should have fewer than 100,000 miles on it. Plan to spend between $10,000 and $15,000 for it.

Before you buy a Step-van, make sure you know what equipment you need to be able to fit in it. Your van's cargo area must have enough space to accommodate your equipment. Visit your local restaurant supply company and identify the best and largest propane or electric equipment. I say "largest" because propane equipment is usually small, and you want to maximize your production space. Only after you've laid out the equipment in the most efficient manner for your concept is it time to start shopping for your Step-van.

The majority of food trucks are repurposed Step-van postal trucks that were used by DHL, FedEx, or other large commercial companies. In fact, the bankruptcy of DHL and the auction of their fleet of vehicles that followed was a direct contributor to the food truck revolution.

For example, the Kelvin Natural Slush Co., created by Alex Rein, a former corporate attorney who spent his childhood craving classic convenience store treats, served all-natural frozen slushies from a Step-van. It was one of the most popular trucks in Manhattan and was voted Best Dessert at the 2010 Vendy Awards. Drink flavors included ginger, tea, or citrus, and a choice of real fruit purée or mix-ins like fresh chopped mint or basil. Alex's truck was a 2000 P30 Chevy Step van he had customized. His advice is to make sure your equipment is bolted down tightly. His equipment wasn't bolted down in the beginning, and he had water leakage issues while traveling from spot to spot.

Sprinters

Sprinter vans are commercial vans, chassis cabs, and minibuses sold under the brands Mercedes Benz and Freightliner. Despite the fact that they're more expensive than Step-vans—four to five times more expensive before customization—some entrepreneurs have started to use them for food trucks. Sprinters are easier to drive and park, which means more of your crew will be able to drive the rig. They're readily available new, and most are more up to date than Step-vans. They're more reliable, have more advanced internal systems, and are generally more comfortable. Sprinters, however, aren't as wide as Step-vans, so they don't have nearly as much space in the cargo area. A new Sprinter van will run you $40,000 to $60,000.

Prefabricated Trucks

Companies like AA Cater Truck, Food Cart USA, Armenco, and Roadstoves rent, lease, and sell prefabricated food trucks. They offer one-stop shopping, and their trucks often come with a guarantee or warranty. Rarely, though, do their deals make good financial sense for small business owners.

The goal of their businesses is to make money off every part of what they're selling. In saving the time and energy of managing the process yourself, you'll actually be spending tremendous amounts of money. A prefabricated truck customized to fit your needs will cost you well over $100,000. This huge expense makes it nearly impossible to recoup your investment without hitting a Kogi-style home run.

Calculating Truck Costs

For the sake of calculating costs, I'm going to assume that you will buy a used Step-van. Purchasing your van should cost you no more than $15,000, and if you can keep the cost to $10,000, which I recommend you do, you'll put yourself ahead of the game. The costs of customizing your rig should break down as follows:

* **Equipment for your onboard kitchen:** $15,000–20,000, depending on your menu.

* **Electrical, steel, awning, and nonkitchen equipment:** $10,000.

* **Labor to customize truck and install infrastructure:** $15,000–$20,000.

* **Pots, pans, grease mats, bowls, hotel pans, and other kitchen goods:** $3,000.

* **High-quality vinyl skin:** $5,000 (a major source of advertising).

* **A brand-new Honda generator:** $6,000.

* **A point-of-sale (POS) system:** Approximately $5,000. This system is important for keeping track of sales, as well as maintaining financial control. New POS options utilizing the iPad, such as ShopKeep, POS Lavu, and Revel Systems, generally cost much less than restaurant systems like Micros & Aloha, and are perfect for mobile food trucks.

Your food truck cost tallies up a total cost of $60,000 to $70,000.

Finding Your Truck

Now that you know what you should buy, you need to locate where to get it. The main sources for Step-vans or used food trucks are eBay (motors.ebay.com), Craigslist (craigslist.org), truck dealers or auctions, and customizers. Check out all of them to find the best deal available.

Before you start looking, create a spreadsheet with price, year, mileage, model, previous use, and any other categories listed that you deem important for choosing your van. Having all the information in one place will make it easier for you to compare the different vans you'll be considering.

eBay and Craigslist

On eBay Motors, search for the terms *Step-Van* or *food truck* from the main page. eBay Motors offers auctions and "Buy It Now" prices for the trucks available. Use eBay's search filter so it only brings up vans/trucks that are within a specified distance from your zip code. No matter how good a deal seems to be, stick to those that are within three hours of your location because you're going to want to see the it and have it reviewed by a mechanic prior to finalizing your purchase. On Craigslist, look in the "Cars & Trucks" section and search for the same terms.

Neither Craigslist nor eBay Motors will provide you with a guarantee for your van/truck. Once you purchase it, it's yours, and you have no recourse if the van or truck breaks down or is a lemon. You should also be aware that Craigslist is infamous for vehicle scams, so be on guard.

Truck Dealers and Auctions

A good truck dealer can provide guidance on which models will best suit your needs, which can be invaluable for someone just starting out in the food truck business. Also, most dealerships offer a guarantee or warranty on the trucks they sell. The problem is that when you plan to customize the truck you buy from a dealer or, in truck terms, "chop it up", you're basically deeming any guarantee null and void. Speak with the dealer about creating a guarantee on certain parts of the truck, like the engine, chassis, transmission, and tires, so you'll have protection on the areas you won't be touching for customization.

Auctions are great places to find incredible deals, but they're a bit of a gamble. Although you're allowed to make sure it starts, you won't be able to have a mechanic check the engine and systems. Auctions are a buy "as is" proposition. I've heard of people getting spectacular deals at auction, but I've also heard horror stories of trucks needing expensive repairs.

Customizers

Customizers purchase trucks and convert them into prefabricated food trucks. Basically, you're paying a premium to have them locate a truck for you, and then do all the work. You'd be much better off finding and purchasing the truck yourself and bringing it to a customizer or metal shop to turn it into your food truck. The only benefit of purchasing directly from the customizer is that they'll usually offer you a guarantee on the vehicle and their work. Though it will be mighty expensive, as always, you get what you pay for. If your truck breaks down or has issues in relation to their work, they should be responsible.

See Appendix B for a list of some well-known truck customizers.

It's well known in the truck business that customizers take much longer than expected to complete the work—sometimes twice as long as expected. It should clearly state in your contract with your customizer the length of time the work should take, along with the penalties for late delivery. Waiting an extra three to six months to get your business started could end up with it never getting started at all. Even if you have a good contract, expect moderate delays and pad your preopening budget to account for them.

Don't forget: if you're planning to buy a customized or used vehicle for your food truck business, spend the money to have the truck tested by a reputable third-party mechanic prior to finalizing the deal. Spending a little bit of money in advance could end up saving you thousands of dollars down the road.

Redesigning an Existing Truck

After you've purchased your truck, the fun really begins. It's time to make it the "right" truck.

The first step is finding a customizer in your area. In most major cities and on both coasts, you'll find professional food truck customizers. However, all you really need to do is locate a quality sheet metal shop. Sheet metal workers have the expertise and machinery necessary to customize your truck, and you should be able to find a local metal shop through a simple online search. I recommend finding someone who has experience working on trucks and is aware of local health codes.

After meeting with the customizer and ensuring that you're comfortable with his or her professionalism and expertise, follow up by asking for references. Check those references to get a feel for the customizer's reliability and quality of work.

Don't forget! Make sure your customizer uses high-quality steel. The preferred type is corrosion-resistant, restaurant-grade 304 stainless, because it lasts longer against wear and tear.

Choosing Your Equipment

Based on the work you've done on your concept, you should have a basic idea of what you'll need to furnish your truck .

Here are important questions to ask yourself at this point:

* **Will you be doing most of your cooking on or off the truck?**

   Are you heating up burritos, serving ice cream, or cooking egg sandwiches? Each one of these items requires very different equipment. Identify your needs and base your equipment on that information.

* **What is your main cooking technique for your menu?**

   If you'll be preparing a lot of fried food, you'll need a lot of fryers and probably won't use a grill or other heat source. A truck that specializes in fried foods can have up to four onboard deep fryers. Also, think about how much storage you'll need, and if it need to be hot or cold storage.

* **Will you have one window or two?**

   If you have two windows, you'll be able to park on either side of the street; with only one, you'll be limited to only serving out of one side. That said, if you're going to be doing a lot of cooking on the rig, it will be virtually impossible to have two windows.

The next thing to consider before you purchase any equipment is how your assembly line will work. Take a minute to outline your *steps of service*. Steps of service are the basic steps that employees perform in food service businesses. You can make changes in the steps as needed to fit the expectations and experience you want your guests to have. What happens when someone places an order? As you go over each step in the process of ordering, cooking, and serving a dish, you'll see what problems might arise and solve them before they happen. I strongly advocate practicing these steps on the truck or a space similarly sized to it. Doing so will give you a real feel for how much space you have, which in turn will help you make better long-term decisions regarding the truck's layout.

The following figures illustrate the basic layouts for a one-window and two-window food truck. Use these diagrams, along with the proper measurements of your truck, as a jumping-off point for designing your truck. Take this information with you to your local restaurant-supply store. Sit down with the supplier to find the best and largest propane- or electric-powered equipment that will fit on your truck. (I highly recommend using as much electric-powered equipment as you can; electric is safer and more reliable than gas.)

When you have your list of equipment, including dimensions, bring it to your customizer to review. Make sure that he or she signs off—contractually, if possible, that all the equipment will fit and function in the truck's design. The last thing you want to do is buy equipment that doesn't fit/work with your rig.

Recommended Truck Internal Layout #1.
This is the ideal layout for a one-window truck.

Recommended Truck Internal Layout #2.
This is the ideal layout for a two-window truck.

One of the best ways to showcase your truck's personality is through your truck's window, with all the conversation, music, and great smells coming from the kitchen. The larger the window, the more action customers can see while waiting. Remember, the customer is coming for the experience and you, so the more of you, your staff, and the cooking process they can see, the better.

Powering Your Vehicle

Your truck's gas and electric lines must be flexible. You're a moving vehicle; anything that isn't flexible or tightly locked in place will eventually move or break.

Don't under any circumstances combine the gas lines for the generator and for the truck. It may seem like a great idea to only have one tank to fill up, but if something goes wrong, you'll lose both and have to fix both, and you won't be able to drive *or* cook.

Budgeting for Fuel and Maintenance

What makes your truck different from a restaurant business? You're a moving operation. Not only must you do standard restaurant maintenance, but you also have to maintain your truck, too. Here's a basic truck maintenance schedule I suggest you follow:

* **After service every night:** Take the truck back to the commissary and thoroughly clean the kitchen and the vehicle itself. No one wants to eat from a dirty truck, inside or out. The care you show with your daily cleaning will directly relate to how successful your truck becomes.

* **Every 100 hours:** Change the oil in your generator. Review the manufacturer's guidelines for your specific model. However, no matter what's recommended, I advocate changing the oil after 100 hours of operation.

* **Every six months:** Get your truck checked by a mechanic once every six months—including an an oil change and checking the tires, transmission, engine, and chassis.

When it comes to fuel, expect to spend about $75 a day on gasoline for the generator and the truck (if it's a gas generator).

Propane costs $20 per 20-pound tank if you own the tanks and $35 per tank if you don't. You can expect to go through one and a half 20-pound tanks per day.

Most cities restrict how much propane you can carry on your truck at one time. In New York City, you can carry one 40-pound tank or two 20-pound tanks on your truck. Check with the local authorities before you build your truck; ignorance is no excuse when it comes to the law.

Finding an Off-Truck Kitchen (Commissary)

Locating a good licensed commissary is one of the most important aspects of creating a successful food truck. Other than your truck, the commissary is where you'll spend the most time, and it will have the most direct impact on the product you serve. Your commissary will be your off-truck kitchen, refrigerated storage facility, dry storage facility, and where you clean the inside and outside of your truck.

Most major cities have multiple licensed commissaries that service the needs of catering companies, food trucks, and other mobile food businesses. With that said, the quality of these facilities varies greatly depending upon the operator. For example, New York City has some great commercial commissaries, such as Casablanca in Hunts Point, but many subpar ones exist as well. A great way to locate a high-quality facility is to ask a respected operator or speak to the local health department.

Using a licensed commercial facility for your truck can be very costly. Two other options are to use your home kitchen or to partner with a bricks-and-mortar restaurant. If you use your own kitchen, you'll have to get it inspected and licensed by your local health department. If you own or partner with a restaurant, you'll save the significant weekly costs of belonging to a commissary, which will greatly increase your profitability. Obviously, that's your best choice if it's a possibility for you.

Depending on the size of your operation, a commissary can cost $500 to $5,000 a month.

Getting the right truck is a seed-level decision. I define those as the ones that affect everything else you do. While you may have great food or a great concept, if you don't get the right truck, you may never get where you are going. Take the time to make the right long-term focused choices and it will pay off down the road.

The Right Location

There was a restaurant in downtown Manhattan that I used to eat at once or twice a week. It was an excellent spot with perfect paninis, tart strawberry lemonade, and wonderful raviolis. When it opened, it was about 1,000 square feet. A couple of years later, as the neighborhood became more popular, it expanded to about three times the size. It was still jam-packed. Two years later, their lease expired and the landlord tried to dramatically raise the rent. They were forced to move to a new location. Initially, customers went out of their way a couple of blocks, but then the restaurant's customers started to fade away. The restaurant lowered prices, shifted hours—anything to rediscover and engage their clientele. But there was nothing they could do. It was a case of location, location, location. Lucky for you, your restaurant is on wheels.

When it comes to food trucks and the restaurant business, similarities abound. The basics are the same: you must consistently serve a high-quality product with attentive service and a side of aspirational marketing. It sounds simple, but trust me, doing this well day after day is no walk in the park.

Next comes the curve ball: in the food truck business, your real estate isn't fixed. Like everything in life, that's a blessing and a curse. But one thing's for sure: not having a fixed location makes things a lot more complicated. In this chapter, we discuss finding the best locations to park your truck, as well as identifying locations to avoid. Then we help you figure out how to make the most of the locations you do choose.

Being Mobile: The Pros and Cons

Let's start with the blessings. You're the food equivalent of a guerrilla army. You can use your mobility to rake in the profits in ways that larger and less mobile food operations can't. If you open up in a spot that's busy during lunch but not dinner, you can just start the engine and move somewhere else for the second half of the day. If you take a risk on a new spot and it doesn't work, don't worry; you can just park somewhere else tomorrow. What if someone wants you to cater a party an hour away in the middle of a field? Just hop behind the wheel, and the gig and the profits are yours. Your mobility provides you with endless opportunities to generate more income.

On the flip side, being mobile creates other issues, and it's your job to minimize them. Let's start with storage. As a mobile food business, your storage is off-site at your commissary. If you run out of hamburger buns, then burgers are *86'd* for the rest of the day. In restaurant lingo, 86 means taking an item off the menu. (Generally, it refers to taking something off temporarily because you ran out of that particular item, but it can also refer to removing it permanently.)

You have to pay extra attention to planning and creating a support system with other trucks and local food businesses. It makes running out of food less likely, and it provides you with options when and if you do.

Your mobility can also create issues with the stability of your business. You may have a great parking spot one day, but what ensures that you'll have it again the next? And, what if a competing pizza truck or shop opens in your spot? Do you surrender it, or do you stay and fight? You aren't paying rent, so other than the goodwill of the food truck community, you really have no claim to that space. That's another reason why being part of the community is so important. When you're part of a group of trucks, you work together to protect each other's interests and share a code of ethics.

When you find good spots, you need to protect and to build them through hard work and fostering great relationships with the local community. Locating and cultivating the right locations for your truck is critical to your success. On that note, let's start identifying prime parking spots for your food truck.

Identifying Where You Should Park

Generally, you want to park in high-traffic and underserviced locations, as well as places that will be in existence temporarily. The following sections identify some of the best places to park your food truck.

Office Buildings and Office Parks

High-traffic office buildings and office parks are ideal locations for the food truck business, especially at breakfast and lunch. Huge volumes of people pour into these locations during the morning and the afternoon, and they're always looking for new and better options to quickly satisfy their cravings. Additionally, such places typically follow a set time schedule, which enables you to hit the area's breakfast and/or lunch rush, and then leave when the rush is over. You can maximize revenue and minimize staffing costs because you'll know exactly when you're going to be busy.

Office locations also offer great potential for delivery business and catering jobs. Areas that are set aside specifically for offices, such as the financial district of Manhattan, are more viable than offices mixed in with other businesses like midtown Manhattan. That's because areas that service several functions have higher rents, and the local food businesses may be contrary if you steal their piece of the customers' spend. If you can get into a spot, make sure you do everything you can to ensure that local food merchants aren't hostile.

Residential Buildings

Large residential developments, especially in budding neighborhoods, are ideal for food trucks. These areas are better for breakfast and dinner because you can catch the traffic of people leaving for and returning from work. During the middle of the day, they'll generally be slower, so I don't advise targeting them for lunch.

Developing neighborhoods are often underserved by food businesses, and residents are looking for more food options. If you gain a following in a developing neighborhood, you'll become a staple and, eventually, be a prime candidate for expansion into a bricks-and-mortar location in the district. Delivery is also a prime opportunity in these up-and-coming locations.

Large Events

Concerts, sporting events, carnivals, festivals, and other events that draw large crowds are perfect for food trucks. These happenings bring tremendous volumes of people to a particular location for a set period of time. With the right location and product, they can spell massive profits for a food truck operator. Depending on the event, you may have to be invited by the organizers or pay an access fee, but sometimes you can just park around the corner and ride the hype.

Recently, food truck operators and local organizations have begun creating large events focused on bringing together groups of food trucks in a particular place and marketing it as a festival. Usually they're advertised in the food press and on food blogs and include additional live entertainment. Such events often sell group tickets that allow customers to sample items from all the trucks for one price. Although you are required to pay a participation fee for these events, they can lead to big revenues outside of your usual spots.

Dorms and College Buildings

Students are the ideal food truck customers. They typically embrace the counterculture, love to try new things, and are looking for a quick hunger fix. Options for food in and around dormitories and school buildings are typically limited to subpar cafeteria grub, making these ideal locations for creating a spot that could be yours for years to come. The key is to create relationships and become part of the school's culture.

For example, the Gorilla Gourmet has been serving the Western Michigan University and Kalamazoo College for over nine years. This food truck has all the foodie favorites. They invent all-original twists on classics like their Killer 20-hour Pork Tacos, a pork belly cooked for over 20 hours and served with corn tortillas and their signature homemade slaw, which includes carrots, cabbage, cilantro, lime, and their secret tomato sauce. These dishes will keep students lining up for years to come.

Seasonal Locations

Boardwalks, beaches, pumpkin patches, and ski resorts are all ideal locations for food trucks. These areas become superbusy during a particular time of year and generally have limited infrastructure to support the traffic they get at those times. They're generally good weekend spots because they receive a lot of leisure business on off days, making them a great balance for spots where you get more weekday traffic. The Ditch Witch in Montauk, New York, is a prime example of this type of spot. It's been supplying grub, such as breakfast burritos, iced coffee, and sesame noodle salad, to surfers on the Ditch Plains Beach for over 20 years.

A word to the wise: vendors often pay a lot of money to operate concessions in seasonal locations like beaches. You won't be popular with them if you cannibalize their business.

Nightspots

When people drink, they love to eat. Parking outside nightclubs and bars is a perfect option for a late-night location. Every city has areas that are packed after 10 P.M., and it's your job to locate them. I suggest parking for two to three hours before closing time. That's when people are looking for food, and you'll be there to serve them.

Food Truck Lots

With the introduction of legislation that regulates and limits locations where food trucks can park (see Chapter 8), food truck lots have begun to spring up. These are typically vacant lots located close to major office complexes. You're required to pay a rental fee for access, but there's no average rate because these businesses are so new.

The lots operate like outdoor food courts, and it's your job to differentiate yourself from the rest of the trucks located in the lot. How successful your involvement in a lot will be depends on its location, the rental fee, how many other trucks are involved, and the amount of traffic it attracts.

Determining Where You're Allowed to Park

Now that you know where you should be parking, it's time for the next step, finding out where you're *allowed* to park. Regulations differ from city to city and state to state. Generally, food trucks can park in metered parking spots, but beyond that, each area has its own laws, often antiquated, that govern street vending businesses. Some actually have no regulations at all.

In Washington, D.C, the rule is that you can only solicit customers who flag you down. Although this law was created 40 years ago to govern ice cream trucks, it's still on the books and very much enforced. Once a customer "flags you down", you can serve them. if no one's waiting, you have to leave. If you don't follow this regulation, you'll be subject to "fines and potential revocation of your license". You can imagine this makes it very difficult to flourish as a food truck operator in Washington, D.C. However, where there's a will there's a way, and the D.C. food truck scene is very active.

New York City had a massive crackdown on food trucks. A judge reinforced an antiquated regulation that states "no vendor, hawker, or huckster shall park a vehicle at a metered parking space to offer merchandise for sale from that vehicle". The police are enforcing the law, and food trucks now have little or no place to park. This is a prime example of backlash from bricks-and-mortar businesses and neighborhood groups, and only time will tell whether food trucks will be able to once again flourish in New York City.

Laws are constantly changing and being reinterpreted based on the food truck revolution. Regulations haven't and probably won't come close to catching up with the boom because politicians and business owners are still deciding whether the industry is good for their interests and those of the surrounding communities. In many cities, food truckers have formed associations, such as the New York Food Truck Association (streetvendor.org), to protect themselves and fight for their rights. The success of the trucking industry has brought attention, both good and bad. It's crucial that the industry work together to be viewed as a legitimate trade.

In order to learn the policies governing locations where mobile food businesses can park in your local area, contact the local department of transportation or similar governing body. (For example, in Miami, it's the Department of Planning and Zoning.) In larger municipalities, you might be able to find the information you need online. For example, try typing "food truck parking regulations" and the name of your city into a search engine to see what information you can find.

In some places, food truckers are being regulated out of business. Check your local parking regulations prior to jumping into the business. You don't want to spend your days fighting tickets and regulators rather than sharing your passion with your customers.

When you're calculating your financials, it's important that you budget for parking violations. They're part of doing business, and tickets can run from $15 to $150, depending on where you are. They can also add up very quickly. Even worse, if you don't pay your tickets, you can end up with larger fines or even jail time. Be aware of local laws and do whatever you can to keep your truck's fines to a minimum. It would be a shame if you worked all day slinging delicious food just to pay your profits to the state or city.

Considering Traffic

The key to choosing any spot for your food truck is to observe the traffic in that location. Rather than throwing caution to the wind and randomly choosing spots through trial and error, it's far better to take a strategic approach.

Pick five neighborhoods and take the time to scout them out. See what days and times they're busy and when they're slow. Observe the competition in the area and consider the following factors:

* **Parking:** Find out the local regulations and choose three spots in the neighborhood that will work for you. See what times those spots tend to be available. Based on what you observe, you may have to send someone ahead of you to hold the spot you most want.

* **Exposure to traffic:** The right location within the neighborhood can make all the difference in gaining exposure to the traffic you desire. It's the same reason people pay extra for corner stores on high-traffic streets; they are exposed to more potential customers. Every day, you're going to act as your own real estate broker, scouting the top spots for your business. You should also consider from where the majority of your customers originate. The closer you can get to that place, the easier it will be for you to service them.

* **Traffic type:** Be on the lookout for businesses that attract similar crowds to your target customers. All the traffic in the world doesn't do you any good if the people aren't interested in the food you're selling. If you sell juices, smoothies, and health food, doesn't it make sense to park outside a popular gym or yoga studio? They service groups of people who are in to eating healthy.

Knowing Locations to Avoid

Just as there are prime locations to park your food truck, there are also locations you should avoid.

Low-Traffic Areas

The most obvious locations to avoid are ones without a lot of traffic. Some people like to buck the trends, believing that they alone can draw the masses with their incredible food and drinks. Please don't be one of them; if you were to succeed, it would be out of blind luck. The reason store owners pay high rents in certain districts is because that's where the customers are.

All the marketing in the world won't make your food truck a success in a bad location on a consistent basis, and you must focus on consistency. Successful food businesses are about moving a lot of product on a regular basis. Weeks of generating a minimal daily profit won't add up to a substantial monthly or yearly profit.

Restaurant Rows

Even though restaurant rows can be very busy, you should avoid them. Areas where a lot of restaurants are competing for the customers' food dollars aren't ideal for food trucks. The average restaurant owner has a bigger budget and larger facilities and will generally be very hostile to someone who isn't paying rent while trying to steal customers.

The most unethical thing for a food truck is to park in front of a restaurant that serves the same cuisine—a falafel truck parked in front of a Middle Eastern restaurant, for example. I can see the logic in trying to attract those customers, but it's so incredibly wrong that obstacles are bound to arise. Anything gained through unethical practices generally is lost through the reaction from customers and the restaurant community. As a member of the hospitality community, it's your responsibility to protect and support your brothers and sisters.

Looking at Other Local Businesses

One of the most important considerations when choosing a location for your food truck is looking at other businesses in the area. Being accepted into the community is key to your success, so do everything in your power to be seen as a positive addition to the neighborhood.

As a community member, your business must add to the long-term prosperity of your district. Not only must you be friendly, but you must become an active member of the organizations that govern local commerce. You should attend meetings and make your presence felt by becoming involved in the actions taken.

To initiate personal relationships, drop off care packages and introduce yourself to all the area merchants. Make sure that if they have an issue with you or your truck, they come directly to you rather than involving the authorities. It will give you the opportunity to remedy the situation instead of creating larger issues.

Take the time to establish mutually beneficial partnerships with local businesses. Let's say you park your sweets truck near a local pottery store that hosts children's birthday parties every Saturday or Sunday. A mutually beneficial partnership could involve you parking in front of their location on weekends and supplying the parties with cupcakes.

If you operate a sandwich truck and there's a construction site in the area that's isolated from local restaurants, strike a deal to show up every day at a certain time to sell to the crew. These kinds of things help your business and also support the community. By focusing on helping the neighborhood—in addition to generating profits—you will experience greater long-term success.

You can also leverage your Twitter following and your email database to build partnerships. You have customers, and other businesses would love access to them. Approach a clothing store with a similar demographic that's planning a big sale and agree to tell your customers about it if they'll allow you to sell your food outside for the duration. With the right store, you'll both benefit without cannibalizing each other's business because your products are distinctly different. If things work out, you'll get yourself an awesome parking spot and a boatload of new customers. Wait till the other stores hear about you!

Building Your Spots

After you've identified your regular parking places, it's vital that cultivate the local clientele to build regular business in that location. Even though you don't have a bricks-and-mortar store, you must use the same methods as that type of business to create local awareness. You want to use the cachet of the food truck while creating the perception of a restaurant that's in the same spot every day. If you do, you'll have your cake—mobility—and eat it too because you will be perceived as being just as reliable as competing food businesses.

Here are some methods for cultivating your business in a particular spot:

* **Social media:** Announce your exact location and the times that you'll be there each day on your Twitter, Facebook, and Foursquare pages.

* **Website:** Have a section called "Weekly Spots", preferably on the main landing page, dedicated to your regular locations. Include a link to a website like Google Maps that shows exactly where you are. Check out korillabbq.com for an example of what a location map should look like.

* **Competitions and promotions:** Establish promotions that are related to specific locations. You might want to offer complimentary cupcakes to the first 20 lunch customers daily, for example. Whatever the promotion, more customers will come when you have a line, so attracting those initial customers to drive business is critical.

  Keep in mind, however, that while promotions are a good way to generate business, don't overdo them. Make sure your promotions don't cheapen your brand with too much discounting; you always want people to think of your product as an object of desire.

* **Menu distribution**: Drop off menus and promotional flyers at surrounding businesses. Invest in printing something that represents your brand positively and will make an impact. Include a coupon to generate a first visit to the truck.

* **Location-based email lists:** Segment your email lists to create separate lists for each place you park, and then send an email blast to the people in that location on the days you'll be there. Build your lists by offering an incentive to customers for signing up, like a free lunch or a catered private party for customer #500 for their office. Enter the emails into a spreadsheet and use an application like enflyer.com to distribute your blasts.

  Mass email applications like mailchimp.com and ConstantContact.com enable you to store addresses and send marketing materials to large groups of customers with relative ease. These applications generally charge a monthly fee, ranging from $30 to $250 per month, based on how often you send out your emails. The software also gives you in-depth information about who is opening your emails, so you can monitor performance. With proper management, these sites are well worth the investment.

* **Sampling:** The first four to six times you visit any spot, you should offer a special or a free sampling of your signature items. Your goal is to create a neighborhood following and what better way to get people hooked on your great product than allowing them to taste it? If you've got it, flaunt it.

* **Location-specific menu items:** Establish menu items that are only available in certain locations. For instance, if you're selling sliders, when you're parked on the Lower East Side of Manhattan, offer a signature Lower East Slider only at that location. Make sure that item is particularly spectacular and you'll end up with press and customers coming from other neighborhoods just to try it.

* **Customer Relationship Management (CRM):** CRM is a widely implemented strategy for managing relationships with customers. Do everything you can to know your regular customers in every location. Keep notes on their preferences, or give them something a little extra with their order. Anything you do to give them the best experience will make them your most valuable advertisers. Create a document explaining how all employees should interact with your customers, and require all of your employees to read it. The goal of CRM is to find and attract new customers, nurture and retain current customers, and entice former customers back.

As a food truck operator, you must embrace change. Nothing proves this more than your location strategy. Where you are today is not necessarily where you'll be tomorrow, and that's the idea. Getting comfortable with this reality and enabling it to become your greatest strength will help you discover your strategy and success in the food truck business.

THE MOBILE FOOD MOGUL

It's time to take your ideas and turn them into a concrete business plan. No one is going to take you seriously unless you're able to clearly articulate your plan to them, and you won't find investors to back you unless you can create financial forecasts that show you can be profitable. You'll need to understand all aspects of the food business, and I'm going to explain them to you.

The next step is to get a grasp on regulations and licensing. The food business involves a tremendous amount of regulation from your local health department. These laws protect consumers from food that isn't properly handled or prepared. Because your business is on wheels, you're also subject to regulation by your local transportation department. Knowing how to navigate these bureaucracies is crucial to your success.

Finally, I get to my favorite subject: marketing. How are you going to get customers to show up at your truck? I'll show you how to use Twitter, Facebook, and great public relations to become the darling of bloggers and foodies.

Preparing Your Business Plan

You don't need to be an architect to appreciate the fundamental importance of having a blueprint to build a skyscraper. Imagine trying to construct a building without detailed plans, measurements, and diagrams: how would you know what materials to buy, how many builders to hire, or even how to lay the first foundational bricks with only a vague vision of the final structure? When building your business, you need to design similar blueprints, which constitute your business plan.

Writing a business plan forces you to clearly define your concept, brand, menu, and market, so that you know exactly where you're going and how you're going to get there. It's also the first step toward finding capital to finance your food truck, which I cover in Chapter 7. Ultimately, a well-thought-out business plan saves you time and money throughout the start-up, launch, and long-term operation of your truck. It also helps you anticipate problems and keeps you from getting in your own way.

In this chapter, I show how a good business plan can help you make important decisions about your food truck. I cover how to predict your costs, sales, and profits, and the pros and cons of different ways to structure your business.

Why a Business Plan Matters

Writing a business plan forces you to make very crucial decisions about your business. It's not enough to have a vision in your head; by putting your vision down on paper, you clearly define for yourself and potential investors the details of your concept and the reality of your start-up costs and profitability.

The four most basic questions a business plan should answer are…

* What is your concept?

* Where is your market?

* What are the start-up and operating costs of your business?

* How much money is your food truck going to make?

As you answer these questions, you'll come across others that you need to consider as well. Answer all these questions in your business plan, so that you're prepared when investors, vendors, and employees ask them later. Your business plan should clearly articulate your experience as well as your goals and ideas for making your business a reality. The more thorough your business plan is, the better prepared you'll be to accurately predict costs and anticipate problems down the road.

Because food trucks are a relatively young industry, you need to clearly explain them as a business concept in your business plan. Here are some of the questions you should answer about food trucks in your business plan:

* What is a food truck?

* Why are you starting a food truck instead of a bricks-and-mortar restaurant?

* What's your long-term goal?

* Do you plan to have additional trucks or open actual brick-and-mortar restaurants?

* What are the local regulations regarding food trucks? Are they changing?

* Will you be working on the truck yourself, or will employees be operating it while you manage?

Even if you intend to finance your food truck yourself, a business plan helps you determine whether your idea can become a profitable business; it also serves as a useful resource when you need assurance that your decisions are consistent with your original intention and associated projections. Having this plan helps you remain focused on your goals and makes it easier to achieve them. If you can't answer basic questions about your business's identity, intended market, and projected financials, it isn't realistic to think you'll be able to build your business. Take the time to analyze things from an investor's point of view. By removing your emotional attachment to your idea, you'll be able to make more accurate analyses. Doing so will save you a lot of time, energy, and money in the long run.

Describing Your Concept, Brand, and Market

In Chapter 3, I discussed the importance of having a clearly defined concept and menu designed with a niche market in mind. In the first part of your business plan, you must articulate what your food truck brand is going to be:

* What specifically is your concept?

* What is your niche market?

* How are you different from other food trucks and neighborhood restaurants?

In this part, don't be concerned with the financial calculations related to your business; instead, try to communicate your food truck's identity as clearly as possible and define your target market.

Your Identity

Your food truck's identity is a fusion of three components that should overlap and inform each other: the menu theme, truck personality, and the truck's philosophy.

Menu theme. Do you specialize in Japanese-inspired vegetarian fare? Guatemalan tamales? Or perhaps you've reinvented the American comfort food favorites of your childhood. Whatever you choose, successful food trucks always specialize in a niche cuisine. Describe how your food is unique in the market and unique unto itself, but be sure that it's consistent with a single theme.

Personality. How will your food truck present itself? What do you envision for its design and food presentation? What message do you want to communicate visually to passersby, and how do you want to communicate it? How will you and your personality integrate into your truck's concept? Whatever your vision, it should be consistent with your menu's theme and attractive to your target clientele.

Philosophy. Every business owner has life stories, beliefs, or a philosophy that informs his or her product. This personal aspect is often the motivation for going into business in the first place. If you're environmentally conscious, perhaps you want your food to be locally sourced, sustainable, and organic, and your plates, cups, and utensils to be 100-percent compostable. Perhaps all of your menu items are your grandmother's original recipes, and you want to honor her in your business. These personal aspects are critical for building a strong brand identity and should be reflected in your truck's menu and design.

If your menu, personality, and philosophy aren't in sync, your target clientele won't get the message. Writing out this section of your business plan helps you discover any areas of your concept that aren't consistent with your truck vision. This is the time to reconsider aspects of your menu, design, and operation to ensure everything is working toward the same goal. As you write, you'll see your food truck's identity begin to emerge. The more detailed the profile is, the more confidence you and others will have in the concept.

If you intend to seek a bank loan or private investment, be sure to include a detailed description of your business experience, especially within the food industry. You're less of a financial risk if you can demonstrate that you know what you're doing or have done it before. If you are a newbie (someone from another industry), you may want to describe ways in which your previous experience can be applied to the food business. You can also make an effort to explain your thought processes in developing this business, exhibiting that despite your lack of experience, you've done the research necessary to avoid pitfalls.

Your Market

After you've clearly defined your identity, you must determine whom your brand is going to attract. Describe your target clientele in your business plan, including where these people typically eat, live, and work in your intended locations.

You want to be sure that a large enough customer base exists in that spot for your niche product. There's no point in selling the best Indian food in Athens, Georgia, if there's no demand for it there. Consider other food businesses near your intended locations and in the food truck market that share your menu's theme or message. Ask yourself if there are enough customers to go around and if you believe they'll want what you're selling.

With that said, some of the most successful entrepreneurs are great at identifying needs that don't currently exist. You need to demonstrate your belief in your food truck idea, back it up with the facts behind the reason, and be ready to supply them when investors ask.

Statistics and facts about the food truck industry and the general food marketplace are very helpful in establishing the need for your product. Unfortunately, it's difficult to locate facts on the food truck business from reputable sources, in part because the industry is still very young. When looking for information for your business plan, you can use general food business resources. Check out the National Restaurant Industry Operations report for detailed facts on all segments of the business. It's produced annually by the National Restaurant Association.

Your Competition

Once you've established that there's a market for your brand, you must determine if you can be competitive within that market.

First, list your direct competitors, which consists of the nearby trucks and restaurants that offer a concept similar to yours. Compare their locations, hours, and prices to your own.

Next, list your indirect competitors—those trucks and restaurants whose products are entirely different from yours but who are still competing for the same customer base.

If you're selling vegetarian lunches, you aren't just competing with all the other vegetarian restaurants in the area (direct); you're also competing with any restaurant or food truck that's open for lunch (indirect). See Chapter 5 for more information on how to analyze the market for your desired location.

After you've listed your competition, you need to explain how and why you're going to gain a competitive advantage over them. Why is your product better? Do you have the email addresses of 50,000 local residents? Do you have a ready-made catering business because of your recent position at a catering company? Whatever it is, use this opportunity to clarify for yourself and your investors why your truck will do better than the competition.

Forecasting Sales

Regardless of how mouthwatering your menu or heartwarming your message, the only thing most investors are really interested in when considering a business proposal is the bottom line. Profitability should also be your primary concern; no matter how in love you are with your concept, if it can't generate enough money to cover expenses, pay back investors, and make a profit, there's no point in even beginning the process. Everything always comes back to the bottom line. Businesses exist to make money. Unless you have a rich uncle who wants to indulge your passions, it's all about the Benjamins, baby.

Learning to project sales and costs is a valuable and necessary skill for any small business owner. Not only will you use financial projections to interest investors in your business plan, you'll also use them to predict sales and expenses every month for as long as you're in business. You can create a simple spreadsheet or use specialized software program like QuickBooks. Your projections don't have to be perfect, and they certainly don't have to be fancy. You're just giving your best guess as to what kind of revenue your business will bring in. Although no one expects you to be Nostradamus and predict the future, you must be able to demonstrate to yourself and to any potential investors that your concept can generate enough sales to cover expenses and become profitable.

Estimate your sales forecast before determining your start-up costs, so you know how much money you have available to spend. To forecast sales accurately, you should've already designed and priced your menu. Begin by determining a plausible *check average,* which is the average amount each customer spends.

Put yourself into your customer's shoes. Would most people have to order more than one menu item to be satisfied? Do you offer appetizers or side dishes? Do you expect dessert to be a big hit? Calculate an average check that includes a beverage. This number should reflect what you realistically expect the average person to order, not necessarily what you would ideally want him or her to order. If your average dish is $7, your sides are $2, and sodas are $1, a reasonable check average for the purpose of sales forecasting would be $10.

Now multiply your check average by the number of customers you expect to serve each day. Because it's impossible to accurately guess the number of customers you'll have on any given day, always pad your sales projections with the following three sets of figures:

* **A best-case scenario:** your sales if everything goes according to plan

* **A worst-case scenario:** your sales if everything goes wrong

* **A split-the-difference scenario**: your sales fall halfway between the best and worst cases

Here's what it looks like in a simple spreadsheet:

Calculating Your Daily and Weekly Check Average

	Sun.	Mon.	Tue.	Wed.	Thu.	Fri.	Sat.	Average	Total
(Best)									
Covers	30	40	40	40	40	40	30	37	260
Ch/Av	$10	$12	$12	$12	$12	$12	$10	$11.43	$3,000
(Worst)									
Covers	5	10	10	10	10	10	5	9	60
Ch/Av	$2	$5	$5	$5	$5	$5	$2	$4.5	$270
(Split)									
Covers	20	30	30	30	30	30	20	27	190
Ch/Av	$6	$8	$8	$8	$8	$8	$6	$7.58	$1,440

Always take the calendar and climate into consideration when forecasting sales. If your food truck is on the streets of a northeastern city, Sales in December through February are going to slow down as people avoid walking in the snow. It must be reflected in your figures, so you can prepare your business for the seasonal decline in revenue.

Forecasting Expenses

You can't expect to be profitable for at least six months after the launch of your food truck, so I can't overstate the value of a highly detailed and well-padded expense forecast. Failure to adequately anticipate every possible start-up and operating expense, as well as emergencies, can be devastating. Fortunately, you can predict most of those costs before you even write your business plan if you're diligent in doing your research.

Your business plan should include at least a full-year forecast of operating expenses, including your salary and a decent cushion for emergencies, repairs, and worst-case scenarios. I prefer to break them down by week, month, and year. As I did with the sales forecast, include three sets of figures: one optimistic, one pessimistic, and one realistic. Your first-year projection must, of course, also include your start-up costs, which I'll show you how to estimate in Chapter 7.

When I say anticipate everything, I mean *everything,* down to the aluminum foil, paper clips, cleaning supplies, debt interest, postage and delivery, gasoline, payroll processing, deposit fees, employee meals, and parking. Many first-time food truckers overlook these things when they plan their businesses. The more you're able to predict now, the less surprised you will be when it's time to pay the bills.

Most of your expenses are controllable, meaning that you can lower or raise them based on your business needs. (However, keep in mind that in less experienced hands, controllable expenses can get out of hand.) Here's a partial list of controllable expenses you can budget for right now:

* **Payroll:** Beyond wages for salaried and hourly employees, you must include payroll taxes, workers' comp insurance, and benefits, some of which won't kick in until you're up and running.

* **Cost of Sales:** These are the costs of the actual ingredients that make up your products, including beverages. I'm not suggesting you compromise quality for cost, but be aware of rising food prices and adjust your ordering or menu accordingly.

* **Utilities:** Water and electricity are considered controllable expenses because all businesses have the flexibility to conserve them.

* **Operating Inventory:** This includes nearly everything that doesn't fall under cost of sales, such as cleaning supplies, order pads, uniforms, paper plates, utensils, straws, napkins, cups, and a thousand other small items that are easy to overlook when planning your start-up costs.

* **Administrative Expenses:** These include credit cards, banking and attorney's fees, phones, office supplies, and postage.

* **Marketing:** Unless you're already famous, there's no such thing as free publicity. Always budget for advertising. Turn to Chapter 9 for ideas on how to design a profitable marketing strategy for your truck.

Determining Your Breakeven

Very simply, your *breakeven point* is when you generate enough revenue to cover all your expenses. Investors will ask you when you expect to break even, so you need to have this information ready. By determining your breakeven, you can see if your sales will be high enough to finance your operating costs.

To determine your breakeven point, you must already have done your sales and expense forecasts. If you've entered these projections into a spreadsheet, generate a line that contrasts both sets of values for one year. You can now see how much you need to make to cover your overhead. If your sales forecast consistently falls below your projected expenses, try to adjust your costs. If that isn't enough, reconsider your menu, pricing, or overall concept.

Estimating Profits

Your estimated profit is the number in which your investors are going to be the most interested. Calculating it is easy: simply subtract your total projected expenses from your total projected sales. The remaining sum is your profit.

If you aren't seeing a profit, stop right there! Try to reduce your expenses to bring them under your projected sales. If you can't break even or make a profit, go back to the drawing board and revise your concept. Your prices may be too low, your menu too big, or your location inappropriate for the niche market you want to tap into. Determining your potential for profit now will save you a lot of time, money, and frustration in the short and long term.

Choosing Your Business Structure

You don't have to decide on a business structure right away, but it's a good time to begin to think about how you want to structure the ownership of your business. How you choose to register your food truck—as a sole proprietorship, a partnership, or a corporation—determines how you'll receive your income, how your business pays taxes, and who will be responsible should your business fail.

It's useful to know in which direction you want to go, so you can tailor your business plan with that goal in mind. Whatever you decide, you should work with an attorney to register your business accordingly.

Sole Proprietorship

A *sole proprietorship* means that a single individual owns the business. If you choose to register as a sole proprietor, you'll be personally responsible for any losses or debts incurred by your business. You get to keep all the profit, but if your business loses $50,000, the bank can take your personal assets to pay the debt. It's a very risky scenario and definitely not recommended in the modern business world. With all the things that can go wrong on your truck, you want to limit your personal liability.

Partnership

In a *partnership*, you share ownership and risk with one or more investors and split the profits according to a predetermined agreement.

A partner may invest time, money, expertise, or a combination of all three. You can set up a partnership in many ways, but be sure you agree from day one on your roles and responsibilities and the expectations you have for each other. You must also determine what stake your partner will have in the company and how you will share the profits.

It's crucial that you agree on a hierarchy and determine who has the ultimate authority when it comes to decision making. There's no room in a food truck for competing egos. Choose someone who shares your vision and decide now who will be in charge.

A partnership won't protect you from personal liability—only a corporation will. A partnership with the right person is always a great idea, though it might not be under this business structure. I talk more about partnerships in Chapter 7.

Limited Partnership

A *limited partnership* is very much like taking on a *silent partner*—an investor who isn't involved with the operation of the business. In the agreement, the limited partner is protected from any financial or legal liability should the business fail and risks only the investment.

Silent partners, however, tend to speak up if they feel their investment is threatened. Be sure to put the terms of your agreement in writing and specify who has the authority to make decisions about the operation of the business. You don't want a panicked investor meddling in your business or fighting you for control.

Corporation

Some small business owners choose to incorporate, forming a corporate structure, known as a *corporation*, that owns the business and pays them a salary. Incorporation offers you a legal cushion should your food truck fail, but you'll be taxed twice: once on corporate profits and again on your income. If you're just starting out, your bank will likely require you to assume personal liability for any loans to your corporation, so your financial risk remains unalleviated even when you incorporate your business.

All things considered, I recommend incorporation. Even though it can lead to high taxation, the protection it gives you is invaluable. Having a corporation is like having another identity; it separates you personally from you the business. If something goes wrong with the business, you, the person, and all your personal assets are protected. You'll live to fight another day, and that's how I like it. Talk to your attorney about the benefits and risks of forming a corporation.

While writing out a detailed business plan for your truck business can be time consuming, it is necessary. You'll learn so much about yourself and your business during the process. Potential problems will crop up that you'll learn to solve and avoid, as well as opportunities you never realized existed. Entrepreneurs, especially those in the food business, tend to keep their plans in their heads. Get them out, write them down, and discuss them with people you trust. The benefits will far outweigh the energy and time you spend. Get started now!

Finding Financing

Now that you've defined your vision within your business plan, including menu, design concept, and possible locations, it's time to secure the cash to make it a reality. Finding financing for a food truck is no easy task. Many people want to invest in hospitality businesses purely for vanity. They dream of hanging out with their friends at their very own restaurant, especially those with monotonous jobs that don't fulfill their passions. The reality is that most outside investors in restaurants and similar food businesses never see their money returned.

From the perspective of investors, food trucks are more attractive than other hospitality businesses because they can be a relatively low investment with the potential for high returns and spin-offs like bricks-and-mortar restaurants. Your job is to sell outside investors on your dream: for a small initial investment, they can get in on the next big thing in the food business. Not only that, but there will be incredible potential for expansion and growth. But no matter how good your numbers or your plan, ultimately, investors will only put their money behind your business idea if they believe in and like you.

Start-up costs vary with the details of your concept, but in this chapter, I help you estimate your initial expenses and set a dollar goal. Then I describe several strategies for reaching that number, including finding an investor, seeking a loan, and the pros and cons of tapping into your own personal savings. Finally, I discuss some creative ways to leverage business relationships to free up capital and even extend your credit.

Knowing How Much Money You Need

Before you can borrow money or approach an investor, you have to determine how much money you're going to need. Estimating start-up costs is a challenge for aspiring and seasoned food truckers alike.

Once you accept money from investors, you must continue to prove to them that you deserve their trust and confidence. As you manage and operate your truck, put yourself in their shoes and anticipate their concerns. Don't allow anything that can be interpreted as wasteful, unprofessional, or potentially threatening to your investors' bottom line spur them to interfere with the way you run your business.

Your expenses are determined by the nature of your menu, locations, and the complexity of your truck's vision. There are, however, many food truck universals and one-time purchases that you can predict to help calculate your start-up total. In general, operators need between $100,000 to $125,000 to properly start a food truck, including purchasing and building a truck and operating capital to launch and manage it until it becomes profitable.

Calculating Your Start-Up Costs

Begin by listing all the inventory items, equipment, and services you require before you open for business. If your menu, design, and overall concept are clearly defined, you should be able to make reasonably accurate cost predictions. Use the following list, with my best estimates provided, to approximate a rough start-up figure if you don't know your actual expenses:

Expense	Cost
Advertising	$5,000
Design	$2,500
Electrical and awnings	$10,000
General operating capital (gas, staff, salary, food and beverages, tickets, insurance)	$25,000–50,000
Inventory (ingredients, beverages, plates, utensils, napkins, etc.)	$2,500
Kitchen supplies (pots, pans, grease mats, etc.)	$3,000
Labor to customize truck	$10,000-15,000
Legal fees	$1,000–5,000
Permits (dependent on location)	$1,500–10,000
Restaurant equipment (stove, sink, fryer, refrigerators, grill, exhaust fan, etc.)	$15,000–20,000
Truck	$10,000–15,000
Truck wrap	$5,000

Calculating Operating Capital

No matter how strong your concept, menu, and advertising campaigns are, you'll continue to need money well after you launch your truck. It's important to have conservative expectations for the amount of revenue you'll bring in during the first few months and to set aside operating capital to cover expenses during that time. Almost every new food business requires time to hone its operation, refine its menu and pricing, and build a loyal clientele. If you give yourself an adequate financial cushion, you can use this period to perfect your concept without unnecessary stress.

When preparing your business plan and start-up estimate, assume that you won't become profitable for several months. Set aside an appropriate safety net—at least $25,000 to $50,000—to cover all your operating expenses, payroll, and advertising, and a weekly salary to cover your own living expenses for the first six months. This cushion should also allow for any unforeseen repairs, upgrades, or changes in inventory as your operation and menu evolve.

Determining Your Contribution

Regardless of how profitable your idea may appear to potential investors, you'll need to invest a considerable amount of your own money into your new enterprise. You must take a corresponding level of financial risk to back your passion if you want investors to take you seriously. With your own money on the line, you'll find yourself even more motivated to succeed, and it's that determination that inspires confidence in investors.

Using your own money has numerous additional benefits as well. If you choose not to seek help from investors, you don't have to divide control of your business with people who may not share your vision. It can be very tedious, not to mention disheartening, to have to answer to others when you're the one doing all the work to realize a personal dream. Should you want to alter your concept, menu, pricing, or locations, those decisions will be yours and yours alone. You'll be able to take pride in knowing that your food truck's success is a reflection of your own dedication, creativity, and the risks you were willing to take.

Be very cautious when using credit cards to finance your start-up inventory and operation. You don't want to incur high interest charges or destroy your credit rating. While credit cards can be convenient short-term solutions with some real benefits, such as frequent-flyer miles and cash points, I recommend saving them for the occasional (but inevitable) crisis: theft, equipment failure, or truck damage. There will be times when you'll have to pay for immediate repairs and seek reimbursement from your insurance company later—a process that can take several weeks or months. Avoid the trap in which too many small business owners have been caught and always regard credit cards as your last and least-desirable finance option.

However, before you invest your retirement savings and your child's college fund, remember that risk also means risk of failure. Should your food truck not succeed, you could jeopardize your savings, your credit, and your assets. Always allow for the worst possible outcome when making any investment. Making a business plan, even if you're financing the project yourself, will help you spend thoughtfully and predictably, and can alleviate waste, confusion, and surprise. (See Chapter 6 for information on writing a business plan.)

Identifying Investors

Don't feel bad if you can't (or don't want to) finance your food truck venture all by yourself. You can seek financing from many different kinds of investors, from partners to friends and family, but there are important things to consider when seeking outside funds to feed some green into your food truck dreams.

Potential Partners

A partner is an investor who actively participates in the formation and/or operation of your food truck, as opposed to an investor or silent partner who is distinctly less hands-on. A partner may invest money, expertise, or some other financial service, or a partner can invest his or her reputation, filling a void and strengthening your overall concept and operation. A partner doesn't just invest money in your success; she invests her skills, experience, and sometimes her name and personality. It's important to choose the right partner for the right reasons. You want someone who won't just bet on you, but will increase the odds in your favor.

If you want to bring on a partner, consider your biggest weaknesses and seek someone whose skills can fill those voids. Here are some examples of areas where a partner can fill a void for you:

* **Culinary experience:** If you lack culinary experience, consider bringing on an accomplished chef as a partner/consultant to help develop your menu, streamline the inventory, and train your staff.

* **Business/accounting:** If you lack confidence on the business and accounting end of the operation, consider finding a partner with strong bookkeeping or fundraising skills who can manage the books, negotiate with vendors, secure loans and investments, or handle legal matters and paperwork with ease.

* **Name recognition:** You might seek a partner because he or she can lend his or her name and reputation to your venture. With a "celebrity" partner attached to your business plan, you can access investors, earn free publicity, and build a tremendous buzz on the local culinary scene.

You can similarly seek partners with marketing expertise, food truck experience, or restaurant management skills.

It's crucial, however, that whoever your partner is, a clear chain of command exists that you both mutually agree upon and respect. While the partnership is a collaborative relationship, one person must be in charge so that decisions can be made effectively and problems can be resolved as efficiently as possible. Many businesses fail because partners haven't clearly defined their roles from the very beginning and later clash, bringing the entire operation to a halt when no decision can be made.

Since its launch in 2010, San Diego–based Devilicious has built an enormous following and attracted more than its share of media attention. Classically trained chef Dyann Huffman partnered with Kristina Repp, a seasoned waitress and restaurant manager, to create mobile fare reminiscent of their childhood comfort food favorites. The friends have turned their combined 38 years of culinary experience into a profitable brand that's widely and wildly blogged and buzzed about and has even competed on Food Network's *The Great Truck Race*. Interviews with Huffman reveal a distinct division of labor based on each partner's expertise and a shared love for "devilish comfort food", as she describes it. They're the perfect example of an effective partnership: two passionate women, two skill sets, and a single vision.

Silent Partners

Outside investors who agree to be silent partners invest cash but have little say in how a food truck is run. Once the business is launched, it's common for investors to break their silence in an effort to protect their returns. It's very important, as with taking on a partner, to clearly define your roles in the business from day one.

Family and Friends

You've probably been cautioned never to do business with family and friends, and for good reason: it's a recipe for financial and emotional disaster. It's very difficult to hold our loved ones accountable, especially when it comes to something as vulgar as money.

Your family and friends are a wonderful resource for guidance and inspiration but not for capital. If you must seek money from them, be sure to put everything in writing, just as you would structure any other business deal.

What You Need to Show Potential Investors

In order to attract outside investors, you'll need to have a business plan. The materials you prepare for them should be concise: What are you doing? Why are you doing it? How are you going to do it? And will it make money?

Potential investors will expect to see the following:

* A business plan of no more than 10 pages

* Estimated start-up costs

* How much money you need from them

* How soon before they'll see a return on their investment

* How much they can expect to profit

* Your vision of a working relationship with them

How to Structure an Investment

Each investor will have his own preferred method for structuring returns depending on his reasons for investing in your business in the first place. Some investors may want to make a quick buck and seek a short-term compensation deal. Other investors—perhaps those who love the food business and want to be involved in your operation—will seek a long-term payment plan.

It's important to negotiate a deal that's fair to your investor, fair to you, and puts reasonable pressure and expectations on the business. The terms of your agreement must be clearly outlined in writing and be vetted by your attorney. Don't accept a deal that could potentially overburden your business with unrealistic payments or timelines; this is where a well-researched business plan can save you a lot of grief, confusion, and money. If you suspect that an investor is trying to take advantage of you, they probably are.

A very common way to compensate your investor is to pay back their initial investment plus interest. There are countless ways to structure these payments, and your investor will have their own preferences depending on how long they want to stay involved in your business. For example, you may agree to pay back the investor's initial $30,000 stake plus 30 percent interest, for a total of $39,000, over three years. You could plan to pay them 15 percent ($4,500) annually for the first two years and repay the $30,000 principal the third. Or, you could agree to pay them $13,000 annually for three years. Whatever you decide, you must be confident that you can satisfy your investor without compromising the business or your own bottom line.

Another way to structure the investment is to offer your investor a percentage of the profits. If the $30,000 investment is worth 30 percent equity in your business, then the investor receives 30 percent of your profits. They may expect their return in the form of *capital gains,* which is the increase in value of a share from the time of the investment to when it's sold, after selling their equity share to you or another partner.

As the business grows, each equity share becomes more valuable, so your investor can sell their stake for more than their initial outlay. Your compensation deal can include a buyout clause, enabling you to regain equity (and control) in your company. You can also structure your partnership, so that you acquire more equity in the company incrementally over time without having to invest more cash.

Whatever you decide, it's crucial that you not lose sight of the business's long-term needs when considering an investment agreement. No amount of start-up capital is worth compromising your company's future with unrealistic payments on an impossible timeline. I'm not asking you to bet against your company's success; instead, I'm suggesting that you bet in its best interest. Always ensure that the terms of your deal are consistent with the most reliable and conservative estimates of your business plan.

Finally, remember that if you have to turn down an investment deal, you'll be able to find another capital source. Don't get discouraged; in business, it truly is better to be safe than sorry.

Getting a Loan

The food truck industry is a risky business, and banks are extremely reluctant to lend money to first-time owners. Those lucky enough to get a loan are usually required to personally guarantee the note, making them responsible for the money regardless of the success or failure of their business.

What You Need to Show the Bank

I'm going to be honest; if you're a first-time food trucker with no other small businesses under your belt, you're going to have a very hard time being approved for a bank loan. You'll probably need to seek private loans, a partnership, or a government-backed loan from the Small Business Administration. Applying for a loan is a critical decision that requires a lot of preparation; make sure you understand all the risks, fees, and procedures before you proceed.

If you're looking for a partner anyway, seriously consider bringing on someone who owns or has owned a successful food truck. Their credentials will significantly decrease the financial risk of your venture and boost the bank's confidence in your business plan.

The bank weighs your financial and business records, credit rating, and experience to determine your ability to repay the loan. Your business plan must be thorough and well researched, and include details of your background in the industry to convince them that your projected earnings are realistic.

Be prepared to demonstrate not only your experience but also how you intend to use the borrowed money. Discuss what equipment and services you'll buy and how these investments will shape the quality and efficiency of your business. Your explanations should demonstrate to the bank that you know what you're doing and have carefully thought out your spending plan. Banks want to invest in people who are business savvy, fiscally responsible, and industry qualified. Someone with a clear strategy is less of a financial risk than an unprepared first-timer simply asking for cash.

The bank will also consider your company equity—the amount of your own money you have or are prepared to invest. The bank regards this as a security deposit of sorts and an indication of your seriousness. They'll likely review your tax returns and credit history for a general impression of your personal risk. If your credit rating is poor, your risk is high, which means you'll have to supply a qualified guarantor who will repay the loan if you aren't able to repay it. The bank will also demand collateral—assets of significant value that can be seized should you default on your loan.

Ultimately, if you're a first-time food truck owner, you're better off seeking a partner or private investor. Once you've built a successful business, banks are a great resource to help you expand.

Small Business Administration Loans

If you don't qualify for a commercial loan, your bank can help you determine whether you're eligible for assistance from the U.S. Small Business Administration (SBA). If you qualify—and most first-time small businesses do—the SBA can guarantee your loan in full or in part, thus alleviating the bank's risk should you default.

Your bank will help to prequalify you and prepare the necessary paperwork in accordance with SBA guidelines. This will include a business plan, your business and financial records, credit rating, equity, collateral, and experience. Even with an SBA guarantee, you'll still be personally liable for repayment of the loan.

You may also seek venture capital from an SBA Small Business Investment Company (SBIC), which partners with private investors to provide private capital for eligible businesses. For more information on SBA assistance and guidelines, visit sba.gov.

Other Ways to Increase Liquidity

Beyond borrowing money or printing it in your basement, you have other more creative ways to free up cash and even extend your credit.

Supplier Credit

Many food truck owners seek an unofficial line of credit from their vendors and suppliers—their purveyors, in restaurant jargon. For example, a supplier might agree to defer the payment of your bills, enabling you to use your cash for other things in the short term. Conventional wisdom dictates that new truck owners would find it difficult to persuade their purveyors to grant extended credit terms, but that's not necessarily the case.

You're already anticipating those first moments of interaction with your very first customer. That person will respond not just to the quality of your food and the cleverness of your design, but also to you, to your passion and authenticity and charisma. The first impressions that are so crucial in building lasting relationships with your clientele are also important to your relationships with your suppliers.

Purveyors ultimately want you to succeed because you're a revenue source for them. There's nothing inappropriate about introducing yourself with a smile, wearing your passion on your sleeve, and asking them to invest in you the same way you'd ask a bank to invest in your business. Invest in your vendor and supplier relationships the same warmth, vigor, and gratitude you will with your customers, and opportunities will become available to you.

Consider partnering with an established restaurant brand. Often, these operators are looking for ways to generate revenues but are too busy focusing on their core businesses. They may consider licensing their brand or partnering with you on a truck business. This gives you instant credibility and a following, significantly decreasing the risk of failure.

You should also consider negotiating with suppliers to get free equipment when buying other pieces from them. As you gain their confidence, they'll be open to haggling, bartering, and renegotiating with you. The bottom line is that while you should never expect to receive something for nothing or on a deferred payment plan, you should never be afraid to ask.

Sponsorships

Anyone who has ever seen a sporting event has surely noticed the preponderance of flashy corporate sponsor logos. Almost any film in your local multiplex and 100 percent of the TV shows incorporate slightly less-obvious logos into their production design in exchange for capital from corporate sponsors. This enables those sponsors to build *brand equity*— the commercial value of a brand based on the consumer perception of it—and positively associate their products with popular consumer trends.

Your first food truck probably isn't going to win the sponsorship of a mega-corporation, and it doesn't need to. You can still take advantage of sponsorship opportunities from companies that are more accessible to you. Any company that sells a product or service— and all companies do—is concerned with building brand equity. It's time to get creative and determine what your food truck can do for them.

The easiest place to start is with your purveyors; you're already in dialogue with them. Instead of asking for capital, offer to feature their names, products, or services in exchange for free or discounted products or services. For example, if you want to buy your produce from Farmer John's Organics, offer to proudly state on your menu and signage that you exclusively use their organic fruits and vegetables. Print up a sample menu and signage and show it to them during your first conversation. Visual aids can be extremely persuasive.

In June 2011, mega-retailer Macy's capitalized on the food truck craze and launched Macy's Chefs-a-Go-Go, a nationwide food truck tour that featured celebrity chefs and that received a lot of press coverage. Macy's cleverly offered special giveaways and other truck-side deals to foodies who visited their website and social networking profiles. It gave the company a huge platform to build brand equity and remind consumers that they specialize in kitchenware as well as fashion.

You need to communicate to potential sponsors exactly why they want their product or service to be associated with your truck:

* Who are you?

* What's your concept?

* What's your company's philosophy?

* Who's your clientele?

Write up a proposal and include visual aids whenever possible.

As your business grows and you build your own brand equity, sponsorship will be easier to secure. In fact, once you're profitable, you may want to be a sponsor yourself, by providing food to a local sporting event, school fair, or charity. It's a highly effective way to leverage your relationships with other businesses and your community to attract more customers.

Regulations and Licensing

My business law teacher in high school, Ms. Sibovits, made a very strong impression on me. She taught us about many aspects of the world of business; lessons I'm sure I still unconsciously utilize today.

I recall a few of Mrs. Sibovits's words with complete clarity: "Ignorance is no excuse when dealing with the law." These words are as true today as they were then. When it comes to legal matters, if you break the law, it doesn't matter whether you knew the law existed or not. You're still accountable.

In the world of food trucks, what you don't know can definitely hurt you. Without knowledge of local regulations and proper permits, you'll end up spending a lot of money for nothing. Food trucks may have begun as an unregulated—or at least minimally regulated—business, but their recent success has made them targets. As a truck operator, you'll be subject to as much and sometimes more regulation than bricks-and-mortar restaurants. In the current environment, regulators are being pressured by restaurants and other businesses to get food trucks out of their neighborhoods. This has put truck operations under a microscope, and local authorities are looking for any reason to ticket, fine, or revoke licenses.

For example, in New York City, you need a mobile food vending license and a mobile food vending unit permit to operate a food truck. The first one is a matter of filling out some paperwork and taking a few classes; the second is a different story. These permits have been capped at 3,100 total since 1979. The only real way to obtain a permit is to purchase one illegally or partner with someone who holds a permit for cash and a portion of the profits. I do not recommend this course of action.

The success and intrigue of the food truck business that led you to purchase this book has also led to a legal standoff that will determine the future of the business. In Chapter 8, I cover how to become a responsible community member and know the laws before the regulators show up.

Knowing Your Local Laws

Prior to making a decision to start a food truck business, you must be aware of local laws; your business plan can be greatly affected by what's allowed or required by your local authorities. Laws and regulations apply to every aspect of your operation. You'll have to deal with regulations that apply to all retail operations as well as ordinances specific to the food truck game. You'll need to deal with taxes, licenses, labor laws, and many other standard hospitality business regulations, but you'll also have to worry about the rules of the road, parking, how much propane you can carry, and other operational components that are very specific to running a food truck.

Most of the laws you'll be dealing with are established by local and state agencies; you'll rarely, if ever, be involved with federal authorities. Your local health department is the governing body that oversees specific codes for serving food in your area. The department of transportation decides where and when you can park your truck. There are even regulations for street food businesses concerning how far away from the curb you should be located or how close to a building's entrance you can park.

Let's use my friend Gelareh as an example. She was planning to sell fruit smoothies in downtown Claudiaville, Wisconsin. The area she chose for her truck is the hottest place for nightlife, so she planned to sell alcoholic smoothies in the evening. She was excited to get started and had purchased her truck and smoothie equipment. When Gelareh was ready to open her smoothie truck, she met with her lawyer, Diane, to apply for the licenses. Diane informed her that local regulations don't permit food trucks to park on Main Street in downtown Claudiaville. Additionally, the liquor licenses for food trucks only allow them to serve before 9 P.M.

Gelareh had to change her entire business plan. Fifty percent of her revenue was supposed to come from her late-night business, and she wasn't sure if she could get the traffic she needed if she couldn't park on Main Street. She messed up big time: Gelareh had already spent $50,000 on her truck! She ended up selling her truck back to Gilda, a local truck dealer, at a loss. Gelareh was done before she even got started.

That's a sad example of what can happen if you don't know your local laws. The best solution is to consult with an attorney because the law is all about interpretation. A good lawyer will save you time and money, so I suggest you reach out to your local bar association.

You can also do your own research by visiting the website or office of your local regulatory body where someone will happily assist you. Easy-to-read guides for beginners are also available on their websites. Remember, they want you to succeed.

Getting Permits and Required Licenses

Licenses are legal documents issued by government agencies giving you permission to do a particular thing or operate a particular type of business. When it comes to food trucks, you'll need a license from your area's governing body to operate, to sell certain items, and even to collect sales tax. If you choose to do any of these things without a permit and/or license, authorities can shut down your business, fine you, and even send you to jail. It's critical that you take the proper steps and obtain the correct paperwork to operate your food truck.

For the most part, obtaining a license isn't something you do once and never have to think about again. You'll need to renew most licenses annually, and the process could include payments, exams, and in some cases, a full reapplication. Work with your attorney and your support staff, if you have any, to establish a system that will let you know when, and if, you need to renew your permits. You never want to be in a situation where you're operating with an expired license. It's a foolish mistake that can cost you and your business money.

Make permitting and licensing for your business a top priority. In doing so, you're not only keeping yourself out of trouble, you're protecting your customers and your employees. Do everything in your power to protect them.

Always keep your licenses and/or permits on board during operation and locked up in a safe place when you aren't on the road. Losing the actual documents can cause major issues when you're being inspected and dealing with authorities, not to mention the time and energy you'll expend replacing them.

Following Health Codes

The Food Code is created and published by the Food and Drug Administration (FDA) every four years as an example for health departments nationwide. It includes the best practices for storing, preparing, and handling food as recommended by the federal government. Your truck is subject to local, state, and national food laws outlined in this code. The actual local codes are adapted from the federal code and vary from state to state and county to county.

The most immediate authority for your truck is your county health department. Generally, their code outlines minimum requirements for safety, but local jurisdictions may have stricter regulations. While you plan your business and throughout its operation, it's important to have open communication with your health department to ensure that you're following the code and not making mistakes that could cost you big time. Each county has clear outlines as to how commercial kitchens must be laid out, and it's better to have this information prior to constructing your truck.

Health codes regulate multiple areas of your commissary and food truck, including the following:

Employee hygiene. Cooks and service staff must be clean and well groomed. If they're sick or have exposed cuts, your customers can be exposed to potential infection.

Inspections. Food trucks are usually inspected at semiannually in addition to potential random inspections. A bad grade on an inspection can lead to your truck getting shut down and result in lost business. Don't take chances.

Cleaning. Health codes tell you what cleaners and sanitizers are acceptable for use in your truck. The code also stipulates how often equipment and surfaces must be cleaned.

Storage and handling. You're responsible for all food that's served to your customers. Once you accept a product's delivery, it becomes a raw material that will eventually be turned into an item you sell. The code outlines how food should be handled and stored. For example, a potentially dangerous item like raw chicken shouldn't be stored above cooked food due to the potential for cross contamination.

Equipment and supplies. The equipment you use in your truck and commissary must be in line with health code requirements. Examples include sinks that have multiple compartments and color-coded cutting boards for meats, poultry, and vegetables.

Obtaining Health Inspections

Every food truck needs an inspection and a permit from the health department to do business. The permit requires you to file an application and pay a fee ranging from a few hundred to a few thousand dollars annually. (This amount is determined by your local government.) Other than the fee and application themselves, the most problematic part of the process is the time you'll have to spend getting them. Health departments can get overwhelmed, leading to weeks of waiting to get an inspector to check your vehicle. Assume the process will take up to four weeks and include the delay in your timeline. As with all legal issues, the health inspection requirements will vary from city to city and state to state. Check with your local health department early in your business's planning stages to be sure you're aware of all the steps you need to take.

In order to get more of a grasp on the process, let's take a look at the licensing procedure for food trucks in Washington, D.C.:

1. **Obtain food protection manager identification from the health department.**

   Food truck operators are required to have this identification with them at all times during the operation of their trucks. To get this identification, you must enroll in a food manager certification course for proper training. After you've taken the course, you bring your certificate, test scores, a payment of $35, and two forms of identification to the D.C. treasurer's office.

2. **Have the health department do a process plan review of your truck.**

   Your process plan lists the food items you'll be serving and how you'll be preparing them. You must submit that plan, along with a payment of $100, to the health department for approval. Only after you've received plan approval should you start building your truck. After you've determined all your truck's equipment needs, you must bring the plan back to the health department for secondary approval. In Washington, D.C., the only requirement for truck design is that the truck be no bigger than 18.5 feet long, 10.5 feet tall, and 8 feet wide.

3. **If you're planning to use propane, schedule an appointment through the fire department to get your design approved by the fire marshal.**

Propane is dangerous and requires an inspection by an expert in the safe handling of hazardous gases.

4. **Submit a vending application to the health department for your vending unit inspection.**

    This is a standard inspection required of all street vendor equipment.

5. **Submit a depot letter to the health department.**

    You must submit a depot letter from a health department–approved commissary to the health department. This letter says that the commissary has the ability to support your operation for food supply/storage, water supply, food preparation, general supply storage, truck parking, repairs, cleaning, and waste disposal. The letter must be approved by the health department and remain on file there.

6. **Have your truck inspected by the health department.**

    In D.C., inspections are performed at the health department's inspection site on Tuesdays and Wednesdays from 9 A.M. to 12 P.M. (It's possible to get an offsite inspection, but you'll have to wait until a field inspector in your area is available.) If you pass inspection, you'll get a 30-day, temporary permit until your permanent license is ready to be picked up.

    This inspection will verify the following:

    * Proof of ownership, proper identification, and driver's license

    * Proof of district-issued food manager identification card

    * Food purchase records and storage

    * Proof of commissary and their license to operate with recent inspection

    If your commissary facility doesn't have prior approval, you'll also need to submit the plan for the facility prior to getting your inspection.

7. **Apply for a Roadway Class-A license for the person(s) who will be driving and operating the truck.**

    Even when fully licensed, you're subject to additional legal issues in Washington, D.C. As I've already discussed, you can only solicit customers who flag you down due to a 35-year-old law put in place for ice-cream trucks that doesn't consider twenty-first-century inventions like social media. Although the regulation is completely antiquated, the authorities must and will enforce it.

In addition to a truck permit, some states require individual employees to be licensed by the health department. The types of licenses required differ by municipality but include food handler's permits, food protection certificates, and certificates of qualification. Employees may be required to take a test and submit to a health check for contagious diseases like tuberculosis and hepatitis.

Are you exhausted? The process of licensing in Washington, D.C., is the rule, not the exception, and if you think it's complicated, you're right. A lot of steps are involved; it's probably one of the most tedious parts of starting your truck. Take your time to ensure that you don't miss any parts of the process. Failing to meet any of the requirements can delay your opening for months, which can greatly affect your profitability.

Staying on Top of Evolving Regulations

The thorniest issues in the food truck business today are the enforcement of antiquated regulations and the possible creation of new ones. Food trucks flourished over the past few years because they existed in a gray area outside standard regulation. They aren't exactly food carts or street vendors, but neither are they bricks-and-mortar restaurants, so it wasn't clear which regulations applied. As long as the number of trucks remained manageable, authorities allowed them to operate under the radar. They were welcome additions to many communities and rarely took significant business from competing establishments.

Pera Turkish Tacos was awarded the first food truck liquor license in New York City in June 2011. Operating out of a food truck lot located in front of Tavern on the Green during its closure, the truck was allowed to sell beer, wine, and cocktails for consumption in their assigned seating area.

But when the revolution began, the number of trucks exploded. Suddenly, there were food trucks on every corner in many cities—a situation that forced the authorities to more strictly enforce current laws and create new ones to police a burgeoning industry. Local businesses became hostile toward the trucks because they began taking more customers from rent-paying establishments.

In almost every major metropolitan area, legislation related to the operation of food trucks is being proposed. Some areas want to expand permitting, while others are talking about charging rent for good spots. Health inspectors are making spot checks on trucks, and cities like Los Angeles are beginning to give letter grades to trucks based on their health inspections.

In response, trucks have started organizing associations to protect their rights and to fight to be heard on the local political scene.

By the time you read this book, regulations will have changed tenfold in most cities and states. So, what do you need to know? Whatever the regulations are, you must be aware of them. You also need to join a trade organization and get involved in the discussion. Speak to local lawmakers, enforcement agencies, and fellow truckers to find out the current situation. Is it friendly or unfriendly, stable or likely to change? You need to make sure you're aware and protected before you invest your hard-earned cash in this business.

In Chicago, New York, Los Angeles, Seattle, Miami, and Atlanta, campaigns continue to change the food truck regulations. The landscape is changing, so know your local laws and become an active community member.

Buying the Insurance You Need

When considering your insurance needs, you need to realize that you're insuring both a mobile restaurant and a vehicle. You need insurance that covers your kitchen and business, as well as your truck. Restaurants can face many potential claims every day, but food trucks face additional risks and exposure to different types of claims.

Here are a few risks to consider:

* Automobile accidents

* Food poisoning

* Slip-and-fall risks around your parked truck

* Kitchen equipment replacement and damage

* Employee injury

I recommend carrying commercial auto and general liability insurance.

General Liability Insurance

Your general liability should have at least a $1 million umbrella policy.

A general liability insurance policy offers specific coverage, such as property and bodily injury, in one policy. You need it because your commercial auto insurance won't cover your entire rig. Many truck operators don't get this coverage, but it's better to be safe than sorry. A general liability policy will protect you from nondriving-related issues, such as property damage or bodily injury that doesn't result from driving. You don't want to have your flourishing food business shut down because you didn't have the right coverage.

Commercial Auto Insurance

Because your food truck is customized and much heavier than an automobile, it's going to need much more coverage. Commercial auto policies offer higher limits, allow modified trucks, and permit different types of uses than the insurance you carry for your passenger car.

You spent a lot of time, energy, and, most importantly, money building this truck; it's critical that you protect it and yourself by insuring it appropriately. You also need to check with local authorities to see if there are insurance requirements for food trucks.

Finding an Agent and Asking the Right Questions

It's important to work with an insurance agent who understands the needs of your business. Many agents deal with traditional restaurants but don't know what's best for a mobile business like yours. Find someone with experience, and make sure to ask the following questions:

* Am I protected if I get into a car accident? If so, for how much?

* Is my kitchen equipment protected from theft or damage?

* Does my insurance permit me to be a mobile business?

* Do I have protection from food-poisoning claims?

* What's my coverage if the truck is stolen or vandalized?

* Am I covered if my employees and/or customers are injured? What if they're injured in the commissary or in front of the truck?

* Are my employees covered to drive the truck?

Establishing a Domain Name and Trademark

Once you choose your truck name, the first thing you should do is purchase the internet domain name through a service like GoDaddy.com or Register.com. The food truck business is based online, and if you can get the domain closest to your truck name, it's almost the equivalent of having a trademark. Even if someone copies your concept or name, the right domain will ensure that the customer finds you before the imposter.

The most valuable thing you'll get from the creation of your food truck is branding. If you create something notable, it will enable you to expand into a bricks-and-mortar establishment through brand recognition. To maintain your brand's integrity, you should *trademark* it. A trademark is a distinctive sign or indicator legally registered by an individual, business, or legal entity to identify their products and/or services to consumers. You can do so via a low-cost service, such as Legal Zoom (legalzoom.com). You should be able to file a basic trademark of your logo and trade name for about $1,500, including fees. It gives you a public record of ownership and the right to file suit if someone breaches your trademark, and it creates exclusive rights to your trademark.

People tend to get frustrated when dealing with detailed regulations, and they sometimes take their frustrations out on local health inspectors and other regulatory authorities. However, such conflicts can make you a target for violations and make life much more difficult than a random inspection or small fine. Always remember it is easier to maintain a positive relationship with authorities and do things the right way from the beginning. Be patient, friendly, and thorough when dealing with bureaucracy. Not only will it make your life easier, it will help you build a growing enterprise.

Creating Your Marketing Plan

Sharing what makes you special while putting the needs of the customer ahead of your own is one of the most powerful actions any business can take. It transforms you from a consumer of energy—a taker—to a creator of energy—a giver. This simple act of unselfishly revealing your creation to the world, adding something to the community experience, and contributing completes the positive energy loop that enables you to make your magic real.

But what does this mean practically? To be a great creator and to market yourself or your ideas effectively, you must share them without selfish intentions. Anything else is manipulation. Consider the current retail conundrum. For years, numerous department stores have had seasonal mega-sales. They had these sales because they were selfish and lazy. Instead of improving their products, building bonds with their customers, and creating value, they simply chose to manipulate customers into action by offering discounts.

The result? Customers only shopped when there were massive sales, which meant profits eroded, loyalty became nonexistent, and, eventually, businesses closed.

In a world where most consumers value meaning over money and experiences over material goods, and crave meaningful connections, the only way to break through is to share, not sell—you need to be selfless, not selfish.

This change in values, combined with new technologies, has created a paradigm shift. The components of an effective marketing plan have evolved. For instance, traditional public relations are much less effective—especially in the world of food trucks—than social media platforms like Instagram and Twitter. What used to be a controlled, one-way message, like a restaurant review or gossip column hit, has turned into an active dialogue between brand and consumer. It's more important than ever to have a well-thought-out marketing plan with room to iterate and test what works.

Marketing Your Truck

Just when you thought you were done setting up your food truck business, you really are just getting started. A successful truck business is a marathon, not a sprint. Getting your truck on the road is only half the job; the other half is making people love it!

Today's competitive environment makes it impossible to rely on luck. The "if-you-build-it-they-will-come" mentality doesn't work anymore. Marketing is critical in establishing a successful truck. Food trucks are no longer novelties, and competition in the business is fierce. The trucks that succeed are the ones with a clear brand identity that saturates every part of the customer's experience. These brands also offer what I refer to as "experiential follow through". They promise something great, and then deliver something even better to get customers to keep coming back.

For an example of this type of marketing and experiential follow through, look no further than your local Apple store. Everything from its logo and advertising to the store's design, employee language, purchasing experience, and the end product speak to Apple's customer-focused brand. Apple customers love their brand so much that they only buy Apple.

You need to take this same focus and apply it to your food truck business. You want to make your customers' trip to lunch the most exciting part of the day, so much so that the thought of eating at another truck never even enters their minds. Let's start by establishing your identity through your logo.

Designing Your Brand Logo

When you think of the logos of companies like Coca-Cola, Nike, and Google, do you have an emotional response? To me, Coca-Cola says classic quality. The Nike Swoosh is hip and athletic. Google is playful, but not too playful. You may have different responses to these logos, but I bet they aren't too far from mine.

Your logo is your chance to create instant public recognition of your brand. It needs to say who you are and what you're like in the simplest and most direct way. So, what are you trying to say about your truck with your logo?

Make a list of three to five core values of your brand. For instance, if you're starting an artisanal ice cream truck, your core values could be high-quality ingredients, locally sourced, and homemade with the help of a master ice-cream maker. How would you say this with your logo? Artisanal reminds me of something more classic or from a small town. The same goes for homemade. If you use a master ice-cream maker, you may want to include the maker's name in your truck's brand.

Korilla BBQ is a Korean taco truck created by Edward "3D" Song. When he asked himself the question, "Who doesn't love Korean BBQ?", he came up with three answers: vegans and vegetarians, people who don't know what Korean BBQ is, and people who don't want to spend $40 or more at a Korean restaurant. That made his decision to start a Korean BBQ truck easy. A Columbia University grad, Edward studied the business, attended cooking school, and teamed up with a great chef. But it was his decision to hire Box Creative, a digital marketing and design firm, that brought everything together and created the ultimate Korean taco brand. The firm took Edward's idea, extracted its core values, and made it a reality. The marriage of Edward's dream and business savvy with the firm's creative talent is what made Korilla BBQ successful, and you need to do the same. Any idea or concept is only as good as its execution, and branding is no exception.

I advocate telling the customer exactly who and what you are in your logo. Consumers see so much information these days that you need to say everything in the few seconds you have their attention. It's best to just spell things out; the words *artisanal ice cream* should actually be included in the logo.

Finding a Graphic Designer

If you don't know any graphic designers, just type "graphic designer" into Google or search the term *logo* on Instagram or Behance. You'll find designers who specialize in logo design and branding. I recommend using someone local with whom you can work closely and who can continue to serve your future design needs. To find someone affordable, contact a local university with a graphic design department. Many students will work for you for little or no money to gain samples for their portfolios.

When you have some designs, go to friends and business associates for feedback. Ask them which designs they like best and why. Then combine that information with your own instincts to make your final choice. Nobody knows better than you which logo best represents your vision for your truck. So, trust your instincts and get cracking!

Creating Your Online Presence

Once you've created your logo, it's time to start building your online presence. Because you're a mobile operation, your website and Twitter account can serve as your home base and the best method for communicating with your customers.

Website

You should think of your website as your storefront where customers come to visit you. If you're mentioned on a local food blog, for example, it will include a link to your website, so readers can click through to find you. And, when they do, that's your chance to make a customer. So, not only should your website be a source of information, but, like your truck wrap (see Chapter 11), it needs to be an advertisement.

Make sure your website works in all major browsers, Internet Explorer, Firefox, Safari, and Chrome. If you hire a professional web designer to create your site, the designer should do this as part of their service.

Here's a list of everything a food truck website should include:

Menus. You should post your food and drink menus in text form. It makes them easily read on standard and mobile platforms, as well as by search engines.

An email list sign-up. Customers should be able to submit their names and email addresses to receive updates about your truck. Building an email database is critical for launching new trucks and promotions.

Don't forget to include sections for customers to include both their work and home locations when creating an email sign-up on your website. You can organize these locations by zip code or neighborhood; either way, the information is invaluable because it enables you to segment your list into areas so that you can target your communications. There's no reason to reach out to people uptown when you're parked downtown.

A Twitter link. The site must have a prominent link so that customers can follow you. The more followers you have, the more people will know where you're parked.

A Facebook link. Your site needs a link so that customers can become fans of your truck on Facebook, and you'll also need to link your Facebook and Twitter accounts, so all information simultaneously posts to each outlet.

A Foursquare link. You'll want users to "check in" to your Foursquare page.

An "About Us" section. Here is your chance to tell your story. Use this opportunity to create an emotional attachment between you and your customers. Tell them how you got to where you are and why.

A "Weekly Locations" section. If you have any permanent locations, list them here with the times and days you'll be there. Your locations will likely change often, so you be sure to keep your customers informed.

A Catering section. This section should include a *lead generator* form for catering inquiries, along with catering menus. A lead generator is a website form that customers can fill out to request specific information about your truck. It's one of the simplest and most effective ways to turn internet marketing into actual customer connections.

A Press section. This section should have links to all the latest mentions of your truck in the media, including the blogosphere. To increase the number of hits you get on search engines like Google and Bing, you should take the time to actually key in the press items as well as include direct links.

A "Contact Us" section. Here you'll provide your email, phone number, and office address, if you have one, so that your customers can contact you directly.

Other cool features include online ordering, a truck locator map, and images of your menu items.

You'll want to work with a web design company or an individual to build your site. I suggest spending no more than $5,000 to build your website, though it is possible to get a quality job done for less than half that amount.

Instagram and Twitter

Your Instagram and Twitter accounts will be the lifeblood of driving customers to your truck. These social networking, photo-sharing, and microblogging apps are the main ways your customers and followers will locate and connect to your truck.

Your Instagram and Twitter accounts will be the lifeblood of driving customers to your truck. These social-networking, photo-sharing, and micro-blogging apps are the main ways your customers and followers will locate and connect to your truck.

To get started, you need to create Instagram and Twitter accounts for your truck. Your account name should be as short as possible, while also clarifying exactly who you are. For example, the Kogi truck's Twitter is @kogibbq; Wafels & Dinges's is @waffletruck.

Building followers takes time, but you can start by inviting your friends and family to sign up for your posts and asking them to share them. Do everything you can to make every customer a follower; include a link to your social media accounts on your website, truck, and materials like napkins and menus.

Your tweets or social media posts shouldn't only be about your location. Be sure to tweet about funny things that happen on the truck, new menu items, family news—all these things will help to create interest in the day-to-day happenings of your business. You want to start a dialogue with your customers. If everything goes right, you'll begin to notice social posts from your customers, like "craving a taco from @kogibbq" or "going to get a Belgian waffle with whipped cream from @waffletruck". Not only is it great to hear, but it also can create action and drive other customers to you as all their followers can see it and click through to check out your truck.

Once you're operating, you should post on social media a minimum of three times a day—morning, afternoon, and early evening. More than that is okay, only as long as you're saying things that are relevant to your audience. Customers will tire of your posts if they're repetitive and annoying, so keep them brief and pertinent. The last thing you want to do is bombard your followers with boring posts, leading them to ignore you.

Some trucks create games using their Twitter account to attract customers. Trucks in Washington, D.C., aren't allowed to park unless there's already a line of people waiting for them, so they entice people to line up and do crazy dances before they'll park and start serving. Establishing games, customer rewards, or discounts through Twitter is a great way to further involve your customers in the experience of your truck.

Facebook and Foursquare

Facebook and Foursquare are also important marketing tools for your truck, though not as pertinent as Twitter and Instagram.

Because you're a business, you need to establish a Facebook *fan page,* which is a page on Facebook dedicated to promoting a commercial interest such as a business or celebrity. You gain Facebook fans through the same techniques that you use to attract Twitter followers. If you link your fan page to your Twitter account, your tweets will automatically repost on Facebook.

Foursquare is a location-based social networking site. People "check in" at different locations using their mobile devices, earning points when they do. You should link your Foursquare account to your Facebook and Twitter accounts.

You can use Instagram, Twitter, Facebook, and Foursquare to create a powerful virtual conversation about your truck—so much so that when people talk, it spreads like wildfire. The key to success is making sure everyone's saying good things. If you handle things right, going to your truck will become as much about eating there as it is about creating a social happening to share with friends, which is an important step in making your truck a success.

Planning a Launch Event

Now that you've established your virtual storefront and built the most awesome truck ever, it's time to begin planning a launch event. That sounds like fun, doesn't it? This is what you've always dreamed about—you and your staff getting saluted by all your friends and hanging with celebrities, all while chowing down on Grandma's famous meatballs.

Not so quick. Your launch event is a marketing tool, not a vanity fest. Keep in mind that first impressions are usually the most important.

The goal of your truck's launch is to make a splash in the local food press and generate buzz among your core clientele. My recommendation is to have two openings: one for press and core clients and another for the public.

The press event should take place in a scenic location where you can park without a problem. Plan for two hours of providing free food and drinks. Try to hire a local public relations agency for as little money as possible to write a press release and invite the most important members of the local press to the opening. Also, invite 50 of your closest friends—the ones who love and support you the most—you'll need their encouragement now more than ever. People with complimentary things to say to the press always help at these events.

Your food and service must be absolutely perfect for this event. If you have to bring on extra staff to make sure you have no problems, delays, or excuses, do it. You won't be cooking or serving at this event; you'll be speaking to the press and your guests, telling them all the reasons why your truck is special. You should prepare two or three stories you think would interest the press beforehand. For example, perhaps you source your one-of-a-kind meat from a butcher you've known since you were a kid, or maybe your truck is the first to ever have a special pizza oven onboard. Get creative and make the most of this opportunity. You'll never get a second chance to make a first impression.

Your public event should be focused on driving sales. After your press event is complete, you'll want to announce when you'll be open to the public. In conjunction with this announcement, you should create a call to action—something that inspires customers to act when they hear you're going to be opening. Maybe it's live entertainment or complimentary food to your first 100 customers. Whatever it is, it should attract crowds to your truck from Day one. Launch this promotion with an event during a time period you know will be busy, and cast your new product in the best possible light. It should get your business rolling, generate some cash, and pique people's interest right from the beginning. Some of the best advice I've ever received is to "throw everything you have at an opening". You never want to hold back when introducing your product, so use everything in your arsenal to drive interest and get the buzz going.

Don't forget to have business cards on hand. From your opening party through the first six months of operations, no one should leave your truck without your business card in hand. In exchange, you should get their email address or phone number. Within 24 hours of their truck visit, you should send them a thank-you email. This type of personal touch will go a long way toward creating goodwill for you and your business.

Reaching Out to Bloggers

Food trucks are different than restaurants, and food bloggers, also known as *influencers*, aren't the same as traditional restaurant reviewers. Why? Food bloggers can say anything they want—and they will. Anyone from the most popular food writer to your neighbor can have their very own food blog.

In a way, food blogs are to writing what food trucks are to restaurants. Culturally, they go hand-in-hand. Someone who loves to write and loves food can start a food blog; someone who loves to cook and loves food can start a food truck. Technology and ingenuity have lowered the barrier to entry more than ever before. If the food bloggers love you, it's a blessing for your truck, but if they don't, you'd better watch out. You need to put the percentages in your favor and play nice with them from the beginning.

The first thing you should do is reach out to local bloggers personally. They're anti-establishment, so as much as a PR firm can help, you personally reaching out to local bloggers to represent your truck is always a plus. You should be able to find the writer or editor's email address on the main page of most blogs, or you can direct message them on their Instagram page. Next, I would do everything in my power to have them sample your food prior to your launch. Ask for their feedback on the product. If they love it, that's great. If they think it can be improved, then improve it. The key here is that you're getting them vested in your success.

Now, invite those bloggers to your private opening event. Even better, get them to invite their readers to it. And, if you can, offer their readers a benefit when dining at your truck, such as a free cookie or a soda with their orders. Anything you can do to get their readers to be part of your army of supporters is great. The people who write and read about food do so because they're passionate about it. It's in your best interest to get them on your team because they'll tell everyone they know how much they love your product. And, it definitely doesn't hurt to give them a shout out on Twitter. A little love goes a long way.

If a blogger writes negative things about you, ignore them. Engaging them in a fight adds attention and validity to their claims. Blogs are trying to gain readership; the less you do to help that cause, the less important you are to them. And, never forget, you'd have much bigger problems if people weren't writing about you at all.

Working with the Mainstream Press

You aren't in this business to have just any truck; you want to have *the* truck—the next Kogi! If you've played your cards right, you have a great website, had an awesome opening, and the blogosphere is buzzing almost as much as your Twitter feed. But how do you get the attention of your local news? Magazines? Newspapers?

After you reach out to the bloggers, your next step is to go after the mainstream press. For food trucks, bloggers are the necessity, while mainstream press is a luxury. PR firms can help, but they're only as good as what you give them to work with. You need to come up with the great ideas that will attract attention and highlight your truck as special. The way to get to the mainstream press is to do everything in your power to establish great relationships with writers. Once you've established these relationships, focus all your efforts on pitching them one great idea.

Reaching out to writers is as easy as surfing the internet. All writers have their information online, and most can be reached through their publication's website. Despite your trepidations, the truth is that writers need things to write about to make a living. They're always looking for good stories for their publications.

You need to become an insider. Invite writers to your truck and become friendly with them. Park outside their publication's building every Wednesday and bring them lunch. Make them aware that you exist and that you are a quality vendor. It's amazing what people will do for you when you're genuinely nice to them.

You also have to do your part. You need to come up with your big idea—the thing that makes you and your truck so interesting and special. What about the creation of a special menu item like a $100 ice cream sundae with gold leaf and the rarest cocoa nibs in the world, or celebrating your ten thousandth meatball sold by creating the biggest meatball ever? You could campaign to have your chicken wings declared the best in the state, or maybe you could take a page out of the Nathan's book and hold an annual hot dog–eating contest. The key is to do something bold that accentuates you and your product. After all, there's no point in having a hot dog–eating contest if you sell pizza.

Remain focused on one thing and scream only when people are listening. Whatever idea you choose, stick with it. Make it your signature and don't give up until you've pitched it to every writer in the county. And, don't forget, timing is everything. It doesn't make sense to try to get attention for your product during the Super Bowl when the big advertisers are spending every dollar they can to maximize the attention they're getting. Look for opportunities when the news cycle is slow or is complementary to your product. For instance, Cinco de Mayo would be a great time to launch a special taco for your taco truck. It's when the press is looking to write about other things related to Mexican American culture.

Remember, your job with the mainstream press is to recognize opportunities and make the most of them.

Treating Every Day As an Event

I'm sure you've realized by now that there's always going to be something to do; some aspect of your truck business to perfect. It's going to take numerous days and nights of hard work for your truck to become a well-oiled machine. It would be very easy to start getting lazy—just doing the same thing over and over again—but that's not an option.

Your energy and passion needs to be infectious to ignite the fire in your staff and customers. You need to make every day on your truck an event—it has to be special. Every single day, you and your staff must be motivated to become better than the day before. Whose job is it to make that a reality? Yours and yours alone.

To make every day an event, you need to add little things to the truck experience that change every time a customer visits. Maybe Tuesday is fried chicken day—the only day you serve your special recipe. Wednesday you could offer free lunch to the first 20 people who reply on Twitter, and at the end of the week, you could have a DJ play outside your truck to celebrate the coming weekend.

To make this a reality, you must apply yourself to create great programming. Take the time to sit with your staff and think of ways to make every day special. Get a calendar and don't put it down until you schedule something different for each day. Create customized promotions that will set your truck apart from the competition, and dedicate yourself to executing them every week.

Making Social Media Your Friend

After you've decided on your programming and promotions, you need to utilize your website and social networking tools to promote these happenings to your customer base. If not, you're the tree that falls in the woods: it made a noise, but no one heard it. You need to activate all your promotions through these tools. They'll be the impetus for creating chatter and dialogue on your Twitter feed and Facebook page. And, this chatter is what leads to customers eating at your truck.

Bloggers should receive news of your promotions in advance of their release on your Twitter. This is because press outlets will provide you more exposure for the promotion, but they will only publish it if the info hasn't been released elsewhere. If they choose to release it on their blogs, I advocate making people sign up to follow you on Twitter to redeem specials and promotions. By doing this, you will gain direct access to the blog's readers and become less dependent on their coverage over time. Even if the blog passes on including the information, you've still established goodwill by offering it to them. The bottom line is that you must be strategic when utilizing your social networking tools, your website, the press, and your email database to disseminate information on your promotions. Doing these things means you maximize your return on investment.

Only speak when you have something to say. Social networking, email lists, websites, and press contacts are great, but only if they're used respectfully. Be mindful of how often you're sending out messages and what you're saying when you do. If you don't use them with care, people will tune you out. Your assets, then, aren't worth anything.

Creating Strong Product and Personal Relationships

The world seems to get more impersonal every day. Products are mass produced and less artisanal. The revolution in the food truck business is a reaction to these factors. Your job as a food truck operator is to break through; make everything about your business personal. Know every customer's personal preferences and ask about their lives. Get them invested in your success by sharing your passion. Your product needs to be as personal as your relationships. The way it's prepared needs to mean something to you. The ingredients you use must be ones you personally choose. Most of all, your food has to taste great, every single time.

Why am I saying this in a chapter on marketing? It's because all the marketing in the world won't get you anywhere if you aren't giving your customers a great product and experience. Remember the importance of experiential follow through in creating a grand brand: promise your customers something great to get them to the truck, and deliver something even better to keep them coming back.

Setting Up
Your Office

All small business owners need an office, and food truckers are no exception. Your business may be on wheels, but it's important to establish a fixed space in which you'll organize all your administrative paperwork and records. With little expense, you can set up an office that serves the needs of your business, keeps your data safe and organized, and helps you run your business efficiently from one central and convenient location.

In this chapter, I show you where to set up your office, what to put in it, and how to personalize a system that keeps you in control of your important information. I explain how to determine your communication needs and design a payroll system that works for you. Finally, I show you where to seek help if you get lost along the way.

Deciding Where to Put Your Office

As a new small business owner, you're going to have a lot of important documents and digital information to organize, including financial and business records, supplier receipts, inventory lists, expense and cash flow projections, and tax forms, just to name a few. Keeping all of this in order is crucial to running a successful business. You don't want to split your administrative data between your laptop and the passenger seat floor of the truck; you need to establish a secure and organized space from which to conduct business while your truck is parked for the night.

When deciding where to set up your office, you must first ask yourself who will be using it most. If you're a one-man show, you're probably the one responsible for all the administrative and accounting duties, including payroll, bookkeeping, ordering supplies, and paying your purveyors. In this case, you can set up a small office in your own home.

Choose a space that's quiet, private, and large enough for you to sit and work comfortably for several hours at a time. You'll need a desk, a computer, and plenty of storage space for your records. Your office doesn't need to be fancy, but it should feel professional, organized, comfortable, and, if possible, inspirational. If you have kids, be sure to set boundaries with them so that they know not to enter your office without your permission or tamper with any of your business-related documents.

Don't store your business or financial records on the family computer. Purchase a separate computer or subscribe to a cloud service, and back up your files regularly to protect your important information. Storing your information on a home computer makes it too vulnerable. Remember, should the IRS audit you, they can look into your past for years, so good record keeping is critical to protecting your business.

If you have a partner, your home might not be the best place for your business office. It should be conveniently located for both of you and large enough for both of you to sit comfortably and work side by side. If either of you already own a related business, you may want to work out of that office. Wherever you choose to set up shop, make sure that you and your partner are equally satisfied with the decision.

Here's a quick list of the basic necessities you'll need for your office:

* **Computer or laptop.** Keep things simple. You'll only need one that supports a basic word processor, a spreadsheet application such as Excel and bookkeeping software like QuickBooks, if you choose to handle the accounting yourself. You should spend no more than $1,500 dollars on this computer.

* **Cloud Storage Service.** A cloud storage service enables you to store your important files and documents on the internet and can be a good option for your truck business. It can save you space, protect your documents, and cost very little. Plus, you can access the documents anywhere as long as you have an internet connection.

* **Internet.** You'll need a high-speed internet connection to quickly communicate with your staff and vendors, send out the week's schedule, and manage your food truck's website and social networking applications.

* **External hard drive.** You'll need at least 256 GB of memory to back up your important data. You can purchase a high-quality and compact backup drive for less than $50.

* **Telephone.** You'll find information on company communications later in this chapter. If you're using your cellphone for your business, make sure your voicemail reflects it. Your image as a respectable and established business is important to those who choose to work with you. Your voicemail should say the name of your company, provide an alternate method of connection such as email, and provide your web address.

* **Calculator.** Get an old-fashioned one with a paper roll that provides a hardcopy of your math.

* **Envelopes and stamps.** Even though you'll be using electronic communication as much as possible, you'll need a supply of legal envelopes and postage stamps.

* **Printer.** Save yourself space and money by investing in a two-in-one fax and printer. It's a good idea to get a unit that also scans *and* makes copies.

* **Ink and paper.** Stock up on printer paper and ink; you'll be printing menus, checks, memos, fax confirmations, spreadsheets, and reports for your own records every week.

* **File cabinet or storage tub.** You don't need anything massive, but you can expect to accumulate many hundreds of pages of records that you need to file. Be sure to label each drawer or plastic tub so that you can easily retrieve documents when you need them.

* **Legal forms.** Keep a supply of W-4 and I-9 tax forms, employee manuals and contracts, and copies of all your own business contracts and insurance policies.

* **Safe.** Keep your cash protected in a small, discreet safe until your next opportunity to visit the bank. Don't keep money in the safe longer than necessary and *never* leave it in the truck overnight. Take care to limit the number of people who have access to the combination.

* **Basic office goods.** Stock up on pens, pencils, legal pads, staples, paper clips, folders, rubber bands, and highlighters. Make sure you have a three-hole punch and a few strong three-ring binders to help keep things organized.

Creating a Communications Hub

As the administrative headquarters of your food truck business, your office must be equipped with the appropriate communication technologies. Vendors, clients, employees, investors, accountants, lawyers, and (hopefully) members of the media need to be able to contact and exchange information with you quickly, easily, and in a variety of ways.

The elaborateness of your communications setup will depend on the complexity of your concept and your expansion expectations; if you plan to have a fleet of trucks, you'll need more infrastructure to monitor the trucks' locations, supply needs, and other necessary components of a larger operation.

Telephone

Running a business requires that you spend many hours on the phone every week. While you'll likely be conducting business via your personal cellphone for much of that time, I advocate having an official landline in your office.

Any standard telephone should be more than sufficient for your needs. Be sure to subscribe to call waiting and voicemail services for both lines and record a very professional outgoing message. You may want to consider a telephone unit with built-in speakers and conference call capabilities, so that you can conduct meetings over the phone with one or multiple vendors, lawyers, investors, or partners.

Internet Services

Internet access is crucial for any modern office operation. A web presence, as discussed in Chapter 9, is a critical tool for expanding awareness of your truck and products. Your vendors, partners, accountant, lawyer, and anyone else with whom you conduct business will expect to be able to contact you via email, which is often more efficient than picking up the telephone or mailing a letter.

Many of your purveyors will allow you to place orders with them via email or through their websites. You'll find that it makes for a much cleaner operation; receipts are automatically emailed to you, and you'll spend considerably less time on the phone. Email also offers an alternative way for customers to contact you with feedback, questions, requests, and catering orders. You'll find that when you provide the option of contacting you via email, more customers will reach out to you than if you only offer a telephone number.

Proactively accumulate customer email addresses, so that you can send out special promotional offers, truck alerts, and general advertising materials. You can offer your customers an incentive for registering with you, such as a free drink or a raffle ticket. The more email addresses you can accumulate and the better they are organized, the more effectively you'll be able to market the happenings surrounding your truck business.

Tablets, like iPads, are incredibly powerful computers in a compact, portable design. You may find it worthwhile to invest in one of these and synchronize it with your main office computer or laptop. It will give you access to all your business information, instantly record customer email addresses, update your inventory spreadsheets, and even place orders from your truck or anywhere, on the go.

Fax

Fax machines remain an essential staple for any business. Many vendors still prefer that you place and confirm orders with them via fax, and you can expect to send and receive legal forms by fax as well. If you plan on sending out your catering menu (and you should) to potential and interested customers, fax or email are the preferred method of delivery.

Handling Payroll and Records

Calculating and distributing payroll can be very time consuming for most businesses. Your food truck probably won't have more than four or five employees, so outsourcing payroll to an expensive service company isn't necessary. You can do it yourself. You can do it efficiently, too, if you follow the procedures laid out in this section.

First, you need to decide on a pay period—the number of days after which a paycheck will be issued. For most businesses, a pay period is either one or two weeks.

There are benefits and drawbacks to both the one- and two-week models. If you pay your employees every week, your payroll expense will remain consistent from week to week, but you'll spend twice the time and energy calculating hours, running numbers, and issuing checks than you would if you paid them every other week. A two-week pay period will save you time and energy, but your expense will jump from nothing to quite a large amount every other week, so you'll have to make sure you have the funds to cover payroll when it comes due.

To calculate and distribute your payroll, follow these simple steps:

1. **Open a payroll account.** You need to have a separate bank account that *only* covers payroll checks. Link it to your main business account so you can transfer money into it online, which will save you countless trips to the bank.

2. **Calculate the total hours worked for the pay period.** You have a small staff, so it shouldn't take you more than 10 minutes to calculate and double check the hours. Have your employees sign in and out on a printed schedule every day they work or on your chosen digital platform. Confirm their check-in and check-out times as they do this and initial their names. If you're on top of this during the week, you'll be able to reliably tally their total hours for payroll with ease.

3. **Tally the gross pay for the week.** Multiply their total hours by their hourly wage to calculate each employee's gross pay.

4. **Subtract taxes and FICA.** Be sure every new hire fills out all the necessary legal paperwork, including a W-4 tax form. Use that information to subtract the appropriate withholding tax, along with Social Security contributions. A payroll company can help you with these calculations if necessary.

5. **Transfer the gross pay to the payroll account.** Once you write a check and transfer money into the payroll account, you must consider that money spent, regardless of how long it takes an employee to cash his or her check.

Your employees will receive net pay unless they are being compensated as an independent contractor. You are responsible for paying the balance, tax payments, and FICA to the government in an interval determined by your accountant.

6. **Print and issue checks.** Each check should indicate the gross pay and total number of hours worked, with all tax and Social Security deductions itemized. Distribute checks at a set time on payday and require a signed confirmation from each employee when they receive their checks. Never fall behind on payroll; always have the paychecks ready at the scheduled time on the scheduled day. You can, of course, pay your employees in cash if you wish, but paying by check has the benefit of leaving a paper trail and verifiable proof that you issued payroll.

Keeping Records

It's crucial that you properly store certain documents, receipts, and information for your business records. You're required by law to keep some of these records. Others will help protect you if you are audited or if someone disputes a charge or bill.

Keep indefinitely all of your financial statements, accounting records, cash and credit card receipts, balance sheets, and contracts of any kind. You should keep tax records, invoices, bank statements, health inspection reports, and payroll records for no less than 10 years.

Remember that the more records you save, the safer you'll be in the long run. Keep in mind that when you're choosing your office location, you'll easily fill a small filing cabinet over the next few years. While backing up your digital files onto an external hard drive is important, it isn't enough. You'll also need hard copies of your records in the event of a tax audit or lawsuit.

Getting Outside Help

Knowing the ins and outs of local laws and regulations is crucial for any entrepreneur. It's very common and advisable for new and seasoned business owners alike to seek guidance from lawyers and accountants as they decide on a business structure, seek permits, and design their business plans. Investing in the expertise of these specialists is something you should be prepared to do if you're starting out with little or no experience in building a business.

You'll want to find a lawyer or accountant who has experience and a proven track record in the food industry in your city. If you know people who own restaurants or food trucks in your area, ask them to recommend someone with whom they have worked. If you're approaching one of these specialists directly, ask them for references and follow up on them. You want advisers who have helped business owners save money, navigate bureaucracy, and make sound decisions about their businesses.

A qualified lawyer can help you understand local laws and regulations and assist you in obtaining all the necessary permits for your food truck. A lawyer can draw up or review contracts, including partnership agreements, and register your business as a sole proprietorship, partnership, or corporation. An experienced lawyer can also provide you with valuable industry contacts.

If you're having difficulty understanding some of the financial concepts involved in developing your business plan and managing the accounting records for your truck, consider hiring an accountant to help guide you through the process. He or she can help determine whether your concept will be profitable and suggest the best way to structure your company. Once you've launched your business, you can retain your accountant to continue managing your weekly and monthly finances to whatever extent necessary.

Lawyers and accountants can become very pricey. Many charge an hourly rate of $200 to $300 that can quickly add up to monstrous fees. It's important that you speak to them up front about the charges prior to engaging their services. I would recommend that you ask them about setting a fee for the work being done rather than their working on an hourly basis. It will help you budget appropriately, and they'll be committed to finishing the job, no matter how long it takes.

The bottom line when working with accountants and lawyers is to choose people you feel comfortable with and trust. These professionals will be handling your most sensitive documents and financial matters. You want to find people who provide great advice and security in these important matters.

3

GETTING ROAD READY

Execution is everything in the food truck business. You only have a small space, so you need to maximize efficiency. And efficiency, speed, quality, and low waste are what lead to profitability in the food truck game. How do you become efficient? Through proper kitchen layout, great design, flawless systems, and many other things I cover in this part of the book.

But even if you have great systems, you still need the right people to execute them. Locating the best employees for your truck could be the most important step in the entire process. I help you get your staff "on the boat," as well as get the best performance out of them.

Last but definitely not least, I talk about what you need to do to make sure your truck is safe. Food safety through proper preparation is vital to protect your customers, employees, and business. The slightest sign of foodborne illness might put your business on life support.

Setting Up the "House"

In most hospitality businesses, there's a front and a back of house. The front of house refers to the areas and employees that deal with customers: dining areas, front desk, servers, and hosts. The back of house refers to the areas and employees the customers rarely see: kitchen, prep areas, cooks, and so on. In general, these areas require vastly different skill sets and personality types. Some people are great at slicing tomatoes but not so good at talking to customers; they're clearly back-of-house people. Others look beautiful and are great at service but can't even fry an egg—these are front-of-house people. Neither of those kinds of people will work for your food truck. You won't have the luxury.

Understanding Your Unique Situation

When it comes to employees for your truck, you need individuals who have an understanding of both your front and back of house. You won't be able to indulge the extravagance of hiring a great cook with a terrible personality. If he's in the truck yelling at the other cooks, your customers will see and hear him, which will negatively affect your customers' experience. And, if that surly chef has to take over the window while you go get supplies, you're in big trouble. You have one truck and one house. There's no such thing as hiding in the back.

Everyone who works for you needs to serve multiple functions. Your employees must be able to work the grill *and* the window. More importantly, you need to apply the one-house philosophy to all aspects of your truck. Your exterior and interior design and how you deal with customers must be put together so that all elements work together to add to the total experience.

In a restaurant or hotel, for example, staff can collect the garbage in an area away from customer view and take it out a service entrance. You don't have that option on your truck. You must discreetly collect garbage and quickly remove it from the truck. A day's worth of garbage in a small truck can become an issue very quickly, chasing away customers with its odor and creating health concerns from cross contamination.

In this chapter, I discuss how you set up your house, which is a very important step in the creation of your food truck. Let's not waste any time getting to it.

Designing the Exterior of Your Truck

The exterior design of your food truck is critical to your success. It serves two purposes: marketing and functionality.

The outside of your truck is the ultimate advertisement for what you're selling. Just as the outside of a restaurant sets the tone for a customer's dining experience, the exterior of your truck does the same thing for your customers. The difference from a bricks-and-mortar restaurant is that your exterior is constantly on the move. The more you drive, the more you advertise. Your truck design must immediately attract the attention of the consumer. And after you grab their attention, you need to convey some important details immediately:

* Your food truck's name

* What kind of food you serve

* Your Twitter handle

Within five seconds of seeing your truck, customers need to recognize that they want what you're selling and know how to get it.

There's no point of having the most beautifully designed truck if nobody knows what you do or where to find you. That's why there are so many trucks with bold and exciting exterior designs. It isn't because food truckers are the most artistic people in the world; their flair is a matter of necessity. Your truck is a mobile billboard, and you need to utilize it to make a statement and attract customers.

The back, right, and left panels of your truck must all include your logo, the type of product you're serving, your Twitter name, your website address, and your phone number. Your job is to find a truck design that includes all of it in a tasteful exterior design. Your truck's name should be sized at 100 percent, the type of food you serve sized at 75 percent, and your contact information at 30 to 50 percent, depending on what looks best.

You have two options for exterior decoration: paint or vinyl wrap. I consider the pros and cons of each option in the following sections.

Paint

Painting your truck is the cheapest way to go, but is generally less effective. To get maximum marketing value from painting, you would need to find someone extremely talented. A talented artist is probably going to be pricey, which defeats the whole purpose of using the cheaper design method.

If you do choose to paint your truck, use contrasting colors for your base and logo. If your truck is black, for instance, use a bright color like fluorescent pink or green for the logo. The best way to add your logo to a painted truck is to either use a stencil or have the logo printed as a sticker at your local print shop. Whichever method you choose, make sure the logo is bold. You don't want to get lost in the crowd.

Painting your truck should cost less than $2,500.

Vinyl Wrap

Truck wraps are the most cost-effective way to maximize the exposure of your brand with the design of your truck.

The company you choose to create the wrap should have an in-house designer who can assist you. If not, reach out to fellow truckers whose designs you admire and ask who wrapped their truck. An experienced designer will understand which areas will be exposed and where seams are located in order to fully maximize the wrap. And, by working with a graphic designer who's done this kind of work before, you'll be able to create any imaginable design. The design fee is usually around $500.

The designer must use high-resolution or vector images to create your truck wrap, with the printing done using a very high-dpi printer. Your customers will see your truck both from far away and close up, so the design must be recognizable from a distance and look like a custom paint job up close. Ask to see a proof prior to the printing of your design, so you'll know exactly what it will look like when it's applied. Review the proof very carefully; you'll have to live with any mistakes you don't catch at this point. Make sure you have the opportunity to sign off on the design before your wrap is installed on the truck.

Not all vinyl wraps are of equal quality. You can get wraps for as little as $1,500, but the vinyl is likely to be thin with no protective laminate coating. These cheaper wraps will begin to peel rather quickly and are much more time consuming to remove.

A thick high-quality wrap with a protective laminate costs anywhere from $4,500 to $5,000. Laminate enhances the appearance of your truck, while also protecting it from fading and scratches.

Protect your investment by choosing a thick 3M wrap with laminate. Your truck will continue to look brand new year after year if you go for the high-quality version. Customers will be attracted to the pristine look of your rig, so a better wrap should lead to more sales. And, if you choose to sell or trade-in your truck in the future, a better-quality wrap will lead to a higher resale or trade-in value. Cheaper wraps are harder to remove and can cause damage to the vehicle.

According to *Outdoor Advertising Magazine,* mobile billboards have a 97-percent recall rate, and 99 percent of survey respondents said they thought mobile advertising was more effective than traditional outdoor advertising. Geopath says that during a single month, a truck can give between 1 and 4 million impressions to potential consumers. Trust me when I say that your vehicle wrap is your most valuable advertising outlet. Don't let that opportunity go to waste.

Window

While there's no standard window size for food trucks I recommend as large a window as possible. The larger your window, the more involved your customers will feel and the more people you can serve at a time. It's always best to have a window on each side, so you have more parking possibilities. If you have two windows, you'll probably need to go with smaller versions than if you had just one. It's a decision you'll have to make based on your own preference and what works best for your concept.

Awning

After you deal with your window size, you'll need to decide what type of awning you want. Most trucks come with a stainless steel panel that you secure in the upward position when your truck is operating. It acts as an awning when you're open and a security cover when you're not. For the most part, you won't really have much for people to steal on your truck. The cooking equipment is heavy and bolted down, and your materials are refilled on a daily basis. I feel the stainless steel cover is unnecessary and suggest replacing it with an aesthetically pleasing awning that you can extend when you park. You can purchase these types of awnings at your local home supply store or from an awning specialist for $1,500 to $2,000. The awning should cover the length of your truck's window and be incorporated into your design.

Drink Fridge

Your drinks fridge or cooler should be accessible to customers from the outside of your truck, so they can reach in and make their choices. This alleviates the need for internal storage and removes one step from the serving process. Make sure the storage container is deep enough to store and cool a sufficient number of beverages for multiple hours of service, and take into account that ice will be an operating expense. Additionally, with the beverages outside, it's important that you make sure all beverages are purchased.

Exterior Menu Holder

You should place a plastic menu holder outside the truck. Having printed menus handy limits the number of customer questions during the ordering process, especially at peak times. Encouraging customers to take menu copies with them also acts as a form of advertising for potential customers and encourages take-out orders. Place the menu holder in a spot that's easily accessible even during busy times.

Menu Board

Your menu board should be located on the outside of your truck to the left of your window. It should be made out of plastic poster board and be large enough to be read from at least 10 feet away. Refer to the menu design information in Chapter 3 when designing the layout and content of your board. The most important point to remember is the item you want to sell the most of should be in the top-right corner.

After you've designed the menu, you'll need to bring it to a printer who specializes in printing on plastic, which will hold up for a long time when mounted very securely on the outside of your truck. This board needs to withstand weather and travel while still maintaining its shine and splendor. It's one of your main sales tools, so make sure it's a beautiful representation of your product.

The Point of Sale System

Say so long to the days of Grandma sitting behind the cash register monitoring the day's take. Nowadays, point of sale (POS) systems (your digital cash registers) manage inventory, process credit cards, calculate food-cost percentages, and handle ordering. Many of them even monitor your business every minute you're operating by generating real-time reports.

Old-fashioned cash registers or manual sales monitoring techniques are subject to human error, leading to inefficiencies, potential theft, and cash loss. A POS system is essential to running a healthy modern hospitality business. Yes, they cost a little more in the beginning, but they pay for themselves quickly by saving you money and giving you peace of mind. A quality POS system not only gives you insights into what your customers are ordering, it also tells you on what days and times they're ordering it, and if they made any substitutions.

POS systems are preloaded with basic reporting options that can assist in monitoring your truck's performance. If you want a report that provides hourly sales breakdowns by item and compares them on a month-to-month basis, so you can monitor growth, your POS system can do it. Here's an overview of the types of performance reports a POS system can help you with:

* **Basic reports.** The system can report on the average spend per person, how much of each item is selling, and percentage of people buying sides and beverages with their orders.

* **Trends.** Monitor the trends within your business; for example, are falafel sales decreasing and gyro sales increasing? Maybe it has something to do with people wanting to eat proteins and not fried foods. You'd better know, because it's affecting your business, and your POS can tell you.

* **Cost centers.** The system will create them for different workers and meals. For example, maybe you do more business when Jason is working the window and Isaac is on the grill? You can use this info to maximize your revenues.

These reports should be more than enough to cover a small operation, but you can also work with your POS company to create customized reports specifically for your business.

A simple POS system for a truck should cost around $5,000, including a terminal with a printer for the kitchen and all necessary installation and setup. Also, you should budget for service and maintenance fees, which for an operation of this size should be less than $50 to $100 per month. To save money, try purchasing a used system from restaurants that are going out of business or through websites such as Craigslist.

Companies like Micros, Aloha, and Squirrel dominate the POS system market. They offer technologically advanced systems and are adding capabilities daily. These systems have endless possibilities and options for customization, most of which aren't necessary for your purposes.

Tablet Systems

Tablet computers offers a much better solution for mobile hospitality businesses. Many companies are making iPad-based POS systems, such as Square, GoPayment, and Clover, that are much more affordable and offer many of the same features as the more advanced systems. You can get a tablet system for between $500 and $2,500 plus a subscription fee of $30 to $50 per month. Try for a system setup for $1,500 with a minimal subscription fee inclusive of the cost of an iPad, iPhone, or similar tablet computer. These usually come with cash drawers and printers and generally take up much less space than traditional systems.

Because social media is so important to your business, you'll definitely need some type of onboard computer. The best option for food truck operators right now is a smartphone, such as an iPhone or Android. These phones have applications that enable you to post on Twitter, Facebook, and Foursquare directly. You can also use one of these phones as the direct number for your truck. Other options include a laptop with WiFi capabilities or a tablet computer, such as an iPad.

Credit Cards

In the modern world, you must accept credit cards. While you will incur some processing fees, simple solutions like Square and Shopify make it easy to take cards from a mobile phone or simple tablet-based system. Just make sure you account for needing internet access and ensure that you calculate fees when pricing your menu items. If digital payments are allowed, you can assume the majority of your transactions will be done that way. On the upside, it makes tracking everything easy and keeps pilfering to a minimum.

When you accept credit cards, you have to set up a merchant account with your bank so that you can accept payment from both credit and debit cards. You can handle your credit card processing through your e-commerce or POS system. You'll also need to contact a credit card processing organization, such as Square, Shopify, or Authorize.net and sign up for an account with them. Numerous kinds of plans exist, so be sure to comparison shop at least three processing companies to find the best rate based on your expected volume of sales.

Don't just look at the transaction fees when choosing a credit card processing company. Some companies lure customers with low rates and hide charges like administration fees in the back end, which makes them more expensive than the normal rates. And, most of these processor agreements automatically renew unless you specifically state not to, so be sure to remove that clause from your contract.

Setting Up the Kitchen

The next step in setting up your house is organizing the design of your kitchen for efficiency. By this, I mean ensuring that you have enough space to prep and plate your food quickly, while also maintaining the quality of your product. It requires military-style organization and precision.

Organization

The first step is making sure that everything within your on-truck kitchen is located in the right place. The storage of your serving materials must be in the same area or right next to where you're plating. You don't want to waste time walking to the back of the truck to get buns and containers every time a burger comes off the grill.

The same rule applies to the way you organize your refrigerated items. If you're making cheeseburgers, you want the cheese in the refrigerator closest to the grill. It's common sense, but not everyone thinks about it.

If you haven't noticed it yet, there are so many moving parts in the food truck business that it's easy to make silly mistakes. If you don't fix these issues immediately, they'll snowball, making day-to-day operations unbearable. Pay attention to details.

Here's a checklist of things to consider when organizing your kitchen for prep and plating:

* Figure out which areas of the kitchen will be used most and least, based on your menu mix.

* Ensure that you have enough refrigeration for a full day's service. If you need to sell 100 hamburgers a day to make money, you'd better have enough refrigeration to accommodate ingredients for those 100 hamburgers every day.

* Make sure the prep area and the storage of prepared materials is close enough to where you're cooking to be quickly restocked during service.

* Make sure there's a clear line of sight and speech between the sales window and the kitchen; the person running the window also acts as your *expeditor.* An expeditor is the person on the truck in charge of organizing the orders. Once an order is taken, the expeditor monitors its progress by coordinating with the kitchen. Then she checks the order to ensure that it's prepared properly prior to delivery to the customer.

* Make sure the cooks have easy access to the plates and take-out containers.

Job Assignments

The bottom line is that everyone on the rig should be able to get his job done without hindering anyone else's ability to get her job done. The best way to figure that out is by creating detailed descriptions of every task needing to be completed by each worker on your truck. Then you can sit down with your initial kitchen design and begin to flesh out the process that each employee must go through to complete his or her job. As you analyze the processes, you'll be able to identify potential bottlenecks and begin to place things in the best possible locations. If you take the time to do this, you'll limit the number of issues you'll run into during your first months of operation.

Don't forget that you need to take into account local regulations. Cities like Chicago have laws that don't allow for cooking on the truck. Windy City food trucks are only allowed to sell pre-prepared or packaged items; even chopping of vegetables is prohibited. Check with your local health department to determine exactly what's legal and what isn't in terms of your kitchen. It could have major impact on how you choose to prepare your food and how you lay out your kitchen. You might've been planning to make sandwiches to order on your truck in Chicago, but now you know that all of your sandwiches have to be packaged in your commissary.

Chicago's original food truck, Chicago All Fired Up, made its way onto the Windy City's streets through some legal maneuvering. Years ago, owner Troy Marcus Johnson convinced the health inspector to approve his truck as a restaurant. Since then, he's been selling baby back ribs and jerk chicken from his truck and cooking them on board. Who knows how he got past the law, but it's great for Chicagoans looking for late-night eats.

Creating an Efficient Workflow

In order to establish an efficient workflow, you need to utilize the assembly line. Assign each truck worker a particular job in the process of getting out orders with ease. The employees can assist one another, but only if they've already fully completed their assigned tasks in the process.

Here's how it works:

1. The employee in charge of the window takes the customer's order, provides him or her with a receipt or order number, and then passes along the order to the kitchen, manually or automatically through the POS.

2. The kitchen then receives the order, and one or two employees begin preparing the food. (In some cases, the cooking process has already begun before the order is taken because the items take longer to fully prepare than you want the customer to wait.) The cooks monitor the order and are in constant communication with the window worker/expeditor, who can update the customer on order delivery.

3. When the food is prepared, the cook plates it for serving and hands it to the expeditor.

4. The expeditor then checks the order and gives it to the customer.

Each truck's system will likely vary slightly from the preceding process, but overall, the process is very similar. The key is to maintain the flow and not create any bottlenecks in the line. If one worker in the process is taking longer than the other members of the team, the assembly line comes to a halt.

Everyone needs to be equally skilled in their part of the process, or the system doesn't work. Skilled employees, combined with fanatic organization and attention to detail, will make your line efficient and consistent. However, unless your setup for the front and back of house are organized correctly, you'll likely have issues way before you even involve truck workers.

Hiring and Managing Staff

Danny Meyer is the spiritual leader of the hospitality business. He has achieved incredible financial success and esteem through his restaurants like Shake Shack and Gramercy Tavern, and books like *Setting the Table*. However, Meyer's contribution transcends hospitality. Since opening Union Square Cafe in 1985, he has transformed into an evangelist of sorts. He preaches and teaches "enlightened hospitality"—the understanding and application of how the delivery of a product makes its recipient feel. Meyer understands that good service—the technical delivery of a product—has become an expectation. Therefore, culture and experience have become the true differentiators. As he puts it, "It's all about how you make the customer feel." Sound familiar? That sounds like emotional generosity to me.

The most important step in creating a hospitable culture is hiring the right people. Meyer calls these people "51 percenters"—team members with a high-hospitality quotient (HQ) and whose skills are 49-percent technical and 51-percent emotional. You can teach someone a technical skill, but it's much more difficult to teach emotional skills. The core skills Meyer looks for are curiosity about learning, an exceptional work ethic, and a high degree of empathy, as well as self-awareness, optimism, kindness, and integrity. As Meyer explains it,

> By putting your employees first, you have happier employees, which then leads to a higher HQ. A higher HQ leads to happy customers, which benefits all the stakeholders. The cycle is virtuous, not linear, because the stakeholders all impact each other.

All businesses are dependent on people. That's because great experiences only occur when one person connects with another, when someone is emotionally generous. When the person on the receiving end of the product or service leaves happier and more fulfilled, the transaction was a success. It's precisely this emotional connection that increases positive sentiment and eventually grows into a successful brand or movement.

Doing this once is quite simple. Almost anyone, for example, can throw one really great dinner party. But when you multiply that one interaction by hundreds, thousands, or even millions, that's where problems begin. How can you possibly make all those connections meaningful and memorable? Organizations like Meyer's Shake Shack manage to do it. Many believe it comes from training, but training is technical. Recruiting—the practice of finding new people to join an organization or support a cause—is truly the most important step in the process. When you empower the right people—emotionally generous people— they will make the right decisions. Or, as Danny Meyer says, "The overarching concern to do the right thing well is something we can't train for. Either it's there or it isn't."

How Many and What Positions?

"If you have the wrong people, it doesn't matter whether you discover the right direction; you still won't have a great company. Great vision without great people is irrelevant," says Jim Collins in *Good to Great* (HarperCollins, 2001), one of the greatest business books ever written. In the book, he researches the greatest companies of our time—those who've shown consistent growth over a long time period.

Choosing the right people to prepare and represent your food is just as important as choosing the right ingredients. A strong team can make your truck a success, while an undertrained or unmotivated staff can sabotage your entire vision. Later in this chapter, I show you how to choose and train the right people and how to create a work environment to keep them motivated.

Food trucks are typically intimate operations, with an average of three to four people on board—one running the window; one or two in the kitchen; and one outside of the truck organizing the line, monitoring the neighborhood, and handling the marketing. The idea is to consolidate as many responsibilities as possible into just a couple of positions.

It's impossible to know how many people you'll need or in what capacity you'll need them until you've clearly defined your menu and concept. The nature and complexity of your offerings largely dictates what responsibilities need to be filled.

For example, a soup truck can usually operate with just two people. The main person takes the orders, handles payment, and serves the soup—not an unreasonable amount of work for one person. The second employee assists during the busy hours, refills soup pots and supplies, and cleans. If the truck operator were to expand the menu to include panini, for example, she would need to hire an additional kitchen worker to prepare the sandwiches and run the panini press.

You should never have more than five people working on your truck, and unless you're operating an ice cream truck, it would be difficult to handle a truck with just one. For a maximum return on investment, you should strive to run your truck with a three-person crew.

To determine the number of employees your food truck requires, begin by analyzing your menu for the following characteristics:

* **Prep time.** How long does it take to prepare all the ingredients for service? How many people are required to prep the kitchen before you open? In the soup truck example, the majority of labor and cooking time occurs before the operator opens each day, so one employee can help the operator once the truck is open and two employees can work to prep the soups prior to service.

* **Cook time.** Do you cook your food to order, or do you merely assemble a plate for your customers? A burger cooked to order requires significantly more time and effort than a meatball sandwich, for which most of the work is done before you open.

* **Complexity.** How complex are your dishes? Do they each require great skill and attention, or can multiple orders be prepared simultaneously? It's much easier to grill several burgers at one time than to properly cook the same number of fish entrées at once. The more focus a dish requires, the fewer orders the kitchen can fill at one time.

* **Variety.** The greater the variety of made-to-order dishes on your menu, the harder it will be to fill multiple orders simultaneously and the longer it will take to fill an order that includes two or more wildly different dishes.

As you analyze your menu, you should begin to get a sense of what processes and responsibilities will require the most time and labor. For example, if you specialize in fresh pastas, plan to spend a significant amount of time preparing the dough and making sauces. Create a list of the major responsibilities that make up the bulk of your operation. Break down each step, from taking the order to serving it, and assign an employee to each role in the process, so you can begin to know how many people you'll need.

Also, consider your own role in the kitchen or at the window. Which of the responsibilities on your list can you take on yourself? While you'll want to do as much as possible, you shouldn't take on too much. Micromanaging is a classic mistake of first-time truck operators. You need to delegate work to your crew so that you can step back and supervise, manage, and interact with your customers.

If you have a partner, you need to consider which role, if any, would make best use of his strengths. One of the best reasons for taking on a partner is because that person brings a special skill set or expertise to the operation. If your partner has a strong culinary background, then his role is clear from the beginning: he should oversee food preparation and determine whether he needs an extra pair of hands in the kitchen.

Once you know what you'll be doing on the truck, consolidate the remaining responsibilities on your list into one or two positions. If you're still unsure how many people you'll need to get the job done, go with your best guess. You'll know very quickly once you start operating if you need to downsize or expand your staff needs. If you communicate well with your employees, you'll be able to implement changes easily.

Getting the Right People On Board

It's time to assemble a qualified team to help make your food truck dream a reality. Depending on the demands of your menu and concept, you'll need experienced and enthusiastic professionals to fill one or two positions.

Notice I didn't include chef on the list of staff positions to consider. At this point, you should have a fully conceived menu, and most chefs won't want to produce someone else's recipes. If you don't have any culinary inclination or just feel uncomfortable designing a menu on your own, consider a partnership with a chef who can create a menu to fit your concept. A food truck has no need for a chef for any other reason than to develop the recipes and for marketing. Your cooks should be more than capable of handling the work with adequate training.

The primary positions you need to fill are as follows:

* Prep cook

* Cook

* Cashier/greeter

The following sections detail the job duties of each of these positions.

Prep Cook

The quality of a kitchen's prep work is a big part of the quality of its finished product. Depending on the truck type, your prep cook might do all the cooking. Prep cooks ready every ingredient for service, from trimming meat to deboning fish to chopping veggies. They make sure the kitchen is fully stocked and that every menu component is on hand, clean, fresh, and ready to be cooked or served. They're often responsible for preparing soups, sauces, and baked goods as well.

A good prep cook should have a solid working knowledge of every piece of equipment in your kitchen and understand the proper way to handle all the ingredients on your menu. She must be highly organized, punctual, and responsible. She should be able to take orders and criticism, and endure long hours on her feet, doing repetitive work. Most importantly, she should take pride in her work and feel motivated to do her job well.

A well-trained and dedicated prep cook can save you countless hours of tedious labor while giving you the peace of mind of knowing that your product is in safe and loving hands. She can also double as an on-truck cook during service, should you need it.

Ninety percent of the people you hire to launch your truck won't be with you six months later. This isn't a reflection on you; it's the nature of the business. The truck is your dream, and you must do everything in your power to protect it, which includes firing someone who isn't right for the job. Constantly be on the lookout for good people and have a file of backups.

On-Truck Cook

The on-truck cook executes the entire menu. Other than the prep cook, the quality of your product is solely dependent on the skill and execution of this individual.

As with prep cooks, you want to find an on-truck cook who is experienced but still receptive to learning and taking direction. Laboring long hours in a truck kitchen can be thankless and exhausting work, so he must be responsible and dedicated, and demonstrate a positive attitude toward his work. Ideally, you should find two people who can work either as a prep or an on-truck cook.

Cashier/Greeter

I highly recommend that you take this position yourself. It's your truck, and you should be the face of it. It's also your money, and at least until you find someone trustworthy, you should be handling it. If you aren't going to be greeting customers and taking orders yourself, you must find a cashier/greeter whose personality and enthusiasm will represent your business in the best way possible. This person should not only care about the product but be able to sell it.

Your cashier/greeter must be familiar enough with the menu to answer any question about the food and to gently *upsell* your customers. An upsell is a casual suggestion to your customers to purchase appetizers, side dishes, drinks, and desserts. Upselling to your guests can greatly increase your revenue and average check. It's a great way to bring attention to menu areas you'd like to push, such as high-profit items.

The Hiring Process

When you're ready to begin the interview process, place an ad in the newspaper or online. I recommend using Craigslist.com, which offers free and paid advertising space for employers to reach out to jobseekers. It's an invaluable resource for attracting food service workers.

In the interview process always take the time to meet multiple candidates and ask for references. Be aware of red flags—applicants who are late for their interview or have a history of jumping from job to job. In the end, rely on your instinct to tell you whether someone is a good fit for your business. Make sure you like them. You'll be in tight quarters with these people, so you'll be better off if you enjoy their company.

Here are a few questions you can ask applicants on their first interview:

* Why did you leave your last job?

* Why do you want to work on our food truck?

* What are your major strengths and weaknesses?

* Why do feel you would be a good fit here?

* What are your personal and professional goals? How do you believe they will affect your employment?

* What is your passion?

For prep and on-truck cooks, definitely include one or two auditions in the kitchen after the initial interview. You'll want to observe their skill, conduct, efficiency, and attitude to see whether you can work comfortably and amiably beside them in small quarters.

Beware of arrogant cooks in the food truck kitchen. You want to work with people who are eager and open to learning, receptive to criticism, and who respect your authority. There's no room in a food truck for people with inflated egos and their own visions of your business. You're better off with someone who's reserved, fastidious, and respectful. Your food truck should be run like an army, and there's no room for dissension among the ranks.

For your cashier/greeter applicants, you'll want to observe them interacting with customers. Ask them to learn the menu and give them a trial period during which you compare their customer service skills and salesmanship with that of your other candidates.

Choose employees who, in addition to their normal duties, are qualified to drive the truck. Make sure they have a license and obtain a report on their driving history from the department of motor vehicles.

Training and Educating Your Staff

After you've hired an experienced, enthusiastic team for your food truck, you need to educate them on your menu, concept, and expectations for the business. Don't assume that just because someone has a strong background in cooking or customer service that he or she won't need guidance and a clear outline of your expectations.

Setting the Right Tone

It's crucial for the team's morale and the overall success of the business that you establish, from the very beginning, an open dialogue between you and your staff. You and your staff should be able to safely express any concern, suggestion, or grievance. Remember that you set the tone for the workplace; if you choose to see and to expect the best in people, they'll usually prove you right. If you choose to see the worst, your employees will prove you right on that, too.

Clearly communicate to each team member exactly what you expect from them and by what criteria you'll be judging their performance.

Training

Taking the time to conduct training sessions and staff meetings not only keeps your employees on top of their game, but it also shows them that they're valuable team members.

Train your on-truck or prep cook one on one. Never throw a cook into the kitchen without giving him the opportunity to learn and practice the recipes. The auditions you hold as a part of the hiring process should double as training sessions. Teach your cook the recipes and ask him to replicate them. You'll quickly sense the skill level of your potential employee.

Consider holding regular staff tastings to familiarize everyone with specials and to review the menu. Product knowledge is crucial for your *front-of-the-truck* staff. Front-of-the-truck is a variation of front of the house, which is restaurant jargon for all the staff members who interact with customers.

Teaching the Importance of Customer Service

Set very specific customer service standards for your front-of-the-truck staff. Customers should be regarded as guests at all times. Your staff should strive to not just serve food, but to also provide an experience to each guest from the moment they're greeted in line to when they walk away.

Studies demonstrate that your guests will remember poor customer service more than the food. No matter how great your burgers are, customers won't come back if they feel your staff was rude or dismissive. Good customer service, on the other hand, can outshine an average meal and make the overall experience positive and memorable. It's by providing a high level of customer service that you connect with your clients and build a dedicated following.

Here are the complete steps of service, including some rules for interacting with your guests. You can copy this list and display it in the truck, or include it in your employee manual:

* Greet every guest as they approach the truck. Smile and ask them how they're doing. Offer to answer any questions they may have, and offer samples, if possible.

* Never have a conflict with other employees in front of the guests, they should never be aware of any problems on the truck.

* Learn the names of your repeat guests.

* Never be distant or too formal. Treat your guests as if they're old friends. Always act excited to see each guest, whether it's her first or thirtieth visit. Doing so will make guests more receptive to upselling, since customers will see you as a friend and not a salesman with ulterior motives.

* Never argue with a guest. If someone is upset, try to accommodate him in every way possible. If you can't, get a manager/owner to deal with the problem. Always smile and remain calm.

* Try to anticipate the needs of every guest. Give extra napkins with a messy item or extra utensils if guests plan to share with friends without their having to ask for them.

* Don't try to save a penny and end up losing a dollar. In other words, if your customer drops her food or spills his drink, give her a new one.

* Know the menu inside out. Be prepared to answer questions about allergies, spiciness, and portion size. This knowledge will enable you to make useful suggestions, helping your guests to pair entrées and sides and increasing their check totals.

* Accommodate modifications to the menu whenever possible. Yes, it's annoying when customers try to create their own dish, but they'll remember that you went out of your way to please them. Knowing the menu well will help you make recommendations to people whose requests you can't accommodate and to help those with food allergies.

* Thank every guest for his or her business, and always say good-bye.

* Never point out the tip jar or mention tips in any way.

Customer response can be rather surprising when these principles are put into action. People respond well to kindness and gratitude, and they'll remember that they had an enjoyable interaction with you and your staff. The key is consistency. You must treat every guest exactly the same way. It only takes one negative experience to lose a customer for life.

Scheduling

The most efficient way to schedule employees is to create a simple spreadsheet. Post a printed schedule in the truck and the commissary, and email a copy to your staff at least three or four days before the start of each work week. Be sure to get your schedule posted by the deadline you set for yourself, so your staff can plan their personal time efficiently. If you can't be punctual, how can you expect them to be?

Making schedules can be really tough for any business, especially when you have multiple part-time employees fighting for shifts or requesting time off. Luckily, your food truck doesn't need a huge staff; making the schedule should be fairly straightforward if you hired wisely and chose people who are making this job a priority.

In general, there are three shifts for workers on a food truck:

* **Prep:** Prepares the food at the commissary

* **Breakfast/lunch:** Prepares and serves meals on the truck during the breakfast and/or lunch shift

* **Dinner:** Prepares and serves evening meals on the truck

Your spreadsheet should list the days you're open, with a row for each position you're scheduling. On slower days, you may be able to cut back on a set of hands in the kitchen or front of house. After you've been open for a couple of weeks, you'll have a better grasp of which days require more help and on which you can do without it (though business will always be changing based on spot availability).

Your staff should generally be able to predict the days on which they'll be working, and their total hours for each week should remain reasonably constant. If you're not consistent, their pay will fluctuate from week to week, and they won't be able to predict their income. It's important to provide your staff with as much stability as possible, so they can focus on doing the best job rather than looking for other work. Regard your staff's scheduling needs as you would your own, and never forget that everyone is there to make money.

Here's a sample food truck schedule:

	Mon	Tues	Wed	Thurs	Fri	Sat	Total Hrs
	6/1	6/2	6/3	6/4	6/5	6/6	
B.O.T. (Back of the Truck & Commissary)							
Henry	Off	Off	10 A.M.–6 P.M.	10 A.M.–6 P.M.	10 A.M.–6 P.M.	12 P.M.–6 P.M.	30
F.O.T. (Front of the Truck)							
Sarah	11 A.M.–6 P.M.	11 A.M.–6 P.M.	11 A.M.–6 P.M.	Off	Off	12 P.M.–6 P.M.	27
Alice	Off	Off	Off	11 A.M.–6 P.M.	11 A.M.–6 P.M.	Off	14

Establish a firm attendance policy from the get-go. Require your employees to notify you at least two hours in advance if they're going to be late or absent. Be clear that it's their responsibility to reach you or another supervisor; leaving a voicemail or text message, or having a coworker explain your absence, isn't acceptable. Request a doctor's note for consecutive absences. If an employee is tardy and/or absent multiple times, disciplinary action may be warranted. Be sure to outline your attendance policies in your employee manual. (See the following section on such policies.)

Setting Policies

Even though you might be a team of only five or fewer, it's important to set official policies and standards for your food truck. Actually, the fact that yours is such a small operation can give the impression that it's okay to treat it less seriously than other businesses. You have to seize the reins from the very beginning and demand respect for your company and authority.

A great way to do this is to create an employee manual that provides information about the company and the standards, rules, and expectations you have for your staff. It should explain the concept behind the truck, the history and inspiration of the menu, and a little background on yourself, so that your staff knows who you are and what inspired you. This information can be especially useful to your front-of-truck people when answering guests' questions. All employees should be required to read and sign the manual, stating that they understand the policies and the consequences of violating them.

Your manual doesn't have to be fancy, but it should be thorough and look professional. The policies and signed statement need to be very clearly worded; you never know when a disgruntled ex-employee will take you to court to dispute the clarity or existence of the policy that got him or her fired. The manual is a way to not only educate your staff and get them excited about your business but to legally protect you and your company.

Your manual should include, but not be limited to, the following:

* **Mission statement.** Introduce yourself and explain the history and concept behind your company. Your mission statement should set the tone, not just for the product and experience you want to give your customers, but also for the work environment you want to foster for your staff.

* **Performance and behavior standards.** Discuss your expectations for professionalism and lay out a code of conduct.

* **Confidentiality.** Agree to guard whatever personal and financial information you, as the employer, must collect from them. Your staff, in turn, is asked to respect any private information to which they're exposed.

* **Drugs and alcohol.** State your policy against on-premises drug and alcohol consumption and identify the repercussions for violating said policy. Illegal activity of any kind cannot be tolerated on the premises.

* **Emergencies.** Identify emergency procedures, including an evacuation plan, and collect emergency contact information for each employee.

* **Sexual harassment.** State your policy that sexual harassment won't be tolerated and warrants immediate termination.

* **Safety precautions.** Provide safety information about driving your truck and operating in your kitchen.

* **Smoking.** Identify an acceptable distance from your truck where employees are allowed to smoke.

* **Menu.** Include detailed descriptions of each menu item, including all the ingredients and identifying the most common food allergies.

* **Customer service.** Feel free to include the customer service outline from earlier in this chapter.

* **Food safety and health department guidelines.** It's crucial that your employees understand and follow all department of health (DOH) food safety guidelines.

* **Uniform, hygiene, and appearance.** Outline your expectations for your staff's physical appearance and attire.

* **Attendance and lateness policy.** State your protocol for reporting lateness and absences, what documentation you may require, and the consequences for repeated lateness and absence. Also, establish a set policy and protocol for requesting time off. Require the request be given in writing before that week's schedule is made. Try to be flexible, but don't tolerate last-minute requests. If you establish a healthy flow of communication with your staff, scheduling conflicts can be anticipated and solved.

* **Disciplinary protocol.** Lay out the steps that will be taken to enforce company policies.

* **Employee agreement form.** Your employees must sign this form, which states that they understand and accept all the policies, guidelines, and procedures in the manual.

Be sure to read the manual aloud with your staff and answer any questions they may have. They will respect you for setting firm policies and should feel valued because most of the policies exist to protect them. Make it clear that these guidelines are designed to provide a safe and comfortable working environment. Keep a copy of the manual posted in the truck, so that you and they can refer to it when necessary.

Motivating and Retaining Your Staff

Once you've assembled a great team and put firm policies in place, you want to keep them motivated and encourage a spirit of camaraderie. We've all had bosses who used fear to control us and make us feel small. You can foster warm, familial bonds between you and your staff and still maintain your authority. In fact, it's the only right way to manage a business.

If you use kindness and reason, instead of threats and shouting, to persuade and motivate your staff, your team will *want* to work for you. Most people haven't been exposed to this managerial style, and I'll tell you from my own experience, it's the only way to build loyalty to your company. At the end of the day, it doesn't matter if the money isn't great; if your employees enjoy being at work, they'll stick around. Not only that, but they'll come on time, avoid calling in sick, and bring their A game 100 percent of the time. An employee who's excited about his job will bring his friends to eat at your truck and spread the word about you to his family, neighbors, and acquaintances.

The number-one way to create a safe and peaceful working environment is to encourage open communication. Your staff should feel comfortable voicing their concerns, grievances, fears, and suggestions. They should never think they have to hide a problem from you or from anyone else on staff. One way to establish a strong communication flow is to hold daily or weekly staff meetings before or after each shift. Open the floor to whoever wants to say something and applaud those who do. Remember, your employees may be aware of problems you aren't; instead of taking these reports as criticism, you should welcome them for the betterment of your business.

This communication style requires humility. You need your staff to respect your authority, and being humble in no way diminishes that. Your staff will respect you more for respecting them and seeing them as individuals. You can reinforce this by openly praising them for a job well done. Nothing—I repeat, *nothing*—will uplift and motivate your staff more than a little praise. It takes nothing away from you and can mean the world to them.

When you need to be negative, offer constructive criticism. Never throw your employees' shortcomings back in their faces. If you're communicating well and offering praise when warranted, they'll have incentive enough to learn from their mistakes without you embarrassing them. They'll appreciate the discreet way in which you point out room for improvement, and will work hard to prove to you that your gentle but firm style is effective.

You might want to take it a step further and express an interest in their personal lives. Don't be intrusive, but inquire about their activities outside of work. Ask about their vacations, hobbies, dates, and performances. Not only will they be more at ease around you, but you'll feel more comfortable leading your staff, knowing that they trust and value your opinion.

In 2007, 23-year-old Tiger Wu founded Veggie Ninja, a vegetarian food truck in Reseda, California. Uncomfortable about managing a staff that was mostly older than him, Tiger encouraged them to express themselves by bringing their talents and personalities to their work. Together, they formed a singing group and later incorporated a karaoke machine into the side of the truck, so patrons could perform while they waited in line. Tiger demonstrated that managing one's staff with kindness translates into big success.

A great way to encourage team spirit is to host company outings outside of work. Take your staff to a theme park or a sports event. Make sure no one ever feels left out; that can happen easily with workers who are less outgoing or assertive. You're all stuck in a small space together, so you might as well like each other and get along.

At the same time, you can't tolerate any behavior that's blatantly aggressive, disrespectful, or illegal. If company policies are violated, don't get angry; simply apply the disciplinary protocol outlined in your employee manual. For many businesses, it goes something like this:

* **First violation:** Verbal warning

* **Second violation:** Written warning

* **Third violation:** Suspension or termination

Of course, some infractions may warrant immediate suspension or termination, such as sexual harassment, drug abuse, or theft. These are instances where you'll need to use your best judgment, keeping in mind that you never want the company to be in any way complicit in the illegal activities of an employee. Don't lose your temper; remain cool and deal with the situation rationally.

If you can incorporate just a few of these principles into your management style, you'll be operating well above the industry standard for positive work environments. Remember, there's no conflict between being kind and being respected, or between humility and leadership. Furthermore, your staff's collective warmth will infect your customers and attract many more.

Inventory and Maintenance

Every action you take when planning your business is a seed. If you plant crab apples, don't plan on harvesting a Golden Delicious. It's especially true when it comes to a project like your food truck. Because it's a relatively small business, all the decisions you make will immediately affect every other area. If you change how you run the window, for example, your kitchen operations will immediately be altered. It's particularly important to take this interconnectedness of your operations into account when you start thinking about purchasing, managing your inventory, and even maintaining your truck. You could be running the most popular truck in the country, but if you're spending too much on food, aren't managing the inventory properly, or aren't taking care of the truck, you won't be able to establish long-term success.

In this chapter, I discuss purchasing food and supplies, managing inventory, and maintaining your truck. Purchasing and maintenance aren't the sexiest part of the food truck business, but they're just as important as the food you're serving.

Purchasing and Managing Supplies

Prior to placing any supply orders, it's of the utmost importance that you have a clear understanding of your concept, staffing, and expected preparation time. By identifying where and when you'll be cooking and prepping your food, you'll have a better sense of the types of products you'll need to buy.

If you're selling hamburgers, for instance, you can purchase regular ground beef, prepackaged and formed hamburgers, or grind the beef yourself from certain cuts. The easiest option is the prepackaged and formed hamburgers, but that decision leads to secondary questions: Will it enable you to produce the best-tasting and highest-quality product? Will your butcher make you a proprietary mix of meats for your burgers? What's the most cost-effective way to get the product you want? That's what purchasing is all about.

Pat LaFrieda is a New York butcher who I credited with reinventing the hamburger. When the recession hit the city in the late 2000s, LaFrieda's restaurant customers were looking to take the best cuts—dry-aged New York strips—and turn them into high-end comfort food such as a signature burger. LaFrieda, now known as the mad scientist of burgers, gave them what they wanted and established a national trend in the process. He created proprietary beef blends for restaurants like Shake Shack, Minetta Tavern, Spotted Pig, and 5 Napkin Burger that have sprouted national chains and been copied by butchers around the country. Thank you, Pat, for giving us the gourmet burger. Our stomachs salute you!

Understanding the Role of the Purchasing Agent

For most hospitality businesses, the purchasing agent is the unheralded champion of profitability. Think of this person as the great offensive line on a football team; he protects the quarterback and is invaluable to the team's success. However, he'll never win the MVP award and is rarely talked about in the press.

After you've decided on your menu and put your systems in place, the work of your purchasing agent—probably *you*—has just started. You know you'll need canned corn or barbeque sauce, but you most likely haven't figured out the brand or size of the order. Now is the time to work all this out.

Researching Your Product Options

To decide your type and quantity, you need to do a lot of research. The first step is to find the products you think are best for your recipes at local grocery stores. Then follow that up by speaking with commercial distributors to see who can supply you with those products at a reasonable price. Most major metropolitan areas have dozens of distributors who supply dry goods, meat, dairy, and other products to restaurants. Contact them, sample their products, and speak to sales reps to find the products that you think are best for you.

Don't waste a lot of money going out and buying samples of different products for your truck, especially if you're on a tight budget. Distributors want your business and will send you free samples of their products. They need you as much as you need them.

Make a list of all the items you'll need to execute your menu on a weekly basis, including the beverages you're selling to accompany your food. Create this list before you start researching suppliers and interviewing sales reps. Break things down into the same categories that distributors use: fish, meat, poultry, dairy, dry goods, baked goods, and so on. Use spreadsheet software, like Microsoft Excel, so you can easily edit and update the list.

Be very specific about the items you're looking to purchase. It may be hard in the beginning, but as you learn more about the products, don't leave any details to chance. Don't just write down "cheddar cheese"; write "Miller's white cheddar cheese, shredded, 15-pound case." If you aren't specific, you'll end up getting something you don't want, which will affect both your bottom line and your end product.

Determining Preparation Time

Consumers want the best product available, not a frozen hamburger or fish filet. You can definitely save yourself time, energy, and money by using frozen or pre-prepared products, but you'll probably lose money over the long run in lost customers. The key is quality: getting the best quality you can at the best price.

The food on your truck should be fresh and cooked as close as possible to when it's going to be served. I also advocate using fresh herbs over dried or prechopped items because they greatly improve the flavor of your final product. Keep in mind that it's very costly to butcher meat and prepare vegetables every day. Doing so may not be a realistic choice for a small business like a food truck.

It's time for another list: breaking down all the tasks involved in your truck's daily operations. It will help you identify which items have the highest impact on your bottom line and which tasks will most greatly affect the quality of your product.

Let's say you serve a chopped salad on your truck. It will cost you $10 an hour to have a prep cook chop the vegetables by hand, and you need 30 pounds of salad per day. It takes four workers to chop five pounds of vegetables in an hour, which costs you $240 a day. It's possible that your local vegetable supplier has prechopped tomatoes, onions, and cucumbers that cost you half what it does to chop them inhouse. Using these prechopped veggies will save you time and money, while giving your clients a high-quality product. To maintain the fresh flavors, however, you decide to chop fresh herbs and add them to the salad. By breaking down the process, you are able to identify which prep you should do inhouse and what you can outsource, while still maintaining the quality level of your product.

The most important thing you need to consider when using pre-prepared items is taste. Taste everything you serve to your customers, especially the things that are prepared by outside suppliers. You have less control over those, and therefore, need to monitor the end product more carefully. Your customers will know if you change an ingredient.

One of the most famous restaurants in New York, Peter Luger Steakhouse, used to serve the most delicious onion rolls. I'd been eating there for years, and suddenly they started using a different bakery. From the minute I saw the rolls, I knew they weren't the same. They didn't have the homemade goodness they did before, and that took a little of the magic of a meal at Peter Luger away for me. It's important to realize that all the little decisions you make will affect how your customers enjoy their visits to your truck.

Locating Suppliers

After you've identified what you need to buy, it's time to choose from whom you're going to purchase it.

Establish a budget prior to reaching out to suppliers. You know your guidelines for profitability. Don't let your eyes become bigger than your wallet, and don't let a supplier sell you anything you don't need.

The best way to find purveyors is to speak with other truck, restaurant, and commissary owners. Your peers know the best people for you to work with and will be happy to share them with you. Locate a truck or restaurant that uses products similar to the ones you're looking to serve. Ask them why they chose one supplier over another, and take notes on who's better at what.

Choose at least three purveyors you can call on in every category, giving you backup if someone is out of an item. Having multiple suppliers also enables you to comparison shop. Don't take anyone's word for it when it comes to finding the best price. The best one for them may not be the best for you.

Set up accounts with each supplier. Call the purveyor's office directly and fill out the paperwork to have a sales representative assigned to your business. All your dealings with the purveyor will go through this representative, so set up a meeting with him or her as soon as possible to establish a personal relationship and outline your needs.

Ask the sales rep to have her boss come along to the first meeting you have. Often, the boss has the true negotiating power, so having a direct relationship with the sales rep's boss will be helpful. It also gives you a second contact if you ever have issues with the supplier.

Also, get your sales representative's cell and home phone number. Your relationship is all about service, and you don't want to be stuck not being able to get a delivery to restock your truck on a weekend.

You should be very clear about the needs of your business with your sales rep. Explain how you plan to operate and give her a breakdown of how you'll execute and serve your menu. Also provide her with a copy of the inventory list you created. You may be surprised at the breadth of the items distributors carry. They'll often be able to help you with more items than you originally thought.

When you review your inventory list with your suppliers, explain what you're looking for in terms of cut, flavor, packaging, and volume. Suppliers may or may not be able to service your needs, but you should always make your desires known. Tell them you'll work with whichever organization can come closest to your preferences. Also, inform them that you plan to place orders on a regular basis, with your money going to whomever can service your needs best. It's a clear and simple way to show them that you're serious and expect prompt and professional service.

Your suppliers should be eager to work with you and understand your business. They should bring you new ideas and products to help improve your business's bottom line and your food's quality. Your purveyors must understand your business's goals, along with your cost expectations and delivery requirements. A great supplier will give you information about local food and business trends that will be invaluable to maintaining a thriving food truck.

Comparison Shopping

Once suppliers get back to you with their pricing, terms of service, delivery schedule, and credit terms, it's time for you to start making decisions. It shouldn't be necessary to get into a contractual agreement with specific order volumes and time periods at this point, because you need to establish your business first. With that said, you still need to work out some logistical details, particularly your payment terms.

Will you pay on delivery or in 30, 60, or 90 days? The longer you take to make the payment, the more money it will cost you. It's your job to balance your cash needs against your pricing needs, and then decide what's best for your business. Additionally, you need to let the supplier know when you need your deliveries and how often. Find out the process for placing orders, and how much lead time the supplier needs to make a delivery.

Always check the items you receive against what you actually paid for and ordered. If the products you ordered and paid for aren't the ones you received, you've got an issue. It's a regular problem in the hospitality business. Additionally, the person who does the ordering should also be the person doing the receiving. And if it isn't the same person, the two of them should be in close contact with one another. If you paid for chopped shallots and received chopped onions, there'll be a vast difference in the taste of your final product, and potentially, your bottom line.

Negotiating

Pricing is the next most important issue when dealing with suppliers. You won't get the best price unless you're able to negotiate. You need to identify the best product for your use, and then push back with the supplier to get the best price. Don't just take the price you've been given; look for an opportunity to get a better deal.

The key to negotiating is establishing volume. You want to purchase as much as you can from as few suppliers as possible. Your purveyor wants to sell as much volume as possible, so the more you're able to purchase from him or her, the better price you'll get.

See if you can enter into an agreement for a fixed price on certain items that you buy regularly. The cost of commodities is in constant flux these days, and such arrangements can add up to significant cost savings. With these types of agreements, your business agrees to purchase a particular item only from one supplier in exchange for fixed pricing and volume-based discounts. Many suppliers love to score consistent business like this and will do whatever they can to accommodate you, including discounts, special orders, and flexible delivery terms.

Inventory

Managing the inventory of your truck and commissary is critically important to your success. If you purchase too much of a perishable item, it can go bad and literally "spoil" your profitability.

Your *inventory* is defined as the stock of supplies you have in your truck and commissary at any given time. Inventory is all potential revenue; you get nothing back from it until you sell it to customers. Therefore, you need to have a minimal amount of money tied up in it, so it won't negatively affect your business's performance. Obviously, you don't want to run out of menu items on a regular basis, but you also don't want to have a year's supply of tomato paste tying up your cash flow. You need that cash to run a healthy business.

Salespeople love to try to get you to buy in bulk with pricing incentives. Make sure you look at these offers closely, so that you can tell whether the cost savings are worth tying up your cash. You have limited storage space, so before you purchase a product, make sure you have somewhere to put it. Sometimes, suppliers offer *bill-and-hold service*, where they store the product for you until you need it; if they do, take advantage of it.

You can manage and track your inventory in any number of ways. The most important thing is to have a system in place and to keep it as simple as possible. I recommend the *par system* for food trucks because it's so easy. The par system refers to the level of stock you need to service your truck over a set time period. If you use two cases of carrots a day, for example, then that's your daily par.

Choose a particular employee to count food every day or every shift, updating a daily par sheet with the amount of prepped and nonprepped inventory you have. Compare your inventory with specified par levels and place orders when necessary. For example, if you need 3 pounds of carrots every day, the amount of carrots you enter on the par sheet is 3 pounds. At the beginning and end of the day, review the par sheet, check inventory, and then place orders for the following day to make sure you're always at par levels.

Inventory Counts

You need to count your inventory for your monthly profit and loss statements (see Chapter 15). Whether you prepare the statements yourself or have your accountant do them, your counts determine the cash value of the inventory you have on hand. It means you have to count the items, and then multiply them by the unit price you paid for them to determine your inventory's cash value. For example, if you purchased 30 pounds of chicken for $200 and have 15 pounds left, the inventory is valued at $100. The total of everything you have on hand gives you your month's ending and beginning inventory values, which is an important aspect of monitoring the profitability of your truck.

You'll also want to utilize purchase orders to monitor purchases and requests for purchases. Have your prep cook check the par on vegetables, so you can put in an order for additional quantities if necessary. It puts one more check and balance into the system. You should monitor your par sheets, purchase orders, and inventory regularly until you establish trust with your employees.

Preventing Theft

There'll always be some theft in your kitchen; how much depends on what you consider theft. An employee eating a carrot or cooking a piece of chicken for lunch is different than taking a case of soda home. You need to clearly communicate what's acceptable in your kitchen. I suggest focusing on theft deterrence, and then matching it with random inventory checks.

Here are some ways that you can deter theft:

* **Accountability.** Put someone in charge of a particular item or duty, and make sure that person is aware of what the punishment for theft will be. By doing so, you're establishing responsibility. If something happens, you now have someone to hold accountable—a partner who should care about that item as much as you do. That employee is going to do everything in his power to protect his position.

* **Security cameras.** Whether they work or not, people usually won't steal if they think they're being watched. The best option on a food truck is an internet-based camera in a hidden location. (Make employees aware that they are being taped, but don't reveal the location of the camera.)

* **Locks.** Put locks on everything you can. People are less likely to steal if doing so requires effort. Make the lock keys a big deal: employees only get keys if they earn them. The fewer people with keys, the easier it is to find the thief.

* **Be present.** It's your business, and the more people see you around, the more they think you're there. It's much easier to steal from someone you don't think is around or will notice.

Minimizing Waste

Waste is the food you throw out because you can't serve it to customers for reasons such as spoilage. Waste is like giving away money. It comes from laziness and poor planning, and it influences your labor, food, and even transportation costs. Once you've been in operation for a month, analyze all aspects of your business to see where you can eliminate waste. The easiest way to limit waste is to be watchful and methodical. Provide incentives that encourage your employees to limit waste in the kitchen and other areas by creating contests with rewards.

Being cheap and shortsighted can cost you as much as being wasteful. People often try to save money in the short term by purchasing inferior packaging or lower-quality food, which ends up costing them more over the long haul. Make the best decision for your business, not the cheap one.

You can take steps to prevent spoilage. Make it unacceptable in your kitchen from Day one. You must become very knowledgeable about the shelf life of the items you're selling. Meaning you need to know how long you can serve food items before they go bad, as well as how they should look and smell upon arrival. You have no one to blame other than yourself if you accept a delivery item that isn't fresh.

Investing in the proper means to store, handle, and extend the shelf life of food also helps prevent spoilage. Covering, labeling, and in some cases vacuum-sealing food can vastly extend its usable shelf life. Finally, make sure your storage facilities are clean. It will not only help extend the life of perishable food, but it will prevent foodborne illness.

Truck Maintenance

You're spending thousands of dollars on your food truck, so it's important that you keep it maintained in the best possible condition. This means maintaining the automobile part of the truck as well as the kitchen.

Have a mechanic you trust and who's familiar with servicing commercial vehicles look over your truck semiannually to check the engine, oil, brakes, and so forth. Doing so will improve your truck's long-term value and will ensure that you won't lose days of business because it's in the shop. Don't be cheap—a good mechanic costs money. Try to arrange a payment or maintenance plan with your mechanic. It would be a shame to have spent all that money, and then not keep the truck in good shape.

Some commissaries offer onsite maintenance, as well as roadside assistance. Look into these options. Maintenance on the truck is crucial to a food truck business. A down truck is time and money lost.

Here are some ways to identify a good mechanic:

* **Ask your friends, family, and colleagues for recommendations.** Someone who has provided them with good service is likely to do the same for you.

* **NAPA, ASP, or Parts Plus certification.** Ensure your mechanic has certification from one of these organizations.

* **Cleanliness.** Look around the shop to see how it's maintained. It's a garage, so don't expect it to look like a hospital. However, how organized and neat it is can foretell the kind of service you'll receive from the mechanic.

* **Manufacturer's certification.** Check to see if your mechanic is certified by car makers like Ford, GM, or Mercedes. It means he or she is familiar with the latest technology and is serious about the craft.

* **Food truck experience.** Food and catering trucks are specialized vehicles. It would be helpful if your mechanic has experience working on them.

Knowing how much profit you are making in your food business is directly tied to keeping an organized and monitored inventory. Often, operators take this for granted when things are going well, and it ends up being the nail in the coffin when things are going badly. Take the time to monitor your inventory correctly, and you'll end up benefiting greatly in the long term.

Food Preparation and Safety

It was October 2013, and Danny Bowien had just received word that his Manhattan restaurant, Mission Chinese, had been shut down by the health department for an array of violations, including an infestation of mice. Overwhelmed, embarrassed, and worried about his employees, Bowien, a rock-star rising chef, didn't know what to do. It was then that his phone rang. René Redzepi—the chef behind the world's best restaurant, Copenhagen's Noma, and Danny's close friend—said, "Chef, are you ready? They're coming for you. They smell blood. You're hurt, you're wounded, and they're going to come for you."

But those weren't Bowien's only worries. At the same time, he was in the midst of opening the Lower East Side taqueria Mission Cantina. The health department issues distracted him, and he canceled a crucial research trip to Mexico. He opened Cantina before it was ready, and the reviews weren't good. Even Redzepi sent him an email saying his tortillas needed an upgrade. After a stretch of being celebrated by peers and customers alike, the once-rising chef was faltering.

Redzepi coached Bowien through his challenges, telling him, "Everything's going to be okay, but you're going to need to handle this. You're going to be fine, but you just need to focus." Bowien was spurred to action by this encouragement, combined with tough love from another close friend, chef David Chang, founder of Momofuku. Despite resolving his issues with the health department, Bowien shuttered the original Mission Chinese and set out to start over in a newer, better location.

Bowien came to terms with his adversity and the realization that it had been his own fault. "I got swept up in the whole thing," he remembers. "Doing events everywhere, getting flown all over the world, not being in the restaurants enough. At the end of the day, my time is best spent in the restaurants. This is what got me here." He retrenched, focused, and went back to giving the kitchen the benefit of his considerable energy. The challenges that once could have destroyed him were compelling him to rebuild instead; a stronger, better Danny Bowien would make a stronger, better Mission Chinese.

After a year-plus of hard work, Bowien reopened Mission Chinese in 2014. The original restaurant had sported a beer keg on the floor and was thrown together and cramped. His new location was more civilized, though it maintained the edgy, creative energy people expected from him. This time, however, it had a more refined expression and ambience. The reinvented Mission Chinese is like an artist's work later in his career—self-assured and polished. He's now spending long hours in the kitchen when he's not with his family, and he's focused on his craft and his fatherhood, not his fame. Danny has become an experienced creative. And ,it shows in the results: the new Mission has snagged three stars from *New York* magazine, two stars from the *New York Times*, and is consistently ranked as one of the best restaurants in arguably the top restaurant city in the world. Just as important, the reborn Mission Chinese is flourishing with more business than it can handle.

Your Food Truck Responsibilities

As a business owner, you're responsible for the safety of your employees, patrons, purveyors, and neighbors. As a food truck owner, you have the additional burden of assuring the safety and cleanliness of your kitchen, food products, and truck. This can be a challenge even for the most seasoned food truckers. As a first timer, always remember that knowledge, planning, and persistent upkeep are key.

In this chapter, I examine some of the basics of food preparation safety, food storage, and maintaining a clean work environment. I show you what to do, what to avoid, and what might happen if you don't pay attention.

It's impossible to overstate the importance of safety in the design and operation of your business, so take your time and take notes. I recommend keeping extra copies of this chapter on your truck and wherever else you prepare food for your business, so you can reference the information easily.

When it comes to food safety, inspections that you perform yourself are as important as those performed by health inspectors. Performing regular random walkthroughs of your truck and commissary is a necessity. Your local health department should have downloadable self-inspection forms on its website that you can use. By doing self-inspections, you'll know your business better than the health inspector and can protect your business and your clientele.

It's easy to take safety for granted because enforcing it properly requires attention to detail. Don't fall into that trap. Nothing is more important than maintaining a safe environment for you, your employees, and your customers.

Working with Your Chef

If you're the executive chef on your food truck, you'll be responsible for overseeing all the food preparation and storage and maintaining the cleanliness of your kitchen. If you've hired or are partnering with a chef, you're *still* responsible for making sure your staff adhere to all the necessary safety and hygiene standards discussed in this chapter.

Not all chefs are created equal. While we automatically expect professional chefs to be obsessively clean and knowledgeable about food safety, many fall far short of the mark. Thousands of people get food poisoning from restaurants and food trucks every year; meaning hundreds of chefs are neglecting this critical aspect of their duties, and hundreds of owners aren't paying attention to what's happening in their own kitchens.

When hiring or partnering with an executive chef, make sure to ask about food safety and cleanliness. Here are some things to look for:

What health department grades/scores has the chef received in the past? Ask your chef to provide this information or research it on your own. Most cities post the details of inspections on their websites, so you can see exactly what your chef did wrong.

Does the chef have a cavalier attitude toward safety and cleanliness, or does he or she seem to truly appreciate the importance of it? A good chef will care about safety, not just out of fear of getting in trouble but because of pride in the operation. Does the cleanliness of your chef's kitchen seem to be a source of pride?

Can your chef demonstrate a solid knowledge of and understanding of local health department guidelines? Your chef should know these by heart and be able to spot a violation without having to refer back to the guidelines.

Does your chef demonstrate outstanding personal hygiene? Does your chef have clean nails? Is his hair groomed and clothing clean and pressed? Often, the care your chef puts into his own appearance will reflect the care he puts into maintaining a clean work environment.

Is your chef someone who can submit to authority and endure scrutiny? Chefs are notoriously hot-headed, which is an unpleasant stereotype that I've found to be largely true. You're her boss (or partner) and she needs to recognize and respect your authority. She should have a thick skin and be able to take criticism, especially when it comes to adhering to food safety guidelines.

At the end of the day, you're responsible for everything that happens on your truck and all the food that comes out of it. If a patron gets sick from your product or if your truck is cited for a health code violation, the blame falls on your shoulders. If you aren't leading the kitchen yourself, you must still maintain a very hands-on approach to ensuring that your executive chef is adhering to all food safety standards.

Too many restaurant and food truck owners turn a blind eye to their employees' neglect of safety standards in their facilities. Their excuse invariably is that they didn't think it was their responsibility because they hired an executive chef to deal with all that stuff, it's her problem. Wrong! It's her problem, and now it's your problem, too. City health inspectors don't care who is in charge of ensuring that everything is clean. Nor do patrons who become ill from tainted food. The blame will always fall on you—the owner— and it should. You're in charge, and food safety is ultimately and without excuse, *your* responsibility.

Learn the health code guidelines and inspect the kitchen yourself. If you find a problem, discuss it with your chef immediately. If he or she tries to make excuses, you may not have chosen the right person for the job. Make it clear to your chef and your staff that laziness and negligence regarding health won't be tolerated. Remember that nothing—I repeat, *nothing*—is more important in the food industry than safety and cleanliness.

Food can be contaminated anywhere along the supply chain. It's important to purchase food only from approved suppliers and personally inspect all incoming deliveries. Learn to identify signs of spoilage in fruit, vegetables, fish, meat, and poultry. You can't afford to let someone else's mistakes ruin your business.

Food safety classes are offered across the country. Require your head kitchen cook and prep cook to take these classes. Cashiers also can take a less intense class.

Keeping Your Kitchen Clean and Safe

Keeping your kitchen free of common dangers and health code violations is a constant battle that requires knowledge, dedicated attention, and diligence. The most common threats, which can be avoided when proper food safety standards are in place, include bacterial contamination of food, food spoilage, and pest infestation (which brings a whole list of additional health concerns).

You must be proactive in your approach to food safety and cleanliness. Don't think you can get away with doing the bare minimum and hope for the best. The consequences of one food poisoning incident, one bacterial infection, or one significant health code violation can be very expensive and potentially irreparable to your business's reputation. You must take pride in how you maintain your equipment, facilities, and, especially, your food.

Health code guidelines vary from city to city. It's crucial that you know your local laws and standards, as your city's health department will evaluate your truck and publish a report. In some cities, like Los Angeles and New York, health officials issue letter grades—A, B, or C—that restaurants and food trucks are required to post in their windows. I've seen the way even a B grade can embarrass and negatively affect the business of a great restaurant, even when it's the result of seemingly trivial violations. Of course, when it comes to health, no risk is ever trivial. Visit the webpage of your city or state's health department for a detailed list of regulations, so you know exactly what to expect when inspectors come knocking on your door, and they will.

In the following sections, I explain the basics of food safety, including how to ensure cleanliness and the easiest steps to prevent cross contamination.

Battling Illness

In *The Art of War,* Sun Tzu wrote, "Know thy enemy" and in the war against foodborne illness, it's useful to know which bacteria pose the greatest threat to your customers and how to prevent the growth and spread of each one. The three major bacteria that you must be prepared to fight are as follows:

* *Salmonella.* Found predominantly in raw poultry and eggs, *Salmonella's* symptoms include cramping, diarrhea, fever, and intestinal pain. In individuals with weakened immune systems, like children, the elderly, and HIV patients, *Salmonella* can result in life-threatening complications. To prevent infection, thoroughly cook all poultry products and disinfect any surface that comes into contact with raw poultry or eggs.

* *Campylobacter.* Also found in raw poultry, *Campylobacter* causes fever, diarrhea, cramping, and dysentery-like symptoms. As with *Salmonella, Campylobacter* can be life threatening for individuals with compromised immune systems. To prevent infection, thoroughly cook all poultry and disinfect any surface, utensil, or food product that comes into contact with raw poultry. (See the next section on avoiding cross contamination.)

* *E. coli.* Found in the intestinal tract of cattle, *E. coli* is extremely dangerous, causing diarrhea, vomiting, and even kidney failure. *E. coli* is almost always traced back to beef products, most commonly ground beef. *E. coli* can be killed by cooking beef to well done. You must be extremely cautious with raw beef so that it doesn't come into contact with any foods that won't be thoroughly cooked.

Bacteria grow and thrive between 40°F and 140°F. Most health code regulators require food to be stored above or below that range. No food, regardless of whether it's particularly susceptible to foodborne illness, should be kept within this temperature range for more than two hours. A piece of raw poultry that's lightly contaminated by *Campylobacter* and *Salmonella* will become exponentially more infected if stored between 40°F and 140°F for even an hour.

The Poppa & Goose food truck along with its sister truck, Goosebeary's, formerly located in Massachusetts, were shut down in November 2001 due to multiple cases of food poisoning. Six people were sent to the hospital. The associated restaurant that acted as the truck's commissary was also shut down because of unsanitary conditions. This incident not only affected the victims and the businesses, but it created fear among customers and gave food trucks a negative reputation in that area. Protect the food truck community and keep your truck safe!

Here are some essential steps to ensuring the safety of your food:

Cook all foods to the proper temperature. It means that poultry must be cooked all the way through, and beef products (especially ground beef) must be cooked enough to prevent *E. coli* from spreading. Once the food is cooked, make sure it's immediately stored well above or below the 40°F to 140°F range.

Never defrost frozen products to room temperature. Move frozen foods to the refrigerator or place them under cold running water to thaw. Because bacteria thrive between 40°F and 140°F, leaving any product at room temperature—even if it's frozen—is a serious health code violation.

If you aren't serving cooked foods immediately, chill them below 40°F as quickly as possible. Divide the food into small containers and soak them in ice baths. Some bacteria are heat resistant, so cooked foods are just as susceptible to breeding foodborne illnesses as raw ones if they aren't stored at the proper temperatures.

Don't reheat foods multiple times. Doing so can actually worsen the presence of certain bacteria. After a few weeks on the truck, you'll get a sense of how much product you'll need to reheat on any given day. Until then, discard any leftovers that have been reheated once. With experience, the amount of waste will diminish in time.

Use thermometers. It's important to monitor the temperatures of stored foods, both hot and cold, and to determine the temperature of cooked meats and fish to make sure they're heated thoroughly.

Establish a rotational system for your inventory, so you always use your oldest product first. This strategy will not only protect your customers from spoiled ingredients but also save you money, because you'll throw away less food.

Implement and enforce a mandatory handwashing policy for all your employees. They should wash their hands after using the restroom; handling trash or raw foods; smoking; coughing or sneezing; eating or drinking; or touching their hair, faces, open wounds, or any bodily fluids. Your staff should use plastic or latex gloves when handling any food products, and you should have hand sanitizer on the truck for their use, as well as for your customers and yourself.

Preventing Cross Contamination

Cross contamination occurs when foods and surfaces that might be contaminated with bacteria come into contact with foods and surfaces that otherwise wouldn't be a potential threat. For example, if you use a pair of tongs to move raw chicken, and then use them to toss a mixed salad without disinfecting them first, your salad is now likely infected with *Salmonella* and poses just as great a danger to your customers as a piece of the raw chicken.

Because cross contamination is, by definition, accidental, you really need to take steps to ensure the safety of your customers. The following suggestions are industry standard for protecting your food and equipment.

* Have separate designated cutting boards for poultry, meat, fish, raw foods, and cooked foods. Make sure they're labeled or color coded, so they're never used incorrectly.

* Use plastic, stone, or rubber cutting boards only; wood boards are porous and can absorb blood and bacteria in a way that can withstand disinfection. Be sure that all cutting boards and cooking surfaces are cleaned after each use with a strong "kitchen-approved" disinfectant.

* Keep poultry, ground beef, shellfish, and other potentially dangerous foods in a separate refrigerator, and if possible, have a separate space designated for prepping them. Never store raw meats, poultry, or fish on the same refrigerator shelf as cooked meats, poultry, or fish.

* Clean and sterilize all pots, pans, utensils, surfaces, and equipment after each use. Be sure to brush your grill between cooking meat, poultry, and fish.

Food Safety On the Truck and Off

You have two main environments to police for food safety: your truck and your commissary. It's important that you have a trained individual present in both spaces at all times, monitoring the work being done. The local health department will spot-check and approve your truck setup and commissary, but it's up to you to enforce the rules and procedures daily. There are no exceptions when it comes to food safety. Just because you're on the truck and busy with all aspects of your business doesn't mean you have an excuse. There's no room for error when the health and safety of your customers is on the line.

Here are some specific issues to think about regarding on-truck food safety:

* There's less space and less access to power, which makes it more likely for food to fall into dangerous temperature zones or to cross contaminate.

* Trucks have a limited supply of water; if you run out during service, it becomes much more difficult to clean utensils, surfaces, and hands and can make for a dangerous situation. Reserve water for handwashing and cleaning truck surfaces. Have extra utensils for service, and wash dishes back at the commissary. Your water supply is your lifeline, so make sure that you always have the maximum you can carry on the rig.

* Many food truck operators are inexperienced and don't know the rules. Always learn about food safety before diving into operations.

* Never offer any medication from the truck first-aid kit or your personal supply to a customer. If he or she has an allergic reaction, you and your company can be held legally responsible.

Cleaning Supplies

Maintaining a clean kitchen is the single most important factor in preventing foodborne illness. It's also the job no one likes to do. It's your responsibility as business's owner and manager to ensure that your truck is thoroughly and routinely cleaned. Diligent cleaning not only prevents contamination, but also keeps you aware of your inventory so that no food ever sits forgotten in the back of the refrigerator. If you clean consistently, you won't have to wonder whether your product is fresh; you'll know that it is.

To do a proper job of cleaning your truck, you'll need to invest in the right supplies. Here are some of the bare necessities for any kitchen:

* All-purpose cleaner

* Degreaser

* Dish detergent

* Floor cleaner

* Hand soap

* Hand sanitizer

* Multipurpose sanitizer

* Oven cleaner

* Soaking fluid for pots and pans

All cleaning agents contain dangerous chemicals. You and your staff must be aware of the possibility of chemical residue on food prep surfaces and rinse them off thoroughly so that no ingredients ever come into contact with any cleaning product. Be sure to store your cleaning supplies far from your food, especially fresh produce, which can absorb toxic fumes from bottled chemicals. In addition, use color-coded towels for different job types. For example, use one color for wiping down food-prep surfaces and another for handling dangerous chemicals.

Enforce a very strict cleaning schedule on every shift. If you allow dirt and grease to accumulate, you're violating your local health standards, and you're putting your customers' lives at risk and inviting pests to nest in your kitchen. It may be helpful to type up a list of what needs to be done and post it on the rig's wall, or you could simply keep a checklist for your personal use. Do whatever works best for you, so long as you see the job all the way through and inspect it afterward.

Do a walk-through of your kitchen and note everything that needs to be cleaned and how often. Some things require an occasional more thorough scrubbing in addition to daily maintenance. If you're inexperienced and don't know when certain equipment would typically need to be cleaned, consult your executive chef or the owner's manual for each appliance. Don't, however, leave it up to your staff to decide when to clean. It's always up to you to enforce a strict cleaning schedule.

Keeping your truck clean should be a source of pride for you. Remember that the safety and cleanliness of your kitchen is a reflection of your leadership and will be reflected in the final product you sell to your customers. Don't wait for a bad report from the health department or for a customer to get sick. Take the necessary precautions from Day one and relax knowing that you've created a safe, clean, and profitable environment for you and your staff.

Shift Cleaning Schedule

Your cleaning schedule for each shift should include:

* Empty the trash multiple times.

* Mop the floor multiple times.

* Wipe down the line and prep areas (constantly, as needed).

* Sanitize cutting boards after each use.

* Clean and sanitize all surfaces.

* Clean the fryer and change the oil.

* Change the water in the sanitizer systems.

* Wipe down the walls and hood vents.

* Empty the waste tank.

* Fill the water tank.

* Rinse the floor mats.

Weekly Cleaning

Your weekly cleaning chores include the following:

* Deep clean the oven.

* Scrub the inside of the refrigerators.

* Clean behind the hot line (if possible).

* Conduct a full inventory as you do the weekly cleaning.

For weekly chores, choose the day of the week when your inventory is lowest; it will speed up the process and help you gauge how much food you need to order from your purveyors.

Monthly Cleaning

One a month, do these chores:

* Deep clean the walls, floor, and ceiling of the truck.

* Recalibrate your oven thermometer.

* Restock your first-aid supplies.

* Empty, clean, and restock your dry pantry.

Semiannual Cleaning

Perform the following chores every six months:

* Clean the hood above your stove.

* Clean the pilot lights on all your gas appliances.

* Test your fire extinguisher to make sure it works.

* Spray your truck for bugs. (Do this every three to six months, depending on your location.)

Emergencies

Every city and state has its own laws and regulations regarding fire exits and emergency readiness. You'll need to research local policies to determine what kind of hardware to put on your doors and what sort of emergency equipment or supplies you may be required to keep on your truck. There are, however, a few items that every food truck must have on board:

* Fire extinguisher

* First-aid kit: Band-Aids, antiseptic, burn gel or cream, gauze, first-aid tape, eyewash, antibiotic ointments, aspirin, and antihistamines

* Clearly labeled emergency door handle that opens the door from the inside regardless of whether it's locked

* Emergency procedures, which should be typed and posted where everyone can see them, outlining what your staff is expected to do in case of fire, injury, severe burn, collision, or if a customer is choking. A copy of this information should be in the employee manual you hand out when each member of your staff is hired.

Food safety is one of the most important pillars of your truck. Operating safely and with clear guidelines will protect you, your customers, and your employees. One negative incident could have a profound effect on your business and the health of your customers. Make sure everyone involved knows how important it is and be clear about the risks based on the product you are serving.

GROWING YOUR BUSINESS

Once your truck is operating, you'll want to protect and grow it into a profitable enterprise. You need clear systems in place for reporting results—daily, weekly, and monthly financial reports that will allow you to monitor the health of your business and make proactive decisions to keep it moving in the right direction.

Controlling your costs and monitoring spending is important, and so is building your clientele. You need to listen to your customers' feedback and make sure they're having an incredible experience every time they visit your truck. And, if you do make a mistake, you must fix it immediately. I'll show you how great service recovery will make you customers for life.

Growth also means exploring opportunities. Food truck festivals, food truck lots, and television shows featuring food trucks are just some of the incredible opportunities available to help you earn money and build your brand. And if you're doing great business, you might be thinking of expanding. What's standing between you and a fleet of trucks? I'll make sure you know before you graduate from Food Truck University.

Protecting Your Business

Once your food truck is open for business, you may find yourself asking if you're running it or it's running you. To be successful, you need to be proactive, not reactive. And, to be proactive, you need to set up an accurate system to evaluate your success.

The only way to determine how well you're doing is to examine the numbers. That's not to say that common sense, intuition, and your business experience aren't valuable tools to gauge the success of your enterprise. But at the end of the day, it's vital you know the brutal truth, and numbers never lie. Don't fool yourself with press clippings, long customer lines, or gross revenues. The bottom-line profitability of your truck is all that matters in the long term. If you aren't profitable, your business is unsustainable.

In this chapter, I show you how to create reports that will help you track your progress. I explain how to create daily sales and expense reviews, as well as how to determine if your business can be more profitable. Finally, I give you tips on reviewing and replenishing your inventory to maximize profitability and minimize waste.

Financial Reviews

The details of your financial reports and the factors determining your performance are fundamental to you making good decisions about your truck. Most importantly, you need to know how much money you're profiting, not how much money you're generating. If you're making thousands of dollars in income, but it's costing you even more to generate that income, you have a problem. Knowing what happens to every dollar that's generated by your truck will tell you whether you're succeeding or in need of improvement.

Acting like a detective and forensically analyzing your business unveils any inefficiencies that exist. Even the most successful businesses in the world have inefficiencies, and you need to find yours to protect yourself. By putting a review system in place to monitor these figures on a daily, weekly, and monthly basis, you'll be able to maintain an accurate perspective of how your business is performing and make the necessary adjustments.

Playing by the Numbers

Numbers reveal the hard truth about the success and profitability of your business. You must have a system for reviewing and analyzing your sales and expenses. Doing this on a daily basis will enable you to spot trends, both positive and negative, and detect waste. Use your experience and common sense to look for irregularities in the reports, and then figure out whether they're business or reporting issues.

Accountants and bookkeepers aren't on your business's front lines. They take information that you communicate to them and put it into an acceptable format. Often, these numbers just don't tell the full story. Take the numbers and combine them with what you're seeing on the streets to make the best business decisions.

Be diligent, even if the truth hurts. You don't want to be surprised by your financial situation, and ignoring negative information only makes matters worse. Use the sales and expense reports you generate as tools. They reveal what's working and what isn't. Use this insight to make meaningful and informed changes to avoid negative situations.

Calculating Your Breakeven Report

In order for your business to be profitable, you have to reach, and then exceed your *breakeven*—the figure you must make in gross sales to cover your expenses for the week, month, or year. Establishing a weekly and monthly breakeven for your business is the primary step in determining your truck's financial health.

Create a list of all your *fixed* and *variable costs*. Add up your fixed costs and divide them by the amount of time for which you're determining the breakeven. If you're trying to figure out your weekly breakeven, divide the total number by 52; for the monthly breakeven, divide the total amount by 12.

Your fixed costs are business expenses that aren't dependent upon the level of goods or services produced by your truck. They stay the same no matter how good or bad business is. Fixed costs include things like insurance and commissary costs. Your variable costs are expenses that change in proportion to your truck's activity: if you sell more food, the amount you spend on the ingredients will be higher.

To determine your weekly or monthly variable costs, generate a sales forecast for an average week or month on your truck. You can do it by reviewing historical data after a few months of business. If you're trying to do it prior to having that information, you'll have to make a conservative educated guess. Add up the costs for food, beverages, and staffing to generate your weekly or monthly variable costs. Due to *inventory rollover*—the inventory's current value from the beginning and ending of a specific time period—it's easiest to deal with food cost on a monthly basis. Counting your entire stock of food on a weekly or daily basis won't give you accurate data.

Now, combine your fixed and variable costs. The total will be your weekly or monthly breakeven. This is the amount of money you need to generate on a regular basis to cover your expenses. Anything beyond your breakeven is profit.

Reviewing Daily Sales and Expenses

Your daily sales and expense reports break down all the money you're earning and spending each day, including your labor and food costs, fuel, tickets, and all other expenses you incur. The sales reports should be broken down by individual menu item. You need to know how many of each product you're selling daily to determine which items are making and losing money, and how you should order for the following day's operation. You should also have a tally of how many customers you served on your daily report.

By keeping detailed records every day, you'll accumulate a history for your business. You can track and compare your sales and expenses on a day-to-day, month-to-month, and year-to-year basis. Being able to refer to what you made on the same day of the previous year enables you to determine trends. The patterns that emerge will help you anticipate these trends with moderate accuracy, so you can adjust your staffing, inventory, and other variable costs accordingly.

If you've invested in a point-of-sale (POS) system (see Chapter 11), it should include a feature that prints a variety of reports. These reports will enable you to better harness the power of historical information and implement changes to your truck that will help you succeed. Have your POS provider program your system to generate the reports you think can best assist you in managing your operations.

An accurate, detailed, and organized history of your revenue generation and expenses will prove useful for several reasons. Here are a few:

Determine whether your business is growing over time, and if not, why. This will be reflected in sales trends, profitability, and cover counts.

Avoid overstaffing. A daily report will help you accurately forecast demand. Being able to predict which days you can do without that extra pair of hands saves money.

Determine the quality of your cashiers' salesmanship. You may notice that your Friday sales are consistently lower when one employee works the window. Either the person working the window on the other days is great, or the one working on Friday is subpar. Either way, you'd better find out.

Determine the profitability of specials. By tracking the sales of your specials and the number of customers that they draw, you'll know which specials are most effective and worth repeating.

Monitor the consistency of your product. Is a lot of food thrown out, burned, spilled, or wasted on days that a particular chef is working? If you find a pattern of food having to be remade, you may need to retrain or replace the chef.

Evaluate promotions and how they affect sales compared to the previous year. What affect does a particular marketing campaign or loyalty program have on your gross and net revenues on a year-to-year basis?

Discover signs of theft. If your cover counts remain constant, but your sales are fluctuating, you may have an issue. Someone might be giving away food or stealing.

Weather. Always include the weather in your daily reports. Inclement weather can have a huge effect on your truck's business. You may have done half the business you did on this date last year, but if it's raining today, that doesn't necessarily mean your business is trending down. Don't draw inaccurate conclusions based on flawed information; make sure you know all the facts before making changes.

Generating an Income Statement

Also known as a profit and loss statement, an *income statement* is a monthly report that reviews your sales, expenses, and profits. It's basically a summary of all your daily financial reports over a 30-day period and can be as simple or as complicated as you like. Naturally, the more detailed your report, the better you'll be able to diagnose problems. With that said, for a small business like a food truck, I recommend keeping things as simple as possible.

Itemize all your expenses, including a breakdown of payroll, inventory, and sales, so that you can see exactly where your money's going each month. Include the figures for the same month of the previous year and your projected figures.

There's no right or wrong way to format your income statement. Again, if you've invested in a POS system, it should come preprogrammed to generate a monthly statement for you. Otherwise, simply plug your figures into a spreadsheet. It's for your own use, so make sure the spreadsheet is clear enough for you to read and understand. The document should be broken down into three sections: revenues, expenses, and profits. Separate your food and beverage sales from one another and the food and beverage costs from the rest of the expenses.

If you don't feel confident dealing with your daily or monthly figures yourself, consider working with in an accountant. You'll still need to keep a detailed and accurate record of your revenues and expenses, but you won't have to analyze the data yourself. Your accountant will take the information, combined with bank statements, generate the necessary financial reports, and give you advice. You can also have an accountant help you set up your systems, and then manage them on your own. That's a good way to save money but still run a professional and efficient operation.

Performing a Cash Flow Analysis

Your cash flow is the rate at which money enters and leaves your business. All businesses strive to maintain a delicate balance between the rate of spending and revenue generation. As you accumulate an accurate financial history of your business through daily and monthly statements, you'll develop a sense for predicting the rates at which you can expect to earn and spend money. It's a very important skill set because you must always be cognizant of how much debt you carry in relation to the income you're generating. You need to know when the bills are due and always have enough cash on hand to cover your expenses.

To determine your cash flow, use as many real numbers as possible, including your current bills for food, labor, and other expenses. Then use the forecast you created earlier to anticipate your sales for the coming weeks. As a truck owner, you must not only be aware of how much money you have at any given time, but also how much you owe. Determining your cash flow involves taking the cash you have in the bank, adding next week's expected revenue, and figuring out what expenses need to be paid at the same time. Perform this calculation for the next four to six weeks to determine your expected cash flow.

When making cash flow predictions, always round up for expenses and round down for sales. It will give you a worst-case prediction. You should always plan for the worst, not the best. If you take the worst-case approach, you'll never have to worry about covering your expenses.

Here are some tips to help you balance your cash flow:

Reduce your staff to lower payroll costs. If your cash flow figures aren't sustainable, you need to cut costs. Use your daily reports and monthly income statement to choose at least one or two days on which you can reduce staff by one team member.

Reduce inventory. Use your daily reports to determine which menu items are the least profitable. (See the next section for help doing this.) Downsize your inventory by limiting the menu or opting for less expensive ingredients. Never sacrifice quality, but aim to operate with minimum inventory until you build up your cash flow.

Opt for longer pay periods with your purveyors. Many suppliers will offer a small discount in exchange for paying within 7 to 10 days instead of the customary 30. Consider the benefit of foregoing the discount in exchange for holding on to your cash.

Never open tabs for customers. People, however well intentioned, are unpredictable. You're in the business of serving meals, not collecting debts. Always require payment up front in exchange for your products. If you do open a tab for anyone, don't count on receiving payment when predicting your cash flow.

Require a down payment for large catering events and parties. This cash can buy you some time by covering your immediate expenses and underwriting the costs of executing the event. As long as you don't misallocate the funds, nothing is better than using other people's cash to earn more money for your business.

Evaluating Operations

In addition to daily cash flow, income and expense reports, and monthly profit and loss statements, it's important to run more detailed reviews of your operations to help find solutions to problems that aren't revealed in the financial reports. You can do this by evaluating your menu and inventory item by item. These reviews will quickly illuminate what's making you money and what's causing inefficiencies in your operation.

Reviewing Your Menu Mix

An itemized analysis of everything on your menu will indicate which items are selling, which aren't, and the profitability of each. It's known as a *menu mix* report. This report is a valuable tool, and it can be as simple to construct as a computer spreadsheet. Include the following columns of information laid out in a horizontal format:

* **Menu item:** The name of each item on your menu.

* **Weekly sales totals:** The total number of that item sold that week.

* **Percentage of total sales by item:** If 10 out of the 100 entrées sold are burgers, they have a 10-percent popularity percentage.

* **Cost of item:** Include the food cost only.

* **Retail price:** What the item sells for on your truck.

* **Item profit:** Subtract the item cost from the retail price to determine the profit.

* **Total cost:** Multiply the item's cost by how many were sold this week.

* **Total revenue:** Multiply the retail price of the item by the total number sold.

* **Total profit generated per item:** Subtract the total cost from the total revenue generated. Now you know how much this item contributed to your bottom line.

* **Total menu costs:** The sum of all your food costs.

* **Total menu revenue:** The sum of all your food revenue.

* **Total profit:** Subtract the total menu revenue from the total menu costs.

After you've completed your spreadsheet, take some time to analyze the information. You should be able to answer some very important questions about your menu, including which items are the most and least popular and which have the highest and lowest profit margins. Often, you'll find that a dish with a low profit margin is one of the most popular and vice versa. Think of ways to make items with higher profit margins more popular. Make those items a special, change the name of the dish, or make your staff aware of the item's profitability, so they'll push it more to your customers.

Your menu mix report will also reveal important trends. You may notice, for example, that your customers prefer lighter dishes in the summer. Use that information to your advantage; change your menu seasonally to offer more of what your customers are seeking. Remember that they're voting with their dollars every time they order from your menu, and as with any vote, there will be winners and losers.

As Gordon Gekko said in the movie *Wall Street,* "Don't get emotional about stock." Your menu items represent potential revenue. If something isn't selling, you're sacrificing potential revenue and increasing your waste. Don't keep an item on your menu because you like it or it's your grandmother's recipe. Keep what sells, cut the rest, and don't look back.

If certain items on your menu are selling poorly, consider making one or more of the following adjustments:

* **Price.** You may be charging too much for these items. See Chapter 3 on how to price your menu to your market.

* **Visibility.** Is the item easy to find on your menu? Consider ways of highlighting your high-profit items to ensure that your customers notice them.

* **Imagery.** Does the language on your menu convey deliciousness, or does it sound bland, boring, or even intimidating? Consider renaming these items or rephrasing their descriptions.

* **Product knowledge.** Your staff needs to be completely familiar with everything on the menu, especially the high-profit items and those that may seem intimidating or unusual to customers. They must be able to describe the items confidently and upsell the higher-margin ones through enticing language.

* **Incentives.** Consider offering an inducement to the employees working the window to encourage them to sell a quota of high-profit items. It's a great way to motivate staff and push the items that add to the bottom line. With that said, make sure what they're pushing will also make the customers happy. There's no point in pushing an item if it doesn't induce them to return to your truck. Repeat business is your number one priority.

Reviewing Purchasing and Inventory

Inventory can be incredibly complicated, and there's no perfect formula for handling it. No two food trucks, even with similar menus, will choose the same ingredients or purchase goods the same way. You need to find out what works best for you and your business in the most cost-effective way possible. It's a matter of trial and error, and making incremental adjustments over time.

While purchasing and inventory are radically different for each food truck, there's one universal tool that can help you maintain a broad perspective of the cost-effectiveness of your purchasing habits. A cost of coods sold (COGS) report measures the true food cost percentage for your menu and inventory as a whole. It isn't very useful as a diagnostic tool, because it just provides a general figure. However, it's the easiest way to keep your finger on the pulse of your total food budget.

To determine your COGS:

1. Determine the total cost of your starting inventory.

2. Determine the total sum of inventory purchases you've made during the time period for which you're calculating.

3. Determine the total value of your ending inventory.

4. Subtract your ending inventory from the sum of your starting inventory and additional purchases.

5. Divide the sum from Step 4 by your total sales.

The figure that you end up with is your COGS percentage.

There are no hard-and-fast rules about where your COGS percentage should be, but I recommend keeping it at or below 30 percent. For a quick service business like a food truck, you'd ideally want your food cost to be even lower, but with the trend toward gourmet trucks, a lower figure may be difficult to achieve.

Controlling your food cost is vital to the health of your business, but you need to find a balance. What you're really doing is determining the point at which price meets value and quality. Your customers will notice minor changes in portion size or the types of ingredients you use, so you need to be diligent in the managing your food while making sure you don't negatively affect the experience you're trying to offer.

The bottom line is really the last word when it comes to operating your business. Generating these reports and using them to make proactive decisions will govern your truck's long-term success. Don't hide from the numbers. Deal with the fiscal realities, and empower yourself to grow and protect your business.

Building Your Clientele

As a seasoned marketer, when I discuss customer behavior, I tend to repeat the old saying, "You can bring a horse to water, but you can't make him drink." Marketing, promotions, and advertising creates buzz about your truck and gets people to show up, but it doesn't turn them into customers.

The product and the experience people have when they visit your truck is what will build your clientele in the long term. It's your job to under promise and over deliver on your customer's expectations. They should leave your truck blown away by the incredible food and service they received. That's the way to not only create customers who will spend money there regularly, but also get the best advertisement money can't buy. The word of mouth spread by a satisfied customer is pure gold when it comes to establishing a new truck.

Developing your clientele isn't about being in the newspaper or sending out Tweets. It's about delivering your customer's desires and surpassing their expectations. Most people know exactly what to do to make someone feel valued or special, but they don't go out of their way to actually do it. This chapter is about establishing a strategy to build and maintain your clientele by putting systems in place, and doing that special thing that your customer remembers. Doing these things creates loyalty and repeat business, which are the lifeblood of any entrepreneurial venture.

Feedback: Listen to the People Who Feed You

Have you ever watched a person or business make all the wrong decisions? We all seem to have the ability to see what's wrong with someone or something else, but when it comes to our own issues, we just don't get it. The same thing is true when it comes to our own businesses. And, in the case of a food truck, you don't have years to come to the realization that you need help. Your business will flourish or fail based upon your ability to quickly accept and implement feedback.

No one is better able to give you feedback than your customers and employees. These people are eating, drinking, and/or working at your truck all the time, and they know exactly what they like and don't like. The key is for you to make it comfortable for them to share this information with you. Why? Because you want to be the best, and you become the best by listening.

Naturally, all the feedback you receive won't be useful. Some of it won't make sense or be practical based on your business structure. After all, you know the intricacies of your business better than anyone else. The key is to approach all feedback with the most open mind possible. Always think to yourself, "What can I do to best deal with this particular point?" Sometimes, the answer will be nothing, but more often than not, you can make your truck more efficient or enjoyable because you chose to hear what a particular employee or customer had to say.

Now that you understand its value, the question becomes how to get honest and valuable feedback without negatively affecting your customers' experience. The most effective ways I've found are truck conversation, feedback cards, and online dialogue.

Truck Conversations

Truck conversations consist of communicating with your clientele to garner as much information as you can. In more simple terms, ask questions. I talked in Chapter 2 about how important it is for you to be a personality and to interact with your clients. This is just another reason why it's so critical to your success. Here are a variety of ways that you can interact with your customers:

Observe and converse. Observe your clients. When you see that they're enjoying themselves, say hello and introduce yourself. Let them know that you value having them as your customers and ask them what's been good about their experience with your truck. And, if you notice someone who doesn't look pleased, introduce yourself as well. Do everything in your power to fix the problem and *listen* to what made their experience negative. Thank them for their feedback regardless of whether you plan to use it. Then get cracking to make sure your truck is the best it can be.

Infuse positivity. It's amazing how you can turn an okay experience into a great one with a bit of positivity and enthusiasm. Say something like, "Isn't that the best meatball you ever had in your life?" This kind of comment makes customers feel special and opens them up to thinking the way you do: like attracts like.

Open-ended questions. Don't ask customers anything that can be answered by a simple yes or no. Ask questions that require a more extensive answer to get to their personal preferences.

Listen attentively. Don't look at your phone or other customers or allow yourself to be distracted in any way. Fully engage the person giving you feedback and respect the time he's spending for your benefit. By giving the customer your full attention, he'll know it means something to you and take it more seriously.

Names and faces. Make an effort to recognize your customers and try to speak to them by name. Recognition will make them feel special and more comfortable with you. Building a relationship with your customers will lead to a regular dialogue, and dialogue leads to honest feedback.

Feedback Cards

Feedback cards are another great way to garner information. I recommend using a postcard-size card with no more than five easy-to-answer questions on it that customers can respond to by rating an item—service or food quality—from 1 through 10. Their experience at your truck is going to be brief; customers won't have a lot of time to reply. At the bottom of the card, have a couple of lines for suggested improvements. You can do this playfully by saying something like "Help us help you" or "How can we better satisfy your cravings?". Customers should feel like they're speaking to someone who cares and that their feedback is valued.

Leave a box with a pen right next to the window of your truck, to make it easy for customers to drop in the cards upon completion. The best time to offer the cards is while the customer is waiting for food or with the package when you make a delivery. Expect only 50 percent of your customers to fill them out, and don't get discouraged by negative results. Use the feedback to get better.

Online Dialogue

Another way to get customer feedback is through the online dialogue you and your customers have about your truck. People will place reviews of your truck on websites like Yelp, Google, Infatuation, and Mobile-Cuisine.com. These reviews will be invaluable to you in monitoring your progress as a business. You need to be aware of what your customers are saying about you, and be registered on the sites, so that you can respond. Always respond positively to reviews, good or bad. Thank customers for taking the time to review your business, making sure they know their voice has been heard. Invite them to email you at your business address, and if they follow up, invite them in for a special visit or truck event. Going the extra step is what makes the difference between a good truck and a great one.

Expect additional chatter through social media applications like Facebook and Twitter. When customers post good or bad comments, you should always reply. A simple thank you, with a contact address for further customer service, is meaningful and will make the customer feel heard. Even more valuable than the customer service element will be the information you garner by monitoring feedback and applying it to your day-to-day operation.

Responding to Criticism and Praise

Criticism and praise are part of any hospitality business. Some customers will think you're the best truck in history, others will leave dissatisfied, and many will land somewhere in between. The key to your business is to do everything in your power to make sure the majority of customers leave happy. This will lead to those happy customers becoming your regulars. Be the best at what you do, and you shouldn't have any problems.

How do you respond when someone tells you that you're great or, more unpleasant, when they say you stink? Even more crucial, what should you do when a critic writes something negative about you on a food blog or in the local newspaper?

Take all reviews, praise, and criticism with an open mind. If someone writes something positive about your business, thank them, put your head down, and keep doing a good job. If someone writes something negative, evaluate, put your head down, and make any adjustments that you believe are necessary. When people are reviewing or critiquing you, it means you're doing something right. You have people's attention, and especially in the internet age, they're going to express their opinions.

The best way to get a positive review is to run an awesome truck. Great food, intuitive service, and a well-kept truck lead to great reviews. Yet, even then you can't ensure that everyone will love it. If you're lucky enough to receive a good or even great review, don't let it go to your head. Satisfaction is a disease—the beginning of the end for any business. Never let your guard down and always aspire to be better tomorrow than you were the day before.

In 2004, the Street Vendor Project began the Vendy Awards to raise money for the organization and protection of the rights of street vendors. In its final year, this annual event attracts thousands of visitors to Governors Island to vote on the best food trucks and street vendors in New York and New Jersey. Awards include Rookie of the Year, the People's Taste, and the best dessert truck, among others. A Vendy award is a badge of honor among street vendors and offers incredible exposure in the food press.

Gathering and Listening to Employee Feedback

Who knows your business better than your customers? Your employees. They see all aspects—front, back, middle, and side—of your operation. Speak with them as much as possible to get feedback on what's going well and what could use improvement. Make time to formally sit one on one with every staff member at least once a month. Also, speak with them informally as often as possible. Enabling communication to flow freely leads to surprising solutions and ideas from the most unlikely sources.

Here are some tips to assist in establishing an open environment:

Create a manager's log where all issues and problems are noted during operations. This record of any and all issues ensures that you'll remember to resolve them and can protect you if more serious issues arise.

Schedule a weekly staff meeting to discuss important plans and allow employees to vent. Meetings can be invaluable to an organization. Employees will do a better job if they feel free to express their concerns and feel vested in the decision-making process.

Allow for anonymous suggestions. Some employees don't feel comfortable speaking up, so create a suggestion box for people to share their thoughts anonymously.

Understanding Your Customers

Your customers are complex beings, not too different from yourself. Once you've identified who they are, it's important that you make an effort to understand what drives them. Ask the following:

* Why do they eat at your truck?

* What is it about your product that attracts them?

* What can you do to make the experience better for them?

* What would make them visit you more often or spend more money each time they visit?

By taking the time to understand your customers, your business will be more effective at servicing their needs.

Observing and Listening

There's no better way to understand your customers than to observe their behaviors and listen to what they say. People are creatures of habit, and watching what they do will give you an eye into what motivates them. Their conversations and comments can give you even more insight into what they're thinking and feeling.

If a customer says, "I love your food so much, but I can't eat here every day because I'll get fat," that might mean you should be including healthier options on your menu. Or, if someone shows up with napkins every time they eat at your truck, it could mean your food is too messy or that you need to supply a better napkin. Whatever it is, you'll gain tremendous insight into your customers by listening and observing.

Here are some additional things to consider:

What do your customers have in common that drives them to your brand? Does everyone who eats at your truck love football? Or, are they all talking about that new show on HBO? Figuring out their similarities will help you cater to your customers more accurately.

Review your menu mix. Figure out what your customers are eating and not eating. Once you have that information, you can speak to some of them to get deeper insights into why they choose one item over another. Maybe they love your meatball hero, but the portion is too large, so they choose the burger instead.

What is the perceived price-value relationship of your truck by your customers? Do they think your truck is a good deal or too highly priced? Are they looking for a lunch or dinner special? Maybe your portions need to be larger or smaller.

Anticipating Their Desires

Reactivity is a recipe for disaster. Food trucks—and businesses in general—must be proactive to be successful. Once you understand your customers, you'll be able to look at the larger environment and anticipate what they might want. If you're selling hamburgers and you read in a food magazine that sliders are the next big food trend, maybe you should add them to your menu. Or, if you're a juice truck and you realize all your friends are drinking coconut water, maybe you should be offering that item as well. Keep your eyes open for opportunities, and then think of the best ways to capitalize on them.

Just because your competition lowers their prices or begins offering an alternative item doesn't mean you should do the same. Take the time to analyze every situation. Make a list of the positives and negatives of any decision, and then make educated guesses. The effects of your choices are cumulative, meaning they increase as you make more of them. Take the time to make the best decisions for your truck's future.

What's important is that you be aware. Just because your truck is successful today doesn't mean it'll still be a hit tomorrow. Doing research, visiting trade shows, and shopping your competition's trucks will keep you ahead of the game.

Exceeding Expectations

When customers come to your truck, they're expecting a certain level of food, service, and treatment. The better you're doing as a business, the higher your customers' expectations will be. It's your job to exceed their expectations every time. To do so, you must make every guest's experience personal.

When I walk into my local coffee shop in the morning, the guy at the counter makes my cup the way I like it without me even asking. It makes me feel like a king. You can do that for your customers, too, by listening to each one's likes and dislikes and committing them to memory. Do everything in your power to ensure that your customers get what they want when they visit you. Some truck owners do it by keeping lists of their best customers' preferences. Each time one of them comes up to the truck, the operator knows what he usually orders. Simply saying, "You want your usual side of spicy sauce?" is a great way to exceed a customer's expectations. The best operators do this every time, and this attention to detail is clearly displayed by their growing profits.

Great customer service is the exception, not the rule. You would think with so many hospitality businesses out there, most would be great, but the truth is that the majority are mediocre.

Here are some simple things that can help you be the best:

Go the extra mile for your customers. Amuse their kids, give them an extra side of fries, or get them that soda they always talk about. Do anything you can to make them leave your truck happy.

Give them something to talk about. Customers love to tell their friends how they're treated like VIPs at a truck. Give them an off-the-menu special taco you keep on the side; they'll tell everyone how amazing it is. Or, tell them about an upcoming food truck festival before the news is released to the public. Make them feel like insiders.

If a customer has been waiting in line for a while, offer them a free item for their next visit. Also, use social media to engage your customers. For example, use a password to get a special discount or item on any given day.

Roy Choi, the Kogi chef, runs nightly specials on all his trucks. Some of the more famous ones include Barbeque Sliders and the Venice Beach Vegan Taco. Specials drive the check average up, keep people interested, and get rid of excess inventory before it spoils.

Find out what they love, and then use the information. If your best customer loves baseball, get him a hat from the local team. Or, if one of your customers always talks about a special type of hot sauce, show you listen and get him a bottle.

Show your thanks. Email or send thank-you cards to your best customers. It's amazing how much a personal note means to people.

Offer preview tastings. Include your customers in your process: let them try the different items you're testing before you add them to your menu. It makes them feel vested in your truck and will provide you great feedback.

Making Amends: Service Recovery

The service recovery paradox is that a service or product failure can offer the chance for a business to receive higher customer satisfaction than if the problem had never occurred.

I promise you, no matter how good you are, you and your employees will make mistakes. The secret to the hospitality business is how you recover from them. Every negative customer service situation is your chance to make a customer for life by quickly and effectively fixing things.

Let's say juice falls off the counter of your truck and spills on a woman's T-shirt. Service recovery would dictate that you quickly make her another juice for free and buy her a new T-shirt. I guarantee she'll never buy juice from another truck.

Service recovery is the way to turn angry people into loyal customers who will tout your virtues to their friends.

Strategies for Earning Customer Loyalty

Events and frequent dining cards are the best ways to encourage customer loyalty on a food truck.

Events. Once you're no longer the new kid on the block, it's important to have special events that encourage people to return to your truck and give them something to talk about. After you've been operating for six months to a year, try to have a special event once every three months. If you have a taco truck, you can host a gathering at a local park with music and all-you-can-eat tacos. Such events will not only garner press coverage, they will also differentiate you from competing taco trucks.

Frequent dining cards. Frequent dining cards are a great way to get customers to return to your truck regularly. Customers love to know that their tenth lunch will be free. It's the perfect motivator, and if you've ever had a card like this, you know that there's a certain satisfaction in getting it punched. Customers will be carrying that card around, and every time they go for their wallet, there you are.

You'll have to make sure your employees actively encourage customers to use them. The cards need to be an integral part of the check-out process, and you must honor the commitments you make. Nothing would be worse than promising a customer something, and then letting them down.

Your frequent dining card should be about the size of a business card. It should have your logo on one side and boxes or stars on the other. The boxes or stars denote how many times they have to eat at the truck before they get their reward. Each time they dine, the card should be punched with a hole puncher or stamped with a custom stamp. Coming up with a unique name for your rewards program, such as "dining all-star" or "meatball maven", is a good way to keep people interested.

Gathering Contact Information

As I discussed earlier in the book, it's critical to gather your customers' contact information. The more information you're able to garner from your clientele, the less dependent you'll be on external sources of advertisement and marketing.

Before your truck's launch, you need to have systems in place to gather email addresses and Twitter followers. The best way to do it is by including your website address and social media application connections on all materials on or related to your truck. After you've driven traffic to your site, capture the information. Front and center on your website, you should have an email submission form and Twitter follow button.

I highly recommend providing incentives to the customers to submit their contact information by offering a monthly sweepstakes for a gift certificate or other reward that involves your truck. In the marketing business, these are referred to as *calls to action*. You should never activate any of your marketing campaigns without a call to action— something that causes the customer to act. Providing incentives for the customer to take action allows you to clearly measure the effectiveness of your campaign and get your client to sample your truck.

Companies like Mailchimp.com help you organize the information customers submit on your website by putting it into an Excel file. Once the information is in Excel, it's much easier to break down by location and other relevant points. Unleashing the power of this information will make you a more effective marketer.

You can also gather your customers' information through direct contact with them. One way to get this information is to have a container where people can drop their business cards to enter a contest of some sort. The other way is to just ask. If you're at the window, tell customers that you want to keep them informed of promotions and your truck location. Most of the time, they'll be honored to be asked to be part of something meaningful by the owner; people like to feel special, so make them feel great and build your business in the process.

Expanding Your Marketing Efforts

If you take some time to count all the burger restaurants, it will blow your mind. Along with In-N-Out and McDonald's, Burger King has over 15,000 locations. Wendy's has over 5,000. And, even with the 56,000-plus restaurants between these four brands, there was enough demand in the market for Shake Shack. Yet, they've opened 136 locations since 2004. It doesn't stop there.

There is BurgerFi, Smashburger, JG Melon, Five Guys, Fatburger, Johnny Rockets, P. J. Clarke's, Umami Burger, White Castle, Bill's, and numerous others. Plus, it's not as if you can't get a good burger in most restaurants serving standard American fare.

How does this make sense? Don't people crave something different or something new? Isn't variety the spice of life? It turns out that isn't entirely true. An overwhelming majority of successful businesses in general, and restaurants specifically, serve and sell familiar items. For the most part, in fact, the point of innovation or differentiation lies in the creative execution of a familiar form, not in the creation of an entirely new form.

Take, for instance, the Cronut, a croissant-doughnut pastry. Dominique Ansel didn't create something new; he combined two familiar forms in a new way. He did the same thing with milk and cookies, transforming the familiar chocolate chip cookie into a cup, and then filling it with flavored milk. Ansel successfully expressed his personal creative vision through a familiar form.

The same could be said of boutique hotels, Airbnb, Uber, Instagram, and many of the most innovative companies in the world. They are all branded reinterpretations or use changes applied to familiar forms. We rarely experience complete disruptions, such as the communication revolution brought about by social media, or the industrial revolution ushered in by the factory system and later the assembly line.

Humans are more comfortable with evolution than revolution. We crave the familiar. We want to be comfortable, we want to understand, we embrace nostalgia, and we're always trying to find our way back to our home, to the familiar.

While I believe deeply that to achieve your food truck success, you must create something that's unique, different, and special, and reflects your true self. However, for it to resonate with your audience and gain traction, the form and presentation must be familiar.

The Myth of the Food Business

The biggest myth about food businesses is that once you're open, the customers just show up, as if by magic. People love to speculate about how much money a truck owner or restaurateur must be making when they see a big line or all the tables filled. They'll pat you on the back, smile, and say, "Business must be pretty good," as they calculate your truck profits in their heads. But that's like thinking that football is easy because you see the players dancing in the end zone after they score a touchdown. The truth is that food trucks don't have lines all the time, and football players spend countless hours training before they score a touchdown.

The food truck business is a marathon, not a sprint. Like football, it's about teamwork, planning, and how many great days—victories—you can put together in a row. In this business, you aren't a champion until you're consistently profitable over a long time period.

In previous chapters, I talked about how to set up, launch, and start your truck. However, once you're operating, how do you keep the lights on and the money flowing in? It takes great marketing, combined with a consistent product. Sounds simple, but what happens after you aren't the new kid on the block anymore once everyone has tried your tacos and four brand-new taco trucks arrive in the neighborhood? What do you do then to differentiate your product and attract customers?

In the past, that was a mystery. Some trucks advertised, some gave out frequent buyer cards, and others discounted. The truth is, there is a formula. None of these methods work alone, but when combined, magic happens.

Strategic Sharing

We all crave the sense of belonging that comes with being part of a community, which enables us to experience that fellowship with others that results from sharing common interests and goals. These connection types engage our spirits. Habitually, we're driven to organize ourselves into groups—by industry, religion, hobby, sports teams, and even the television shows we watch. Therefore, to effectively share your food truck ideas, it's critical that you recognize the importance of your community and how they've evolved.

In the industrial age, communication was primarily a one-way road where messages went out from those controlling the distribution channels and were consumed by the watchers and listeners. The places where people could comment or criticize were also limited. The only way to amplify your message was to spend more money on advertising. The more you spent promoting your message, the more exposure your message received. Whether the audience liked the message was a guessing game.

Today, the cost of communicating is far less, and digitally, the reaction is instant and measurable. While you can still buy distribution, the more you advertise or sell, the less engaged the communities you reach will be. Trust has replaced money as the most valuable commodity in communication; in a saturated environment, we only pay attention to messages from trusted sources. Additionally, that one-way road has become a multilane expressway, with trending messages that are circulated and recirculated by communities with overlapping interests.

Instead of sending out one-way messages—i.e., traditional advertising—you must now relate to these overlapping communities by appealing to their shared beliefs, values, and struggles. We call this *strategic sharing*—putting the needs and desires of the audience ahead of your own while maintaining your intention to achieve a desired outcome. When you find the communities that share your belief system, you must contribute meaningfully and consistently. For some, this may mean sharing information or creativity, while for others, it may mean throwing food truck events or giving to charity. While it requires patience and time, anything worth doing requires that you make significant investments. This type of cultivated amplification is the result of doing the right thing over a long time period, and consistently and strategically doing right by your audience is the special sauce of modern marketing.

However, you don't have to be a global brand to apply strategic sharing. In Manhattan's Soho district, there's a restaurant named Jack's Wife Freda that applies strategic sharing beautifully. While their food is consistent and high-quality, they aren't serving high-end cuisine and haven't spent tons of money on décor or marketing. Yet, Jack's Wife Freda is jammed all the time—so much so that they had to open three locations. The owners, Maya and Dean Jankelowitz, are restaurant veterans who trained for many years under the legendary restaurateur Keith McNally of Balthazar fame. They're present, attentive, nice, and involved with their community.

Their goal has always been to run a great, comfortable, and successful restaurant and take care of their regulars—their "true fans". They've done an incredible job of tapping into overlapping communities by simply doing the right thing. Over the years, their friends and customers have become influential in the communities of fashion, art, media, and hospitality. These people posted regularly about Jack's on their social media channels, which led hordes of young professionals to flock to the restaurant. Maya and Dean did the right thing, combined it with good strategic thinking, and over time the communities amplified their message.

Unlocking the power of strategic sharing and your community all comes back to the quality of your contribution. The more giving you are, the more likely a community will embrace your message and amplify it. Once you've earned their trust, you must continue to contribute by delivering on the promises you've made, even if that's just serving a hot cup of coffee. When you do the right thing, strategically and consistently, the universe will reward you endlessly.

The Creative Element

Creative (as a noun) encompasses everything from your logo to your social media photos to all the content you produce—videos, photos, blog posts, email newsletters, printed flyers, business cards—and even the way in which you communicate your food truck's message. Creative is expressed through content, which is directed toward specific audiences via any form of media, from television to the internet, smartphones, books, ebooks, magazines, and live events. Creative is the product of transforming your idea into sharable forms of messaging that people can interact with, relate to, and use any of the modern platforms. However, what does it mean for you?

Consumers, especially those under the age of 40, don't pay attention when they're being sold to directly, especially when the source isn't a trusted one. It means your only way in is to entertain and creatively engage them with your truck's brand. Your brand must be a wellspring of inspiring, beneficial, and interesting content that reinforces your core value and beliefs. Once you have that, you have to amplify your creative and get it in front of the right eyes, which brings us to distribution.

The Distribution Element

> Sharing is good, and with digital technology, sharing is easy.
> —Richard Stallman, internet activist

Distribution refers to how you share your creative with consumers. How do you get the word out about your food truck? Think of your creative as a tree falling in the woods. You can have the best content ever made, but if you can't get eyeballs on it, no one will ever know about it. In the modern world, digital content is the primary way for you to get that message to the most people for the least expense. It is highly efficient, requires minimal investment, and provides instant feedback.

For instance, 17 percent of the world's population is on Facebook, with many people using the site daily. They provide gobs of information, from where they are hanging out and eating, to what they are watching, to what they are planning to do and with whom. It's a marketer's bonanza, a strategic sharer's ultimate playground. Google search is similar. If you're signed into your Gmail account when you are searching and using Google Chrome as your browser, then Google basically has access to everything you are doing on the web.

While from a user standpoint, this is less than desirable, it provides amazing information to marketers, and for you, that is an enormous opportunity to promote your food truck. Digital channels are by far the most effective, efficient, and measurable way to disseminate your food truck idea. The challenge in digital marketing is matching the right message (your "creative") with the right customer, demographic, or psychographic. While there are some amazing tools available to help you do that, like Facebook Business Manager and Google Analytics, it really is a high-tech game of trial and error. Test, test, and test again until you find your audience.

Distribution Channels

The kinds of distribution channels you'll be using generally fall into four buckets:

* **Paid:** Distribution you purchase on any channel, such as Facebook or Google advertisements or just plain old ads or billboards.

* **Owned:** Distribution points that you're in full control of, such as your website(s) or in-room advertisements at a hotel.

* **Shared:** Your social media channels where you're part of a community and can actively share your content with that community.

* **Earned:** Mainly refers to other people talking about you because they like what you're doing. If someone writes an article about your new ice cream on Eater or blogs about you, that's earned media, public relations, and referrals.

All these channels work together to reinforce your message. Think of your messaging like items on the food truck's menu. Certain items, like burgers and pizza, will be sure sellers, while others won't sell, like tripe or snails. You need to determine which of your messages—your menu items—are the sure sellers and which are not. You'll know this through both anecdotal feedback and hard data from your analytics platforms and website usage. Tools like Google Analytics and Facebook Ad Manager are free and easy to use, so you have no excuse not to know more about how your messages are performing. Once you have this information, even if it's just a hunch, you need to combine your messages to yield the best results. Again, think of this like a menu; you're trying to figure out the combination of an appetizer, entrée, and dessert that most people will order. Your goal is to filter and refine your feedback, so you can focus your resources on the most effective channels and messages. The greater your distribution, the more amplified your message.

The Experiential Element

The third element of modern marketing is *experiential*. Experiential is where your idea comes to life in some physical form with which your audience can interact. It can be in the form of an event, a live marketing activation, or a retail store. Even if your business has no brick-and-mortar presence, it's still very important that customers be able to experience who you are and what you do. It may mean hearing you speak, tasting or sampling your product, or visiting a pop-up location. Whatever you choose, this physical manifestation of an idea helps people understand what you do and gives them permission to believe more deeply.

Influence isn't a new concept born from influencers; all advertising and marketing has always been based on influence. It's why we used to buy full-page magazine ads, TV commercials, and vied for the attention of magazine editors. But with the democratization of communication and technology, the owner of that influence has shifted, and it continues to evolve. While some influencers, magazines, and newspapers are highly valuable, some are not. As marketers and entrepreneurs, you need to move away from relying on any one outlet or person who may have the power at the moment, and instead build your own influence. You can do that by establishing a strong direct relationship with your audience.

In an ever-changing landscape, the best way to build influence is through a direct relationship on platforms you own, like a website or email newsletter. Secondary platforms like social media, or YouTube are amazingly impactful as well, especially for building awareness about your food truck and finding new customers. However, you are at the whim of the company running the platform. The more direct your relationship, the more you control your influence, and the less dependent you are on intermediaries who will eventually cost you money and dilute your message. Remember, your platform is there to generate food truck profits and please all users, not just serve you and your needs. Shareholders will eventually force publicly traded platforms to monetize.

Influence equals freedom. The more you have, the more opportunities you have to create value for yourself by making people aware of your truck brand and getting them to come experience it. This thought must be paramount in every interaction you have with your followers. If they trust you and engage with you, then your influence is growing. Influence is critical to your success in the modern paradigm, no matter your pursuit.

Storytelling

Right now, you are a legend in your own mind. Though you can see your truck idea in your head or even in your hand, the greater universe is not yet aware of what you have to offer. Through strategic sharing, your audience will awaken to who you are and what you have created or intend to create. The goal is for you, your ideas, and your creations to become legendary in everyone else's mind. Let me explain.

A legend is a compelling, especially well-known individual, group, or narrative. Legends are often associated with an exceptional skill, capability, or event. Take, for example, the story of how Steve Jobs and Steve Wozniak founded Apple. This origin story ends with the creation of the most valuable company in human history and made Jobs, Wozniak, and their brand legendary. What started simply as an idea eventually transformed all involved into legends through great storytelling. It is no different than the story of how Barack Obama became president, the story of the founding of our country, or the story of the parting of the Dead Sea. These stories transformed the people, ideas, and things involved into legends. Storytelling is the most effective form of communication we have, and learning to do it well is a critical tool in your strategic sharing toolbox.

The story you tell about the origin and development of your food truck idea will play a big role in whether your audience engages. For example, without a doubt there were extreme amounts of death, destruction, and massive shifts of wealth and power that went into the formation of America. Yet, the story we're told conjures an upstart nation fueled by democratic ideals overthrowing an exploitative empire.

The stories people like to hear are ones that make them feel good, and that are entertaining, exciting, inspirational, and easy to remember. Keep this in mind as you craft your origin story, consider the following:

* **Simplicity and positivity.** Keep your story and messaging simple, direct, and positive. You have mere seconds to grab a customer's attention, so make your message clear. Keep your messages upbeat, focusing on the solving aspect of your creation's problem-solution equation. As for negativity, no one wants to hear someone complain.

* **Repeatable.** Give your customers something they can and want to easily share with their friends. A New York bar recently made a spicy chicken wing covered in hot sauce made with liquid gold. While this is clearly ridiculous, it's also very easily repeatable. "Did you see those hot wings made with gold?" Insert opinion, share video. A short, impactful story is easiest for us to remember and repeat.

* **Relatable or aspirational.** Can you see yourself doing the same thing as the people in the story? Do you want to see yourself doing it? If you want to engage a particular audience, make sure they are able to connect with your story or maybe even aspire to be part of it. Your audience should hear your story and say, "Yes, I agree," "I have felt like that, too," or "I want to do that."

* **Struggle.** Nobody is perfect, and knowing that everyone experiences struggle is a notably comforting feeling for someone who is struggling. Beyond that, it's appealing to root for the underdog, a position most of us have experienced. When you tell your story, remember that people want to know something about a challenge or struggle you've encountered or are encountering on your journey to success. Because living a fulfilled life and manifesting astonishing success invariably requires overcoming a struggle, it shouldn't be too hard to find your own stories of struggle that people can relate to.

* **Redemption.** All struggle ends with some form of redemption for the hero. Give your story a happy ending. If that's hard to do because you're still struggling, then point to the light at the end of the tunnel. Illuminate the knowledge you've gained and the challenge you're on your way to overcoming. This will provide a payoff to your audience and enable them to further invest in your successes.

Humans crave stories—it's how we share and connect with one another. We constantly tell and share these stories, so getting yours to be part of the conversation is important to the sharing and amplification of your idea. For that to happen, your story must be told and reinforced on all your channels, both owned and paid. The more your story is repeated, refined, and accepted by your tribe, the more a groundswell of support will grow for you and your pursuits. This support will eventually form a community, or as some call it, *a tribe*. The more your story is told, the closer you will be to becoming a legend ... and as they say, legends never die.

The Compounding Cycle

The key to unlocking the power behind your food truck brand is using a *layered marketing* approach, which is a method in which multiple marketing techniques are utilized in one campaign to reinforce the brand's message and intentions, thereby generating tangible results. I call it the *compounding cycle*. It combines public relations, advertising, social media, experiential follow through, and personal relationships to reinforce a singular message to the target market. I call it *compounding* because it's similar to compounding interest: the marketing message and momentum get exponentially more powerful with each repeat of the cycle.

Determining Your Message

The first and most important step in the process is determining your message. And, there's no point in drilling a message into the minds of consumers unless it's the correct one.

Let's say you're selling meatballs. Is your message that you have the best, the highest quality, the cheapest, or that you'll deliver your meatballs the fastest? All those are potential marketing messages. The question is which one will work? How do you determine the answer before you spend thousands of dollars on a campaign?

Figure out who your consumer is and what motivates him when he makes a buying decision. If your truck is parked on a college campus, the price and taste of your product will usually be more important than the nutrition. But if you're in a hip downtown business district, nutrition and quickness may be your customers' main concerns. Identify, to the best of your ability, what motivates your clientele, and then tailor your marketing message to those factors. You're looking for the point where motivation meets marketing.

In the 1970s and 1980s, Domino's Pizza built their brand on speed. Domino's promised they would deliver your food in 30 minutes or less; if not, you got your pizza free. Domino's realized that when their customers were hungry, they wanted their food quickly. They focused on that motivating factor and built a billion-dollar business on it.

The Campaign

Once you've determined your marketing message, you need to design an effective campaign around it. That means packaging the message into flyers, emails, social media messages, and consumer experiences that encapsulate it. The goal is to make the information in your materials as easy to consume as possible, motivating your customers to make a buying decision. Unless you're an artist yourself, creating your marketing materials will involve hiring a graphic designer to take your words and present them alongside your truck brand.

For instance, if you're selling the highest-quality beef hot dogs at the best possible price, your slogan might be, "Artisanal quality at artist prices. Who says an artist has to starve?" Then you'll integrate your slogan into every aspect of your business. No one should make a purchase from you without being aware of that slogan.

The Steps

Once you have your message and your slogan, the compounding cycle really takes effect. You must constantly repeat the program outlined here to reinforce the message and grow your customer base:

1. Distribute the promotional materials for your event or promotion via email, social media outlets, your website, and other methods of direct contact with your customers.

2. Reinforce your marketing message through trusted sources: television news, newspapers, magazines, and other reputable communication outlets. Most consumers believe what these sources tell them because they don't seem to have ulterior motives. The value of press coverage from a trusted food blog or association with a notable personality can lead to much more business than an email blast or Twitter message on its own.

3. Give your promotion life with experiential follow through (see Chapter 9).

4. After any successful promotion, you must thank your customers. They're your lifeblood and, like a relative, they want to feel appreciated. Make sure you send an email, Tweet, or post a sign on your truck thanking your customers. Your thank you should also be personal. The extra effort you make with a phone call, email, or handwritten note will come back to you tenfold.

The compounding cycle is about generating repeat business by forming consumer habits related to your brand.

Let's assume you're planning to offer a special green hot dog for St. Patrick's Day. Create digital and print flyers and distribute them through your communication outlets in as close a timeframe as possible to when your customers will be making their buying decisions. You don't want to send out a St. Patrick's Day food truck promotion two weeks ahead of time. No one decides what they'll eat for lunch that far in advance. It makes more sense to distribute flyers two to three days before the holiday, and then send an email message the morning of St. Patrick's Day.

The best way to ensure press coverage is be friend local writers or employ an effective public relations firm. Another way to get a trusted source on your side is to purchase advertising. That ad space purchase might include editorial coverage or the event's sponsorship as part of the package. Getting a news source to copromote your truck will greatly enhance the message you're sending to customers.

When partnering with media outlets or notable personalities, make sure they represent the image you want for your brand. Often, businesses partner just to create buzz but wind up creating the wrong kind of buzz, which could end up with your brand being less trusted than it was before.

Let's say 1,000 people show up for green hot dogs and you only have 300 to sell. That's bad experiential follow through. Good experiential follow through involves being prepared by gauging the demand, setting up a system to deliver the green hot dogs quickly, having entertainment to distract the waiting customers, and making sure the green hot dogs taste better than any hot dog you've ever served before. Now you have the opportunity to turn this into an annual St. Patrick's Day promotion. People will talk about the promotion and look forward to it every year.

Never overpromise. It's always important to underpromise and overdeliver in the hospitality business. Your marketing efforts should be enough to motivate a buying decision, but not too much beyond that. If you promise the best meatball in the world or your money back, you're setting yourself up for failure. It's inevitable that someone's going to be disappointed. Manage expectations so that you can comfortably surpass them and leave your customers thrilled, not disappointed.

The best advertising in the world comes through word of mouth. You can't buy it; you have to earn it. Repeating the compounding cycle hundreds or even thousands of times is the only thing that leads to long-term success in the hospitality business. Some people will tell you otherwise, but they either don't know what they're talking about or they're lying. Great hospitality businesses are a combination of meaningful marketing that speaks to the customer and great experiential follow through. Rinse and repeat.

Social Media

In Chapter 9, I gave you a basic breakdown of how you should utilize social media to start your truck business. Here, I elaborate by giving you some examples of successful food truck social media campaigns.

Doubletree CAREavan

Doubletree is a famous hotel brand owned by Hilton. They're known for giving out chocolate chip cookies—almost 21 million a year. For the 25th anniversary of the brand, Hilton created the CAREavan, a food truck that's mission was a "10-week, 10,000 mile, 50-city journey to deliver hundreds of thousands of smiles to weary workers, tired travelers, and local charities across the country through the pleasant surprise of a chocolate chip cookie treat."

Social media played a massive role in the campaign's execution and its eventual success. The Doubletree Facebook page featured an application that tracked the truck's location in real time, as well as videos, tweets, and an entry form for a CAREavan contest to win free hotel rooms. The Doubletree Facebook page vastly increased the number of "likes" they received after the campaign was launched.

Doubletree used Foursquare to update the truck's location and teamed with Topguest to offer Hilton rewards for checking in. On Twitter, they offered a contest in which followers had the chance to win a delivery of 250 cookies for using the hashtag #sweetbreak when posting. Finally, they used YouTube to capture "Cookie Confessionals"—people talking about why they love cookies.

The campaign was multilayered and blanketed the internet with a very clear message: Doubletree is welcoming, hospitable, and accessible. They got all of that out of combining social media with a simple cookie.

Made for Mexicue

Seasonal items are a great way to encourage visits from your clientele. One summer, New York truck Mexicue started a "Summer Market Special" contest in which customers submitted recipes for an item to be featured on the truck. The promotion became so successful that the boys decided to continue the promotion every season. Using a Facebook app, Mexicue announced a different seasonal ingredient every couple of months. The truck accepted recipe submissions and posted them for Facebook users to vote on. The winner received a truck card, and Mexicue featured the winning recipe on its menu the following season. The campaign was a great way to engage customers in the brand. It also helped make Mexicue so successful that it has now become a chain with multiple brick-and-mortar locations in New York and Washington D.C.

Chil'lantro BBQ

Chil'lantro BBQ is Austin, Texas's version of the venerable Korean taco truck. The owner, Jae Kim, is an avid fan of Twitter, Facebook, Yelp, and Foursquare and uses them for communicating with customers and marketing the happenings of his truck (and now restaurants). His most successful social media campaign happened during the South by Southwest festival. Kim teamed up with mobile payment system Go Payment, an iPhone credit card processing company, to offer tacos at a greatly reduced price to customers who signed up to follow the truck on Twitter and paid for the tacos with their credit card. It turned out to be a huge motivating factor for the customers at the festival; many were technologically savvy and weren't carrying much cash.

What made this an awesome campaign was the way Kim matched his desire for more Twitter followers with the target market's desire for cheap eats and fondness for paying through credit. Jae Kim listened to his customers and was rewarded in the process.

Beware of becoming overly dependent on social media. There's no replacement for a sound business plan, personal relationships, and great planning. Social media is part of a good marketing plan, but it isn't a good marketing plan on its own.

Publicity

Using public relations properly will lead to a positive perception of your food truck in the blogosphere, local community, and media.

In order to do proper press outreach for your truck, you'll need to prepare a press kit, which should include information on the key players, photographs, and a general description of your truck, menus, and possibly a special promotional item related to your business. I've seen press kits delivered by butlers and include chocolates shaped like the logo of the business. You should do whatever it takes for the media to have a positive connection with your product. Place your information in a clean folder made from high-quality stock with your logo on it. Make sure your business card is prominently placed on the front of or inside the folder.

When it comes to publicity, there are two ways to go: handle it internally or hire an outside company. It all depends on your budget. I suggest hiring a professional for your first three to six months of operation at no more than $2,500 per month, and then go it alone. If you can't afford to hire a publicist, don't worry; you can make it on your own.

The main advantage of putting publicity in an expert's hands in the beginning is that it will enable you to focus on refining your operations during those critical first months.

Handling public relations yourself can be very effective, as long as you live by one rule: avoid being negative. As I've said before, like attracts like, and negativity will only attract more negativity. Never say anything bad about your competition, the authorities, or anyone else for that matter. As far as you're concerned, everyone is spectacular, and you're happy to be part of this great industry.

The upside of doing your own publicity is that no one knows your business better than you. You created the project, and no one will talk about it with more passion than you. The downside is that you won't have the benefit of working with a professional who has experience and an outside perspective. Interview several PR firms even if you don't plan on hiring one; it's a great way to generate ideas and make connections. Don't worry about wasting someone's time. As long as you're relentlessly positive and cordial, something good will come out of the meetings.

PR firms generally work on a monthly retainer, though some will work on an event basis as well, meaning you don't have to pay them when you have nothing in particular for them to promote. For a start-up business like a food truck, paying on an event basis is a great way to work with a PR professional without making a major commitment.

Community Outreach

Your publicity will form the public's perception of your truck and you. My advice is to make a positive contribution to your community. There's no better way to generate positive PR than doing good and sharing. By positively contributing to your surrounding neighborhoods, you'll generate goodwill for you and your business.

Your food truck should be involved in as many charity events as possible to build relationships in the community while enhancing your brand image. Use these opportunities to let people try your grub, sampling what you've worked so hard to create. The people you're helping will become word-of-mouth advertisers, espousing the virtues of you and your business. You should spend a minimum of a few hundred dollars a month on sampling your product through charity functions. If you become super successful, I recommend using up to 10 percent of your income on assisting the community. I promise you, it isn't something you'll regret over the long haul.

It's one thing to donate your assets and those of your employees; contributing your own personal time to the community will be even more meaningful. Volunteer for the local chamber of commerce, food truck association, or other groups. An even better option would be to join a group your customers admire or that has a high-profile image within your community. As a leader in the food truck or hospitality community, you'll have a forum in which to promote your views and protect your business.

Advertising

Advertising isn't generally useful for food trucks due to the cost. It's very difficult, especially for a small business to gauge the performance of an advertising campaign.

If you do choose to advertise, you need to be focused. Taking ad space in *The New York Times* doesn't make sense for a food truck. You'd have to sell thousands of falafels or hot dogs to pay for just one advertisement. However, if there's a food festival going on in downtown Manhattan and that's where you park, you could advertise on the ticket or program. The cost will be relatively reasonable and the exposure is targeted to people who love food and will be near your truck.

Sponsorship is a great way for food trucks to advertise. Local athletic teams and charity events will give you maximum return and generate community goodwill at a comparatively low cost. There can also be opportunities for you to sell your product by parking at the games or events.

When you're a new food truck operator, your primary objective should be to create awareness within your target market. Your advertisements should include all the relevant information about your truck and a call to action. Before running an ad, make sure it covers the following five most important aspects of your business:

* Name

* Type of product

* Why it's special

* Website address

* Twitter hashtag

Customers can't act if they don't know what they're looking for. Mystery makes for great books, not great advertising.

Repetition and Consistency

When it comes to the sharing strategies I've been discussing, repetition and consistency are crucial to using them effectively.

Repetition is the performing of an action over and over again. Messages can only break through to our deeper consciousness when they're repeated. As Schopenhauer said, "All truth passes through three stages. First, it is ridiculed. Second, it is violently opposed. Third, it is accepted as being self-evident." The only way to get past ridicule and violent opposition is to practice repetition.

Consistency is when the quality of a product or service doesn't vary greatly over time. Every great brand is consistent. The practice of brand management is actually defined as managing what makes you consistently different. Name any product you think of as great and you'll realize the consistent delivery of quality is what makes the product that way. Coca-Cola? Google? Mercedes? The reason people use their products is because they've consistently met or exceeded their promise over time. If your Coca-Cola didn't consistently taste the way you expected it to, or Google didn't consistently provide the search results you were looking for, you'd find another product that did.

Brands, products, and people can only manifest their full potential when they're able to combine repetition with consistency. To unlock your potential, you must show up every day and reinforce what you want the world to know about you and your truck. You must repeat your message consistently until your audience begins to embrace what makes you different.

Trust

Your goal is to be a trusted brand and that results from practicing strategic generous sharing. Trust is, as I've noted, the most important connection you need to establish with your community.

You're constantly taking in information and categorizing it based on your level of trust for the source. As an example, let's look at New York newspapers. The *New York Times* is the king of NYC papers. The newspaper has been reporting the news for more than 150 years and is widely considered the pinnacle of reliable news outlets. The *Times* will only print stories if there are multiple reputable sources. For the *Times*, getting it right is more important than getting it first. On the opposite end of the spectrum is the *New York Post*. The cover of the *Post* is regularly strewn with over-the-top headlines and is filled with sensational tabloid stories. It's famous for its gossip column, and the content is more entertainment than education.

The *New York Times* is the friend you reach out to for serious advice—more trust; the *New York Post* is the friend you have fun with—less trust.

The continuum of trust is directly related to value. When trust for a brand is high, you're willing to pay more or make purchases with less consideration. For instance, Mercedes starts convincing you of the superiority of their automobiles when you're young. The intention is to build your trust in the brand so one day, when you have the means, you'll purchase a Mercedes. It's crazy to think, but the sales cycle of a Mercedes actually starts 30 or 40 years before you make a purchase; people buy promises, not products. When trust exists, you don't have to manipulate customer behavior with discounts or sales; you only have to effectively and consistently communicate your story. Trust is a long-term play.

The same theory applies to individuals. Your name and reputation make up your brand. Your coworkers, friends, and even family value you similarly to the way you value a product. While this may sound clinical, it's true.

Being considered trustworthy may be the single most important factor toward achieving your goals in the new paradigm. Ironically though, how you evaluate trustworthiness has barely changed since the beginning of time. You make these decisions almost entirely based on your instincts and emotions. What do they look like? What do they sound like? What is their reputation? Therefore, all the sharing strategies we talked about, from storytelling to collaboration to repetition, are fundamentally about building trust. You must understand your audience, and then package your truck's message in a way that makes your customers feel an emotional connection.

Once you've won their trust, protect it, because if that bond is broken, it's nearly impossible to fix.

Believe

Manifesting starts with believing. Pablo Picasso's mother said to him, "If you are a soldier, you will become a general. If you are a monk, you will become the pope." Instead, he became a painter, and eventually became "Picasso". But he wasn't anointed Picasso when he woke up one morning. He became Picasso after years of art school, brushes with severe poverty, decades of hard work, and a bunch of luck. He became Picasso because he believed he could become Picasso, despite those obstacles. He manifested his creativity because despite every challenge he encountered, he continued to believe in himself and his vision. This same principle applies to your journey. You must believe.

Ninety-nine percent of the stories we tell ourselves are limiting. While they satisfy our sense of self-importance by explaining our past, they set limits on what we believe is possible for our future. These narratives define how we think about ourselves, which directly impacts what we're capable of manifesting. Yet, there's good news: these stories are completely made up. You can change the story any time you like.

It's generally accepted that action is what makes successful people different. What not everyone considers is that action is preceded by thought, and how successful people think is what truly differentiates them from everyone else. Successful people believe. They believe in themselves, they believe in their people, and most importantly, they believe that no matter what happens, they'll figure things out.

As Steve Jobs said,

> When you grow up, you tend to get told the world is the way it is and your life is just to live your life inside the world. Try not to bash into the walls too much. Try to have a nice family life, have fun, save a little money. That's a very limited life. Life can be much broader once you discover one simple fact: everything around you that you call life was made up by people that were no smarter than you.

Food Truck Events and Opportunities

It's mid-August in New York City's South Street Seaport. The sun is shining, and beats are pulsing from a DJ booth overlooking the water. South Street is usually a destination for tourists, but today it's twice as busy as usual and filled with what seem like actual New Yorkers. Why are they spending their summer day in the city rather than at the beach? The answer: food trucks. More than 30 food trucks have descended on the seaport for a festival. The event, organized by the New York Food Truck Association and covered by the *New York Times* and food blogs like Eater.com and *New York Magazine's* Grub Street, has created a frenzy, with Manhattanites ready to line up for a taste of what everyone is talking about.

Did that fire you up? I know it got my juices flowing and taste buds watering. Walking the festival that day, I noticed that some trucks were jam packed with people, while others were pretty barren. So, I sat down at a table for an hour to observe. Why were some crowded and others not? My conclusion is that it came down to branding and marketing. The trucks that were doing well were putting on a show. They were living their brand, enjoying the process, and engaging the customers. Not only that: the truck operators who seemed to be enjoying themselves were clearly putting out a better product. Trucks like

Korilla have the whole package—branding, personality, process, colors, music, and food—all working together to create a better food truck experience, the kind of experience that produces memories. And, as you know by now, memories create cravings.

Festivals

Food truck festivals are becoming modern-day food courts, featuring the best gourmet grub you can find in one location. No longer are trucks just showing up in high-traffic areas; they're now planning events and happenings that create their own high-traffic locations. Thousands of people attended the festival in New York City, translating into extra income for the food trucks involved.

A food truck festival is similar to a music festival, but it's centered on eating. As food trucks have become a phenomenon, they've run into parking problems and difficulties in supporting the growing number of trucks on the road. There used to be plenty of business on the street, but these days trucks need to figure out new ways to build their businesses and new places to sell their products. The food truck festival is a fabulous result of American ingenuity that has sprouted from these issues. The truck community and/or event organizers with connections to the world of food have created and promoted these events as a secondary revenue option. They usually involve 10 to 50 trucks in an open-air location combined with live entertainment, other vendors, and sometimes contests for the best truck or the best of a specific item. Prime locations for these festivals include harbors, parks, beaches, and urban squares.

Festivals are organized, marketed, and promoted weeks or months in advance of the actual date. The event often sells passes that enable customers to sample one item from each truck for a set price. A festival can attract tens of thousands of foodies and can generate big revenues for the organizers and the trucks involved. Trucks also get tremendous publicity through public relations outreach and inclusion in distributed marketing materials. The ability to expose your product to thousands of potential clients can be both a blessing and a curse; your product will be under a microscope. The key to maximizing the exposure is to provide the best product and service and showcase your brand's culture.

Getting Noticed

You can't afford to be quiet when there are dozens of other trucks surrounding you. You want to ensure that you make money at the festival, and more importantly, generate repeat business for the future. Go out of your way to make a statement. Here are some ways to do that:

Offer samples of a signature item. Make sure your samples are just large enough to entice customers. Samples will draw a crowd to your truck, and at these festivals, the action around your truck is what draws in more people. Keep people crowding your truck, and soon enough, you'll have a line around the block.

Music. Play great music at your truck through a speaker system, live performer, or DJ. It will generate attention and is a great way to display your brand's energy.

Signage. Make sure your signs are big and bold, especially at a festival. Make a larger than usual, brightly colored menu board to help you stand out from the crowd and focus on the items you want to sell.

Specialty items. Create a one-of-a-kind taco or meatball that will only be available at the festival. Spend the week before promoting it to your loyal clientele, and then offer it as an add-on to your more traditional items at the event. It's a great way to increase what a customer spends during a food festival.

Combo meals. Create a combination of entrée, side, and drink for a special festival price. It works for McDonald's and Burger King; it can work for you.

Festivals are incredible places to gather contact information for your email and social media followings. Most of the people attending the festival are avid food truck fans and foodies. They represent your most dedicated client base, so make sure you get their information and thank them immediately for their support

Getting Involved

You can find out about festivals through food blogs, city websites, your local chamber of commerce, and food truck trade organizations. When you find out about one that you're interested in joining, email or call the organizers to find out how trucks become involved. Don't seem too eager; an event producer will sense desperation and take a hard line on your deal for involvement. If you can swing it, find a friend in the industry who's involved and try to get him or her to recommend you to the festival organizers.

To make festivals as beneficial as possible to you and your business, you need to generate a lot of buzz about your truck. That buzz and a strong following will make you more valuable to festival organizers. Before long, organizers will start calling you to capitalize on your popularity, and you'll be able to decide which festival best suits your needs. It's only a dream until it comes true.

Review the list of trucks involved in any festival before signing on. If you're a pizza truck and several pizza trucks are already committed, you may want to reconsider your involvement. Make sure all the elements are in place for you to be a success before you agree to participate.

Also, see what their marketing avenues are. Check their social media pages and see how many people are following them or "like" them. To be successful, the event must be well promoted..

Covering Costs

Most of the trucks involved in festivals must pay an entrance fee and sometimes a percentage of total sales as well. In some cases, organizers will invite better-known trucks, like Kogi, to be involved for free, and these trucks might even be guaranteed a minimum amount of sales. When you're first starting out, that won't be the case for you, and you might actually end up losing money from a festival. Entrance fees can be up to $2,500 for the day, and you might end up not generating enough revenue to cover them.

When you agree to attend a festival, make sure there's a weather contingency. You don't want to spend money entering the festival and preparing your food only to hear that the event is being cancelled due to rain. Make a deal with the event organizers that you'll pay a lower entrance fee if it rains, and make sure they have a rain date planned.

Food Truck Lots

The mini backlash against food trucks has created a need for safe and friendly environments for trucks to ply their trade. When bricks-and-mortar businesses and the authorities are coming after you, there's comfort in being part of a herd. Food truck lots are popping up all over New York, Los Angeles, and other areas throughout the United States.

A food truck lot is a piece of real estate, like a parking lot or an empty lot, that acts as an outdoor food court. Trucks pay $25 to $60 per day for access to the property. For that fee, they're provided with a daily spot, access to customers, and in some cases, infrastructure support and restrooms. For many trucks, a lot creates the opportunity for steady income and a welcome sanctuary from daily parking tickets and other issues.

The key for any food truck lot is to attract large amounts of steady traffic. It will be a shared responsibility between the lot organizers and the truck operators. All parties need to work together to create awareness within the local community. I highly recommend not depending on the organizer; work with the other trucks to create hype. Canvass the area with promotional flyers, send out coordinated email blasts and Tweets, and do local public relations outreach. Another very effective method is to reach out directly to surrounding businesses and offer their employees an incentive to come check out your truck. You would be surprised at what you can get with a free soda or side of fries.

Food truck lots aren't typically located in developed neighborhoods. Real estate values are too high, and food truck lots don't generate enough profit. Instead, truck operators should seek out neighborhoods where there aren't already a lot of restaurants. These neighborhoods play to their strengths as mobile business operators who can choose to be in a location only when the traffic is present.

Lots are also placed in cities where food trucks may rarely travel, too. As in a large city such as Los Angeles, it may be difficult for those living in surrounding cities to get to LA for a food truck. Find lots in areas where your customers are and where there is a want/need for food truck love.

For example, Rockrose, a major New York development company, launched a food truck lot in Long Island City (LIC), while the area was being developed. LIC is home to many major businesses, including Citigroup, but at the time was empty in the evenings, which has made it a difficult place for restaurants to develop. Rockrose and other developers built multiple apartment buildings and had a vacant lot that wasn't scheduled for construction for a couple of years. To attract attention to the neighborhood and more infrastructure for potential residents, they decided to open a temporary food truck lot. And boy, is it the perfect spot for one. The food trucks gain access to a bustling yet underserviced lunch business and drive off to greener pastures in the evening. This is the perfect opportunity for a truck operator to create stable income in the neighborhood and develop a following for a potential bricks-and-mortar location when it gentrifies.

On the West Coast, the Southern California Mobile Food Vendors Association, with its 130-member food trucks, runs 5 food truck lots. They're currently in talks to develop additional lots, many in partnership with institutions such as the California Heritage Museum. What could be more perfect than institutions with tons of visitors offering better-quality, diverse food? That's what food trucks are all about. Because food trucks are mobile, they don't have to wait for opportunity to find them; they can go out and look for it themselves!

Note, food truck lots are often the target of city health departments. They're an easy way for inspectors to review multiple trucks in a short time period. If you choose to be involved in a lot, make sure you're prepared. Make sure the lot meets the local health department requirements as well. They will go after the vendor, not the organizer.

Developers use food truck lots as short-term ventures to attract interest in the properties, just as they do with pop-up restaurants and flea markets. Once the area develops and there are more lucrative options for the properties, the food trucks will have to move on to other locations. The key to your success as a truck operator will be to find the best opportunities and exploit them to the best of your ability. But that's why you have a restaurant on wheels, right?

In Austin, Texas, they call their food truck lots *food truck trailer parks*. The Picnic next to Barton Springs Pool, houses Kebabalicious, The Mighty Cone, Trudy's, Hey Cupcake and has a BYOB policy! There are resident trucks like Chef Kevin Gambino's Cajun Creole Gambino's Gourmet Exchange, from-scratch Italian truck Cannone Cucina Italiana, Brazilian-inspired Açaí Hut, and Steel City Pops. There is ample parking, lots of beautiful trees to rest on, and actual restrooms.

Television

Long gone are the days of Julia Child. The Food Network, founded in 1993, combined with the incredible talent of Emeril Lagasse, changed how Americans think about food forever. Although they're a relatively young industry, food trucks have found their way into your homes via TV. The lure of the mobile gourmet has been too great for TV executives to ignore.

Television is a great way to gain massive exposure for your food truck brand, but you want to make sure it's positive exposure. You wouldn't want to appear on local or national TV unless it was a positive portrayal of your product, brand, and self. There's no way to make sure of that other than to trust the people you're working with and control your actions while filming. If you have the opportunity to take your truck to the airwaves, be aware of everything you're saying while the cameras are rolling, and only do business with producers you feel make content that's in line with your beliefs. A positive TV piece should showcase your truck, not the conflicts and drama that go on within your organization. If you choose to go the way of a show like the *Real Housewives* series, producers will find a way to encourage drama and conflict. Don't be naive. Protect your business at all costs.

Television can be a very powerful tool to promote your business, but make sure you aren't doing it for your ego. Any time you're focused on promoting yourself, the viewer will know. The camera never lies.

The following sections offer a sampling of the greatest moments in food truck television to date.

The Great Food Truck Race

The Great Food Truck Race premiered on August 15, 2010, on the Food Network. Hosted by celebrity chef Tyler Florence, seven specialty food trucks competed in a multiweek competition in different locations including San Diego, New York, a truck stop, and a farm. The trucks traveled across the country from west to east, selling their food and competing for the highest total revenues. The truck that earned the least amount of money each week was eliminated. The winner of the competition received a cash payment of $50,000, along with many prizes given out throughout the competition.

Season 1 teams included:

* **Austin Daily Press:** Originally from Austin, Texas; serves hot sandwiches wrapped in a sheet of newspaper from the *Onion*.

* **Crepes Bonaparte:** From Fullerton, California; serves Parisian-style crepes.

* **Grill 'Em All:** From Los Angeles, California; serves gourmet burgers.

* **Nana Queens:** From Culver City, California; serves banana pudding and chicken wings.

* **Nom Nom Truck:** From Los Angeles, California; serves Vietnamese style sandwiches and tacos.

* **Ragin Cajun:** From Hermosa Beach, California; serves Cajun cuisine.

* **Spencer on the Go!:** From San Francisco, California; serves French cuisine. Through a legal loophole, Spencer can set up chairs so customers can sit down to eat in front of the truck.

Top Chef

On Episode 8 of Season 3, *Guilty Pleasures*, each team was given a food truck and asked to create late-night grub at the Miami nightclub Nikki Beach. Contestants used their trucks to create items such as Oysters in a Half Shell with a Spicy Watermelon Ceviche Taco and Bacon Wrapped Shrimp with Cheese Grits and Tomato Chipotle Butter. Chef Sara Nguyen was eliminated for her take on Beef Sliders, while Chef Tre Wilcox won the competition. He took home a first-edition signed copy of guest judge Chef Govind Armstrong's book and a platinum access card to all Nikki Beach locations.

Throwdown! with Bobby Flay

The premise of this Food Network show is that celebrity Chef Bobby Flay has an impromptu cook-off with a chef or restaurateur known for a specific food item, such as meatballs or hamburgers. The contestant thinks he's going to be on a Food Network show and instead is challenged by Chef Flay in front of a large group of people, many times the contestant's closest friends and family, and Flay and his team create their own version of the food item. The episodes follow the cook-off, and dishes are judged by two local chefs to determine the winner. Since commencing the show, Flay has challenged two trucks.

First, Bobby was challenged by Jerome Chang and Chris Chen's DessertTruck to make a better chocolate bread pudding. The DessertTruck boys put Bobby to shame; the contest wasn't even close!

In his second food truck challenge, Bobby took on the boys of Wafels & Dinges. Once again, the truck bested Bobby, as Chef Thomas Degeest made his famous Liege Belgian Waffles. Doesn't Bobby know not to try to out-do a Belgian when it comes to waffles?

What's Next

The food truck revolution is just beginning. Although big cities like Los Angeles and New York are saturated with food trucks, secondary cities are just beginning to be hit by the wave. The opportunity for new trucks now lies in these areas. Established brands have the opportunity to open new trucks or offer licenses and franchises in these cities.

It's incredible to think that what started as a way for people to enter the business with a small investment has become a booming industry all its own. With many of the successful trucks opening their bricks-and-mortar locations, it's not crazy to think that the next big fast-food restaurant could come out of what once was a food truck.

In major cities, food trucks are in what I call generation 2.0. The streets are saturated and backlash is rampant; but despite all this, many trucks are still thriving. How? The opportunity lies in events and catering. You work in the streets to pay your expenses, generate a modest profit, and pay your staff, but establishing a catering or events business is the way to profitability. Restaurants have known for a long time that catering is where the big money is.

Now that the truck business is maturing and there's more competition, trucks need this second revenue source. You can generate the same profits from catering one corporate function or working a day at a music festival as you can an entire week on the streets. It's especially important to promote your catering services in November and December when businesses are looking to spend money. You should maximize your share of the pie by making direct contact by phone, using social media, and sending emails to your targeted list.

Off the Truck

Food Trucks are quickly moving beyond the truck into food halls, airports, catering events, and large-scale brick and mortar locations. It's now clear that food trucks and pop-ups are the leading incubators of new food concepts for the industry.

Remember the mall food court where they used to give out an endless supply of chicken teriyaki samples? Well, they have been replaced by over-the-top spectacularly themed gourmet food halls that sell food to order, food to take home, and related food merchandise—anything and everything a foodie could desire. From Eataly to Urbanspace to the outdoor Smorgasburg, food halls are the natural extension of a food truck's operations. They're a great way to expand profitability and promotion. It's amazing because they need you, the operator, to provide them diversity, yet the food hall is largely responsible for bringing the people. Your interests are very much aligned.

Concept Testing and Promoting

Another trend that has risen among well-established franchises and brands is *concept testing*—a means by which businesses use food trucks to test new business concepts and products before bringing them to market. According to the New York Food Truck Association, companies like Whole Foods, Olive Garden, and Outback Steakhouse have used food trucks as test kitchens to try new food products and serving concepts, in some cases, without putting their names or logos on the trucks (most likely to get unbiased feedback).

Community Building—Your Part of Something Bigger

As real estate developers continue their expansion into new and unexpected locations, specifically opportunity zones, and retail undergoes a difficult period of transformation, opportunity exists now more than ever for food trucks to expand their profits and influence by bringing people together. For example, many large-scale urban developments lack infrastructure as they are constructed. This means despite the completion of apartments or office buildings, they have yet to open restaurants, coffee spots, and other necessities of modern life, which is where the opportunities come for food truck operators. Quite often, developers will invite food trucks in to service these communities during the developmental phase, and developers may even subsidize their operating costs to keep them around. That is, they'll pay your expenses to be there. Additionally, if things go well, they'll offer operators advantageous deals on brick-and-mortar spaces to stick around and service the community. You see, their money is made on the apartments and offices, so they view these amenities as a necessary cost of operating and marketing their communities.

If you have read the paper in the past five years, you'll know, without question, that retail is suffering through a hard time. Once again, it's an opportunity for food truck operators to leverage the brand they built for expansion. Whether it's activating a location that has yet to be filled or was recently vacated, or taking over a space at below-market rent, opportunity exists for recognized brands to grow their footprint due to the challenging retail environment. Build your experience, and customers will come.

Stockton Street, a highly dense area of San Francisco near Union Square, has been under major construction for numerous years. In response, local government worked with community development partnerships to organize events during the construction breaks. Food trucks and retail vendors put together an experiential holiday market, complete with a live performance that attracted more than 1.7 million guests. It added up to a lot of found money for the food trucks that took part.

Food Trucks in the Classroom

Schools around the country and the world have taken notice of food trucks and have begun to offer programs to enable to mobile food industry. There are online courses, government resources, and even actual classes with real in-the-flesh food truck operators. Even coworking companies like WeWork have begun to offer mentoring and incubator programs solely focused on the food and beverage industry. Students can learn about every aspect of the food truck biz, from how to operate and market to the ins and outs of catering events and handling government licensing. Florida International University offers a program called StartUP FIU Food that specifically aims to train and assist entrepreneurs in growing their food businesses beyond one unit. Everywhere you go, help is one click away, so don't be afraid to ask.

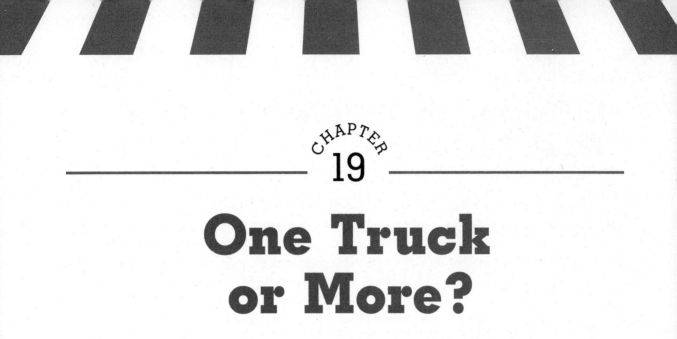

One Truck
or More?

To expand or not to expand? Once you have one successful truck, this question will inevitably start popping up. Expansion is serious business and brings with it some very important thoughts to explore.

Following are just a few of the questions you'll need to ask yourself before considering an expansion of your food truck business:

* Is expansion the right thing for you personally?

* Is your business ready for expansion?

* Does the demand exist for multiple trucks?

* Do you have the infrastructure to support more than one truck? If not, how would you need to build or change your infrastructure to support this expansion?

* Are there enough parking spots in high-traffic areas to support the expansion of your fleet?

Is Expansion Right for Your Food Truck Business?

Let's look at what I consider the four most important questions to consider:

1. **Talent.** The first and probably most important part of the expansion equation is to hire quality people. When you're expanding, hiring the right talent is everything. As James Collins says in his book *Good to Great*: "Consider the idea that charisma can be as much a liability as an asset. Your strength of personality can sow the seeds of problems." A charismatic founder can be very involved in what is happening when the business is local, but when it expands over large distances, it's the people you hire who will be left to make the decisions. No matter what infrastructure you have built, the right people are the ones who make the right decisions for your business.

2. **Simplicity.** When Thomas Keller opened Per Se in New York and French Laundry in California, he installed cameras in their kitchens, so he could accurately monitor what was happening in real time at both locations. This approach, though admirable, is not a strategy for large-scale expansion. Simplicity equals consistency. The more complex your product, the less likely it can be duplicated. The moral of the story: keeping it simple keeps the odds of success in your favor.

3. **Measured pace.** How many things can you do well at once? Very few people can successfully multitask, and you're likely not one of them. When expanding your business, you must move at a measured pace. If history has taught us anything, it's that no one can win a war fighting on too many fronts. The supply lines eventually get cut off, bad weather sets in, and things start falling apart. Whatever can go wrong, will. Slow and steady always wins.

4. **Location.** The majority of dining decisions are made based on location. You may try a destination spot once or twice for a special occasion, but if you're hungry, odds are you are going somewhere close. Being able to access high-traffic locations in great neighborhoods will help your food truck business tremendously. Remember, if you are spending time looking for customers, you'll have a lot less time to spend impressing them.

As you ponder the decision to expand your food truck business, you'll inevitably come to what I call the "expansion dilemma". One of my favorite stories sums this dilemma up perfectly. There was once a big executive who went on vacation to an island. He was on the beach and saw a small shack where the local fisherman and his family were eating lunch. The fisherman invited the executive to join them. When the executive tried the fish, he was amazed. It was the best fish he had ever eaten. He told the fisherman that he should sell the fish. The fisherman asked how to do that, and the executive explained that first he should get a bunch of boats and start selling to the other islands, and then, after a while, build a factory and start shipping all over the world. "And then what?" the fisherman asked. The executive said, "Then, you can sell your business and do whatever you want all day." And the fisherman replied, "I already do that." Bottom line? Everyone has his or her own taste for life.

The Lifecycle of a Hospitality Business

Before considering expanding, you need to understand the lifecycle of a hospitality business. By grasping the stages a truck goes through, you'll be able to make more educated decisions about a potential expansion of your truck empire.

Stage One: Market Introduction

The first stage in the life of any hospitality product is the market introduction. It's when you're launching your truck and making the market familiar with the product you're offering. There are no shortcuts; you may have the most amazing concept in the history of food trucks, but you can't avoid the introduction phase.

During this period, which can last from three months to a year, you're performing a delicate dance with your customers and the press to create positive buzz about your truck. Every customer experience is magnified because these people are the seeds of your word of mouth—the major source of your buzz. Every mention in a local newspaper and food blog forms the public's perception of your business.

The characteristics of the introduction phase are high costs, low sales volume, and minimal direct competition in your niche. In this stage, there's little existing customer demand, and you need to create that demand. You'll also most likely be making little or no money. You may actually be losing money because of all you're spending on marketing to drive sales and operations to establish a great product.

Stage Two: Growth

The characteristics of the growth stage are reduced costs, increased sales, moderate profitability, and increased customer awareness. As the business grows, you're becoming more efficient and shedding the costs related to launching and training. This, combined with increased sales, should lead to some level of profitability. Expect this stage to begin at the end of Year one, perhaps continuing into Years two and three.

As the market becomes more aware of your product, you may find you have increased competition within your niche and parking locations.

Stage Three: Maturity

You've reached the maturity stage when your truck is a known brand and has a consistent customer flow. You may be able to go on your first vacation during this stage. The key in the hospitality business is to maximize the length of the maturity stage and rake in the profits. Your costs should be at their lowest and your sales at their highest. Your hard work is paying off, and the customers are showing up with minimal money being spent on marketing. This stage should begin in Year three and continue as long as possible.

If you've reached the maturity phase, it's because you're successful. You should expect increased competition, which may force you to lower your prices or offer more value, cutting into your margins. Your most important initiative at this point is to be creative in implementing programs that differentiate your brand from the rest of the pack. It could mean new menu items, weekly special events, or partnering with artists to do installations on your truck's façade. Whatever you choose, it must appeal to your audience, giving them a reason to talk about and visit your truck.

Stage Four: Decline

The final stage in the life of a hospitality business is the decline. There's not too much to say about it, and I hope you never reach it. If your truck arrives here, I have only one good piece of advice: don't hold on too long. Sell if you can, so you can leave gracefully and with a couple of bucks in your pocket. Shutting down a business you've put so much of yourself into is more painful if you build up debt while hanging on too long.

You're in the decline phase when your costs become too prohibitive to continue operating your truck. If you're selling corn and all of a sudden the price goes up 10 times with no signs of falling, you might as well shut down unless you're able to increase your retail price 10 times. The other way you'll know you're in decline is a consistent decrease in sales volume. If your sales are dropping regularly over a three- to six-month period, you have a major problem.

When considering which stage your business is in, you must also consider the stage of the food truck industry in your area. The food truck business may be a mature industry in Los Angeles, but in a city like Indianapolis, food trucks may still be in a growth stage. If you had the first food truck in Indianapolis, you might be in the growth stage because the overall market is growing.

Making a Living from a Food Truck

Making money from your truck needs to be your main goal. It's a simple matter of getting a reward for your hard work. Passion is important and admirable, and enjoying your work is great as well, but your excitement will disappear very quickly if you aren't generating enough profit.

What constitutes "enough"? That's a very personal question. Let's define enough profit as the maximum income you can generate working in a business you enjoy. So, if you love being in the food business, and you can make $60,000 working in a restaurant, and you're only making $20,000 running your own food truck, you aren't making enough profit. If your truck is reaching its full capacity and generating only $20,000 in profits, you need to either expand or get out of the business.

Let's assume you want to expand. One truck is never going to make you rich. A food truck business at its most profitable will generate $500,000 in gross revenues annually. With that kind of revenue, you'd be considered an extremely successful operation. At that level, your profit margin would be no greater than 15 percent. (I'm being generous here.) It means you'd be making about $75,000 before paying taxes, so your take home would be around $60,000. It's a respectable income, but after paying back the initial investment—and especially if you're sharing that money with partners or investors—is that enough? You can increase your income by working the truck and paying yourself a salary, but that isn't a strategy for expansion, which requires delegating authority effectively to your employees. Trying to do everything yourself is a recipe for disaster.

Assuming you live a middle-class lifestyle—or aspire to—and you're planning to support yourself from your food truck business, you'll almost definitely have to expand your operation. But if your truck is an investment or passion project, expansion probably isn't the best option for you. It will quickly make this more of a grind and less about pursuing your dream. The stakes will go up, and so will the stress.

The key to deciding whether you should expand is to determine whether expansion is in line with your goals as an individual and a business owner. There's no way to expand without increased stress and responsibility.

Some people aren't motivated by material wealth. Anthony Mangieri, the owner of Una Pizza Napoletana, was noted for his obsession with his craft, his high-quality product, and his dedication to classic Neapolitan pizza. After reaching the height of his popularity in New York, Mangieri abruptly shut down his parlor and moved to San Francisco. He could have stayed and reigned supreme over pizza in the biggest city in the world or expanded to multiple locations, but Anthony walked away because he had different goals for himself. He opened a small pizzeria in California and followed his desire to spend more time with nature. Mangieri's personal plan didn't call for a multiunit expansion.

Am I Ready to Expand?

If you've decided that expansion is right for you and your business, the next thing to determine is whether you're ready. Every truck you add will require more staff, inventory, prep time, maintenance, gas, cooking fuels, insurance, and the list goes on.

Demand

The first issue that you need to consider is demand. Is there enough demand to support an expansion of your product? You can find out the answer to this question pretty easily by answering some follow-up questions:

* Is there always a line for your truck?

* Do you have more locations at which you think you can generate high revenues in one day?

* Are you getting more catering requests than you can handle?

If the answer to all of these questions is yes, then there's enough demand for you to expand. If it's not, think twice about it and thoroughly analyze your business. If you're not operating your first truck perfectly, what makes you think you can operate two?

Look at the macroenvironment before seriously considering an expansion. If the economy is in recession or local businesses are closing, it may not be a good time to expand. Speak to local businesspeople about their performance for more insight into the general marketplace.

Capital Resources

The first question you need to ask yourself is whether you have the capital resources to support an expansion. As a rule of thumb, you should have a minimum of two months' operating capital in the bank to support your business. That can be hard for many people, but if you want to expand, it's an absolute necessity. You should have that capital in addition to the fixed costs related to expanding, including an additional truck, commissary, insurance, and other costs that don't vary with consumer demand.

Let's say a second truck costs you $50,000 plus an additional $10,000 to operate it for a month. You'd need $20,000 a month to operate both trucks, so that means you need $40,000 in the bank at launch to cover the second truck's introduction and the operation of both trucks for the two months after expansion. That also assumes you'll be generating positive cash flow within the first couple of weeks of the new truck's operation.

Staff

Once you know the capital requirements of expansion, you need to make sure you have enough great people to expand your operation without negatively affecting the original or expansion product. An expanding enterprise immediately comes under the watchful eye of consumers and the media. Your competition and critics will be waiting for you to make a mistake, so you need to be entirely confident that you, your management, and your facilities can handle the increased capacity.

During an expansion, you'll be putting much more stress on your business, staff, and systems. A poorly planned expansion can end up ruining a thriving enterprise. Ensure that you protect your core with a strong capital and talent base before thinking about any growth.

Systems

In addition to great people, you also need foolproof systems. As you expand, you'll have less time to oversee the day-to-day operations of the truck; the only way to make sure your customers' experience is the same every time is to implement systems for all aspects of your trucks' operation. Systems will also protect the costs of goods sold and transportation, keep waste at manageable levels, and protect you from employee theft.

Adding a Bricks-and-Mortar Location

Expansion doesn't necessarily refer to additional trucks; it can also mean a bricks-and-mortar location. One of the best parts of being in the truck business is that you have a chance to showcase your talents with a minimal initial investment, which is something that's never been available in the food business before. Right now, the media loves food trucks, so it's an optimal way for you to build your brand. Once the public recognizes your name, it has value and can be used for expansion. Opening an actual restaurant can be an optimal way to expand.

A bricks-and-mortar expansion is complementary to your food truck business. You're already paying for a commissary, storage, and staff, as well as infrastructure costs like an accountant and a lawyer. A bricks-and-mortar location would share those costs, and in many cases, absorb them. Excess food could be used in the restaurant before it spoils, and cooks can prepare in the morning for both truck and restaurant. This will vastly decrease your operating costs for the truck and might increase its profitability by 25 to 50 percent. The restaurant on its own should be a profitable venture because of the positive brand association with the truck and your built-in following.

Finally, when you have a restaurant, rainy days are nonissues. You don't have to take the truck out when the weather's bad and customers don't want to stand in line on the street, so days that would have created a loss for you in the past are no longer a problem. With two sources of income, you only have to take out the truck when the demand exists. When it doesn't, you can ride out the storm in the comfort of your very own restaurant.

If you do expand into a bricks-and-mortar restaurant, make sure you open in a high-traffic location. If you've learned anything from food trucks, it's that location is one of the most important aspects of a successful hospitality business.

Identifying the Benefits of Expansion

Expanding your food truck business has the potential of bringing you increased sales for higher profits and further expansion. Potential expansion opportunities could include licensing/franchising, packaged food products, and catering services. A successful expansion plan combined with high consumer demand will most definitely add profit to your bottom line. Those profits, combined with additional exposure, will help further establish your brand in the marketplace, which will assist in extending the life of your business. The additional profits and branding will also make your business more attractive for a potential sale.

Avoid the ego trap, though. Expand because you think it's the best thing for the health of your business, not because you want to have the biggest truck fleet on the road. Many of the most successful businesspeople I know made the most money when their companies were small and regret expanding. They ended up with more revenues, less profits, and a bunch of headaches.

Watching for the Pitfalls of Expansion

If it were easy to build an empire, our society wouldn't spend so much time celebrating those who succeed. Your expansion will come with increased expenses, stress, and a more complicated organizational structure, which means you'll need more capital and better management. Proper capitalization and the hiring and training of new staff will be critical. After that, you'll need to worry about maintaining the quality of your food and service. But the biggest concern is the exposure you're creating by leveraging your current business. Your expansion is putting additional stress on the original operation, and if it isn't successful, it will threaten the health of the entire enterprise.

Before you choose to expand, examine every part of your organization, determine what point of the truck's lifecycle you're in, gauge consumer demand, and put together a clear plan. Once you've prepared the plan, sit with it for at least a month. Speak to your staff, trusted advisers, other operators, and take some time to think. If expansion still feels like a good idea after that, go for it!

Selling Your Business

Whether your truck is a great success or runs into difficulties, the most viable exit strategy is to sell your business. If your truck has been a success, you can sell it for the value of the business plus the value of the truck. If the business hasn't been profitable, you'll only be able to sell it for the truck's value.

My rule of thumb for determining the value of a food truck business is 40 percent of annual revenues: that's what your brand, website, trademarks, concept, customer lists, databases, and anything else related to the business other than the truck itself is worth. If your truck is making $500,000 in revenue, the value of the business side of things is $200,000. If your truck is worth another $50,000, you should price the entire operation, including equipment, at $250,000.

To determine the worth of the truck itself, reference the Kelly Blue Book, Edmunds, or another guide to valuing automobiles. These guides price used automobiles by their make, model, year, and mileage/condition. Once you've done your homework, it's time to visit some truck dealers. Get a proposed valuation from at least three. They'll let you know whether they're interested in brokering a sale or purchasing your truck. Dealers may know people looking for trucks and will put the two of you together for a percentage. There's no standard for that, but the fee shouldn't exceed 10 percent.

Try online bulletin boards like roadstoves.com, auction sites like eBay.com, and classified sites like craigslist.com to sell your business and truck. Putting them up on these sites will help you test the market. You can gauge interest at different price points and get a good feel for the questions potential buyers will ask.

The guidelines I've provided for the valuation of your business and truck are only that— guidelines. Also, take into account the unique attributes of your particular truck and the motivations of potential buyers. Certain things can drive up the value. For example, if you have a pending contract to serve as the exclusive vendor for a local stadium or arena, your business could be worth more to buyers, and selling for 40 percent of annual revenues might be too low. Some buyers want to purchase a food business to fulfill a lifelong dream, and that could mean they'd be willing to pay a higher price because the intrinsic value is more than the market value.

Here's a brief list of the steps you'll need to take if you're considering selling your food truck business:

1. **Initial review.** Discuss potential pitfalls with your lawyer and your accountant. They'll give you an outline of the process and what legal and tax issues you need to take into consideration. Once you have that information, you can do the market review already discussed.

2. **Valuation.** Check out the automobile guides, speak to truck dealers, and review your financials and other items that may add value to your truck operation. Now's the time to decide what you think your business is worth.

3. **Locate a buyer.** Utilize your personal network, place advertisements online, and speak to customizers, truck dealers, and other operators who may be interested in buying your truck or know people who might be. Be discreet!

4. **Structure a deal.** Get as much money as you can up front. The only benefit to not getting all of your money ahead of time is that if the new operator defaults on payments, you can take back your truck. But if you're selling your truck, you don't want it anymore, so it's best to get all your money and be done with it!

5. **Complete the deal.** Sign a letter of intent immediately upon agreeing on terms. Both sides can then perform their due diligence while creating the purchase agreement. At the closing, contracts are signed, checks are exchanged, and you're off to the next stage of your business career.

The Myth of Success

A few years ago my therapist asked me, "What do you want out of life?" I said the first thing that came to my mind: "I want to be successful." He looked at me, puzzled, and replied, "What do you mean?" "You know what I mean," I said. "I want to be successful. I want to be wealthy, powerful, and recognized." In other words, I framed a conventional vision of success—the one drummed into us by popular culture and other social dimensions.

My therapist chuckled at my naiveté for a moment and then asked, "Alan, why do you believe that wealth, power, and recognition are the definition of success?" He then went on to explain to me that success is defined as "accomplishing an aim or purpose", but the definition of that aim or purpose is up to the individual. My mind was officially blown.

Up until that day, I had never really thought about why I defined success that way. Instead, I'd been obsessed with how I would attain those things. That focus on the how instead of the why had really tripped me up. It had led me to make some very bad decisions and to experience some very unhappy times. When you follow the influence of mainstream culture—television, movies, magazines, and more—to elevate the goals of wealth, power, and recognition above all else, it becomes logical to take selfish or negative actions in order to attain them. After all, that kind of approach—playing the game, playing for keeps, as they say—is put forth as the way to achieve success and happiness. Machiavelli's writings are often referenced to support this point of view statements like "The ends justify the means." However, it should be noted that Machiavelli died alone and in exile.

It's only when you free yourself from external definitions of success that you're able to comprehend the folly of this type of pursuit. Ask yourself, "What's the point of attaining a goal if it isn't going to satisfy my internal needs?" All you're going to end up with is some form of a trophy, such as money, a big house, a nice watch, or some press clippings, alongside a big bowl of unhappiness and dissatisfaction. You can only define yourself as a success if the result of your actions is the satisfaction of your internal desires, not that of some superficial, outside force.

It isn't relevant if society deems you a success—it's whether you believe you're achieving success that matters. For some, this may mean fame and fortune, but for others it may just mean putting food on the table every night for their families and having a loving relationship with their spouses. The determining factor is how you feel and what you desire on the inside. The first and most powerful step is realizing you have the power to determine what success looks like for you. Only then can you free yourself from the myth and begin the journey of living your truth.

Glossary

added value   Characteristic of a product or service that has exceeded the customer's expectations by providing something more at little or no cost.

aspirational   A product or service a user believes has positive characteristics, inspiring a strong desire to obtain or to associate with it.

assembly line   The process in which parts are added to a product in sequence.

average cover   The typical amount of money a customer spends to feed one person.

blog   A website or part of a website maintained by an individual containing commentary, descriptions of events, and sometimes, graphics or video.

blogger   A person who writes a blog.

bricks and mortar   A business that serves customers from a permanent physical structure.

cash flow   The rate at which money enters and leaves a business.

catering   Providing food to a customer at a remote site or preparing prepackaged food for a large group of people.

check average   In the food business, the typical amount of each customer's check.

commissary   The location at which a food truck operator parks, cleans, and stocks a truck; often also the location of the kitchen.

compounding cycle   A marketing cycle combining public relations, advertising, social media, experiential follow through, and personal relationships to reinforce a singular message to a target market.

consistency   In the food business, the delivery of a product in the same way over an extended period of time.

cook time   How long an item takes to cook.

corporation   A legal entity that has its own privileges and liabilities distinct from its members.

cost of goods sold (COGS) report   A report that measures the true food cost percentage for a menu and inventory as a whole.

cross contamination   When foods and surfaces that might be contaminated with bacteria come into contact with other foods and surfaces that otherwise wouldn't be a potential threat.

cultural perspective   The underlying message your truck communicates to the customer. Also known as *point of view*.

customer relationship management (CRM)   A widely implemented strategy for businesses to manage their relationships with their customers.

customized truck   A truck that's made to your specifications for the use of your business.

delivery sales   Sales made when a customer orders through the phone or internet and the food is delivered to their location.

demand   The willingness of a consumer or group of consumers to make purchases at any given time.

dry goods   Items such as tea, coffee, sugar, flour, and paper products that don't require refrigeration.

eighty-six   Restaurant lingo for taking an item off the menu. Generally refers to taking it off temporarily because you ran out of the item, but it can also refer to removing it permanently.

emotional attachment   A feeling of closeness developed through a long-term relationship.

enlightened hospitality   The positive feeling that the delivery of your hospitality product—food from your truck—makes the recipient feel because of the positive and generous way you operate your business and share your passion.

expeditor   The person in charge of organizing orders.

fan page   A page on Facebook dedicated to promoting a commercial interest, such as a business or celebrity.

fifty-one percenters   Employees who will go the extra step every time to get the job done, with skills divided 51 to 49 between emotional hospitality and technical excellence.

fixed costs   Business expenses that aren't dependent upon the level of goods or services produced.

Food Code   A document created and published by the Food and Drug Administration (FDA) every four years as an example for health departments nationwide. It includes the best practices for storing, preparing, and handling food as recommended by the federal government.

food truck   A mobile kitchen, canteen, or catering truck that sells food or drinks.

foodie   Aficionados of food and drink who don't work professionally in the food and beverage industry.

forecast   The process of making educated guesses or statements that predict events not yet observed.

general liability insurance   Specific coverage for property and bodily injury, for instance, in a single policy.

gourmand   A person who takes great pleasure in food.

income statement   A monthly report that reviews a business's sales, expenses, and profits. Also known as a profit and loss statement.

inventory   The amount of food, beverage, and other saleable materials a business has on hand at any given time.

labor costs   The amount of money spent on labor to run a business over a set period of time. This can be turned into a percentage by dividing the total labor cost by the total revenue.

layered marketing   A method in which multiple marketing techniques are utilized in one campaign to reinforce the brand's message and intentions.

lead-generator form   A form on your website customers can fill out to request information on your business. It's one of the simplest and most effective ways to turn internet marketing into actual customer connections.

menu mix   The calculation of how much of your gross sales each item accounts for.

niche   The subset of the market you're focusing on to sell your goods.

on-truck cook   The person in charge of preparing the food to be served to your truck's customers; similar to a line cook in a restaurant.

operating capital   The amount of money you need to have on hand to run a business.

operating costs   Expenses related to daily operation of a business, including fixed and variable.

par   The level of stock needed to service a business over a set period of time.

partnership   Two or more persons agreeing to carry on a business, each sharing the profits and losses.

plating   The act of placing prepared food onto a serving dish to be presented to a customer.

point of sale System (POS)   Manages and monitors the checkout process, sales, and financial reporting of a business.

prep   Work such as chopping vegetables or marinating meat that's done prior to service.

prep cook   A kitchen employee who prepares food for service.

prep time   The amount of time it takes to prepare ingredients for service.

price-value relationship   The connection consumers make between the price and quality of a particular product or service.

profitability   The efficiency of your business at generating net earnings.

reverse truck   A food truck business that began as a bricks-and-mortar food operation.

service recovery   The paradox that a service or product failure can offer the opportunity for a business to receive higher customer satisfaction than if the problem had never occurred.

simple food cost   The wholesale cost of the food purchased for a business. This can be turned into a percentage by dividing the total by gross sales.

sole proprietorship   A business owned and run by one individual who assumes responsibility for all profits, losses, and liabilities.

start-up capital   The amount of money needed to begin and continue to operate a business.

steps of service   The basic steps employees perform in a food business.

target market   A defined group of customers to whom a business is pitching its product.

trademark   A legal term for a distinctive sign or indicator owned and used by an individual, business, or legal entity to identify products and/or services to consumers.

true food cost   Food cost that incorporates factors such as waste, menu mix, and discounts.

upselling   Casual suggestions made by service employees to customers to attempt to increase the amount of money spent.

variable costs   Expenses that change in proportion to the activity of your business.

volume   The amount of product your business sells in a given time period.

Resources

In this appendix, I provide resources to help you navigate the world of food trucks and help you run a small business. I've also included some direct links to notable trucks and websites for the latest news.

Websites

eater.com

Food blog with a national site and 22 city sites: Atlanta, Austin, Boston, Charleston, Chicago, Dallas, Denver, Detroit, Houston, Las Vegas, Los Angeles, Miami, Nashville, New Orleans, New York, Philadelphia, Portland, San Diego, San Francisco, Seattle, Twin Cities, and Washington, D.C.

findlafoodtrucks.com

Centralized site for Los Angeles—food truck twitter feeds, as well as a blog.

Grubstreet.com

National food blog specializing in the culinary scene in New York.

theinfatuation.com

International food website bringing you the most honest and trustworthy opinions on where to eat around the world.

mobimunch.com

A total solutions provider to the modern street food industry.

mobile-cuisine.com

A complete online resource for the mobile food industry.

Food Trucks

Big Gay Ice Cream Truck

biggayicecream.com
Exotic soft-serve ice cream, New York and Philadelphia.

Eddie's Pizza Truck

eddiespizzany.com
Thin-crust pizza, New York

Kogi BBQ

kogibbq.com
Korean BBQ, Los Angeles

Korilla BBQ

korillabbq.com
Korean BBQ, New York

Mighty Cone

mightycone.com
Cones and sliders, Austin, TX

Roxy's Grilled Cheese

roxysgrilledcheese.com
Grilled cheese, Boston

Skillet

skilletfood.com
Seasonal comfort food, Seattle

Souvlaki GR

SouvlakiGR.com
Greek, New York

Taim Mobile

taimfalafel.com
Falafel and smoothies, New York

Van Leeuwen

vanleeuwenicecream.com
Artisan ice cream, New York

Wafels & Dinges

dinges.nyc
Belgian waffles, New York

Truck Customizers

AA Cater Truck

750 E. Slauson Avenue
Los Angeles, CA 90011
323-235-6650
aacatertruck.com

Armenco

11819 Vose Street
North Hollywood, CA 91605
1-800-345-0104
cateringtruck.com

Food Cart USA, Inc.

Miami, FL
foodcartusa.com
866-274-6935

Shanghai Stainless

78–82 Gerry Street
Brooklyn, NY 11206
800-253-4815
shanghaimks.com

Worksman Cycles

94–15 100th St
Ozone Park, NY 11416
1-800-BUY-CART
worksmancycles.com

Hospitality and Small Business Organizations

Legal Zoom

legalzoom.com
An online legal documentation service that provides low-cost legal services for processes such as trademarking and copywriting.

National Restaurant Association

restaurant.org
The largest organization of restaurant and food businesses in the United States.

Small Business Administration

sba.gov
A government organization that provides support to entrepreneurs and small businesses.

Southern California Mobile Food Vendors Association

socalmfva.com
An organization representing food trucks and street vendors in Southern California.

Street Vendor Project

streetvendor.org
An organization dedicated to protecting and promoting street food vendors, including food trucks. They also are responsible for the Vendy Awards, a New York–based food truck awards event.

United States Patent and Trademark Office

uspto.gov
The agency within the Department of Commerce that issues patents to investors and businesses for their inventions and trademark registration for product and intellectual property identification.

APPENDIX C

Truck Tales

Our society has an obsession with telling the stories of brave pioneers and their journeys from relative obscurity to fame, fortune, and success. Watching shows like *Biography* and *60 Minutes,* we mimic these pioneers and entrepreneurs to get closer to achieving our own dreams. The world of food trucks is no different. There are stories that include great success, tremendous obstacles, unique partnerships, creative genius, and sometimes, catastrophic failure. In this appendix, we will share the stories of some notable trucks. Take some time to examine the stories and glean as much information as you can. You may find something that makes the difference between your success and failure. As the Greek writer Euripides said, "Leave no stone unturned."

The Big Gay Ice Cream Truck

Does the name sound funny to you? You're definitely not the first person to enjoy a giggle or smile when hearing it. But when it comes to ice cream, the Big Gay Ice Cream Truck is as serious as it gets. Doug Quint, the founder of this gourmet ice cream truck, is actually a classically trained musician. After earning degrees from the Manhattan School of Music and Juilliard, Doug decided to follow his passion. He purchased an ice cream truck from a flutist who played in an orchestra with him and set out to make ice cream even more delicious.

After taking some time to customize his truck, Doug went from musician to ice cream man with partner Bryan Petroff in early 2009. And the name? It came from the way they used to refer to their truck during its creation. One day when setting up the truck's Facebook page, Doug said to a friend, "It's just me and my big gay ice cream truck," and the brand that launched a thousand cones was born. Doug figured that even if the truck failed, people would walk by and laugh. But that ended up being far from the case. The Big Gay Ice Cream Truck spawned an ice cream empire, and their biggest problem became keeping up with demand.

Doug's truck is part old-school Mr. Softee and part mad flavor science. The Big Gay Ice Cream Truck is known for its wacky combinations and even wackier names. Would you like a Bea Arthur—vanilla soft serve, crushed Nilla wafers, and dulce de leche—or a Salty Pimp—vanilla ice cream, sea salt, dulce de leche, and chocolate dip? The truck pairs creamy soft serve ice cream with even crazier toppings such as Sriracha hot sauce, bacon marmalade, and crushed wasabi peas. The truck has become so popular that Doug and Bryan now have four first bricks-and-mortar shops in downtown Manhattan and Philadelphia. On top of that, they've become media darlings with feature segments on Anthony Bourdain's *Layover* and the *Rachael Ray Show;* a write-up in the *New York Times;* and attention in many of the biggest media outlets in the food universe.

Through a combination of creativity, personality, and plain old-fashioned deliciousness, the Big Gay Ice Cream truck has become big business.

Schnitzel & Things

While the 2008 recession hit many companies hard, some people used their unemployment as a chance to start their own businesses. Oleg Voss was one of them. The Ukranian-born Voss went from international investment banking to food trucks. Voss got his start in the hospitality business at a restaurant, but he "hated it". He decided to get his business degree from NYU instead. He had an opportunity to go to Austria to become an investment banker and took it. He packed up his fancy suits, expensive watches, and was all set to become an international businessman, but six months in, the crisis hit, and he was unemployed. "Last one in, first one out" is how he puts it.

So, he started researching the food truck trend and came up with the idea for a schnitzel truck because "Who doesn't like a fried piece of chicken or pork." With that, Schnitzel & Things was alive and frying—frying so well, in fact, that the truck won Rookie of the Year in the 2009 Vendy Awards. Oleg's menu consists of four types of schnitzel including chicken, veal, pork, and cod, as well as German-style bratwurst sausage and his very own deep-fried Schnitz Burger. The schnitzel is served Austrian style with sides such as potato salad, beet salad, cucumber salad, and even Oleg's own sauerkraut. Combine that with a little spicy sriracha mayo or ginger scallion relish, and you have one of the most delectable lunches in Manhattan.

Schnitzel and Things is a perfect example of taking something that you love and turning it into food truck gold, and I am not talking about the crispy skin on your schnitzel.

Mmmpanadas

Empanadas are fried pastry from Latin America that are stuffed with meats, cheeses, fruits, vegetables, and any other edible delicacy you can dream up. Mmmpanadas is a food truck in Austin, Texas, founded by Cody and Kristen Fields, a couple who absolutely love empanadas. Cody fell for the pastry while building wastewater plants in Costa Rica. After working the grind at a local bank, the Fields began to think of ways to become self-employed. That's when fate came knocking on their door. While speaking to a bar owner, he mentioned that his empanada guy fell through, and the Fields offered to provide the product. They delivered six dozen, and the bar owner and his customers instantly loved them. From that one account, they began a business as wholesalers of fresh empanadas. From there, it took only six months for the couple to enter the food truck business.

The Fields' truck was originally a pizza truck that they purchased on eBay. They replaced the pizza oven with a convection oven and installed warming cabinets to hold their cooked empanadas. For the first year, Cody worked every single shift that the truck operated. He learned a lot, and he became an expert on things like fixing a diesel engine. Most importantly, he always trusted his belief that the empanada was the perfect street food.

Since then, they have served green chile chicken and spicy black bean empanadas to luminaries such as the Stone Temple Pilots and Matthew McConaughey. They even serve experimental items such as the "ham and cheese experiment" and a sweet empanada based on s'mores. My mother used to always say "find what you love and get someone to pay you for it," and that's exactly what the Fields have been able to achieve.

Skillet

Every food truck has elements of the city in which it was founded. Seattle is known for rain, coffee, and grunge rock. So, what type of food trucks does this city produce? The answer is an awesome one named *Skillet*. Way back in the beginning of the food truck revolution (circa 2007), Josh Henderson founded Skillet, an airstream trailer serving high-end American comfort food using the best local ingredients available. And boy, is it good!

Josh spent the years prior to launching Skillet finding his way. For a while, he worked in restaurants and hotels, but was tired of working long hours and "missed his dog". So, he spent the next couple of years working with photographers handling the food for photo shoots in faraway locations like the Mojave Desert. Even though he loved the experiences, he knew he needed something closer to home. With that in mind, he began searching for something, and stumbled upon a truck while browsing Craigslist. Once he struck a deal, it was off to the races.

For Josh, it has been a downhill journey. From the moment the doors opened, there has been an onslaught of press and lines of people. The main battle for Skillet has been getting the city of Seattle to change their legislation and make it friendly for food trucks to operate. This finally happened three years into their operation. At one time, the city only allowed trucks to park on private property, but with Skillet's help, food trucks now can park virtually anywhere with the right permits.

Skillet still operates today, but has expanded into several bricks-and-mortar locations known as, the Skillet Diner, and a line of products including bacon jam and pumpkin Sauce. Josh also recently released *The Skillet Cookbook: A Street Food Manifesto*. In a 2011 interview with *Seattle Weekly*, Henderson said, "Street food was never going to be the foundation of at least a financial empire—it'll be the foundation of our business and the brand and who we are as DNA, but it's never going to take us to our bacon jammer yacht we planned." This is a clear example of how important it is to use your food truck to expose your skills and establish your brand so that you can generate supplementary opportunities.

Marcelo's Ceviche

There's nothing more refreshing and tropical than a well-prepared ceviche. And there are many things that are more refreshing than losing your job. That's exactly what happened five years ago to Marcelo Florindez when he went on vacation from his position at a Miami restaurant. After that gut check, Marcelo, the eternal optimist, wanted to open his own restaurant. But a restaurant was too expensive, so he decided to take his idea mobile. We happy he did!

Marcelo's first step was to purchase and build the vehicle, which he did completely by himself. Next, he had to obtain a license, something that most ceviche trucks in Miami don't usually take the time to obtain. Marcelo is by most accounts the only licensed ceviche truck in Miami, and he has a stellar record with the health department. That is something any truck would take pride in, but it's especially difficult when you are serving raw fish. Marcelo operates the truck alone or with one employee four days a week and also caters private events.

All the ingredients that Marcelo uses, aside from the fish, are sourced from Peru, the ceviche capital of the world. The fish are sourced from Costa Rica and Panama, as well as some local suppliers. Marcelo's fish ceviche is marinated in lime juice, cilantro, red onions, and Rocoto chiles. All the ceviches are made to order, and he makes custom items based on special requests.

Marcelo's ceviche is an example of taking darkness and turning it into light. He was given a challenge when he lost his job, and he turned it into opportunity. In the process, he established a market-leading product that is nationally recognized. Go, Marcelo!

Mexicue

What do you get when you combine the spicy deliciousness of Mexican food with the smoky goodness of BBQ? The answer is Mexicue. Founded by David Schillace and Thomas Kelly, Mexicue got its start when the owners started experimenting mixing spicy and smoky flavors in their Brooklyn kitchen.

Prior to deciding to start the truck, Dave was at a corporate sales job and looking for something different. He had spent some time in Los Angeles and was inspired by watching Kogi explode onto the scene. David and Thomas were close friends, and Dave knew that Thomas was very talented in the kitchen and was also looking to make a change. So, Dave approached him with the idea, and they both knew it was the perfect opportunity. But what type of truck would it be?

The first step was to find a truck, and they had a rough time of it. Eventually, they located a partially built truck on eBay. After bidding online, they traveled a few hours to Woodstock, New York, and picked up their rig. They spent the next four months testing, planning, and customizing their truck in Long Island City, just outside of Manhattan. The original concept was tamales, but as Thomas began experimenting in the kitchen, he decided to expand the menu. After finalizing their Mexican BBQ fusion concept, they expanded to a commissary kitchen on the lower east side of Manhattan and developed a system to prepare their signature smokes and braises.

When Dave and Thomas were finally ready to launch the truck, they decided to spend their first day in Park Slope, in Brooklyn. The traffic was light that first day, and so the next day, they felt ready to challenge themselves by heading into the Midtown business district. They had no idea what was waiting for them. From the minute they started serving, a line developed. It got so busy that during the lunch rush, it reached three city blocks long. That shocked their system, and they knew it was time to develop operational procedures. Once they got the system in place, things became much easier, so much so that after only six months, they launched their first bricks-and-mortar location. Currently, they have a six locations and are continuing to expand. They capitalized on their truck to take part in the hottest trend in today's restaurant market gourmet fast, casual, quick-service restaurants.

When asked what the key to their success was Thomas said, "My personal tip—what has been most beneficial for us—is to develop a strong brand, the sky's the limit; then you can take that brand and do whatever you want with it." Moral of the story: Think through your branding and marketing efforts at the beginning to maximize your long-term value.

Crepes Bonaparte

Gaston. You may think that is the name of the owner of Crepes Bonaparte, but that's actually the name of the truck. The brains behind this creative stunt are Christian and Danielle Murcia, a husband and wife team from Fullerton, California. The Murcias started Crepes Bonaparte as a catering company in 2008, providing French crepe stations to private events. After seeing the opportunity and growth in the food truck business, the Murcias decided to join the party in 2010.

Christian and Dannielle purchased Gaston, their Morgan Olson Step-van, from a local Chevy dealer. After finding the rig, they worked with MSM Catering Trucks in Southern California to customize it. Some of their special requests included a crepe grill and service window large enough to allow customers to see their crepes being prepared. According to Christian, the most important step the Murcias took was to include a clause in the contract requiring MSM to finish the job in three months. They chose to go with a completely custom interior for the truck because prefab trucks came with a lot of materials they wouldn't need to execute their menu. By customizing the truck and purchasing the chassis, Christian estimates they were able to save $30,000 to $40,000.

The Murcias offer their delicious sweet and savory crepes throughout Los Angeles and Orange County. Their menu consists of breakfast crepes, savory crepes, dessert crepes, and traditional crepes. The most requested crepe is the HazelBerryAnna, a classic sweet crepe filled with strawberries, bananas, and Nutella. Christian's favorite crepe is the PCH, which is a decadent mix of peanut butter, Nutella, and honey, which he prefers with a big scoop of ice cream. They say the biggest challenge is working out of such a small space. Not only do they serve their customers from the truck, the Murcias actually run their catering business from the truck as well. This makes for major storage issues, especially when it comes to refrigeration. But good operators make the best of situations, and that's exactly what the Murcias are.

Even with the challenges, Crepes Bonaparte is flourishing. The Murcias goal is to provide crepes like they do in France, "simple, cheap, and on the go." Their commitment to this goal has made them a leader in the business and carried them all the way to become a contestant on *The Great Food Truck Race* with celebrity chef Tyler Florence. Even though they only made it to the third round of the competition, the exposure has increased business and helped make them local celebrities. With huge amounts of media exposure, passion, and a great product, Crepes Bonaparte should be satisfying people's crepe cravings for years to come.

Souvlaki Boys

Mike Kambouroglos, the co-founder of Souvlaki Boys, is extremely excited about all the delectable food options provided by his food truck. Started by Mike and his cousin Pete Alexopoulos in the summer of 2012, Souvlaki Boys was concepted as a truck that would bring authentic Greek cuisine to the Lancaster, Pennsylvania. This idea of authenticity and passion literally drove them to start their food truck, and it continues to be the core of the business today.

Mike spent a lot of time in Los Angeles and Portland, traveling and tasting, only to come back to Lancaster and dream about what he could create at home. "Cuisines from around the world were represented in their [LA and Portland's] food truck scenes. Immigrants got a shot at the American Dream through their native cuisine—it was awesome!" A couple of years later, he raised some money and finally got his idea for a truck off the ground. "Looking out at an hour-long line of people waiting to order our food—it was simultaneously humbling and validating," said Kambouroglos.

The menu at Souvlaki Boys consists of signature pitas filled with market fresh toppings like gyro meat, chicken souvlaki, fresh feta cheese, tomatoes, red onions, tzatziki, and French fries.

"Real Greek Food was the tagline from the start because I serve the food and experiences that I know so intimately from my time spent in my homeland," Mike explains. "I've been to almost every part of Greece and eaten plenty along the way and particularly spent a ton of time on the island of Kos where most of my family hales from." This authenticity comes through in the product. Mike has been successful because he reflected himself and his love for Greek food in his truck creation.

While the food truck continues to operate today, Mike has expanded to a 26-seat brick and mortar, a testament to his passion for sharing authentic Greek cuisines with his hometown.

Koi Fusion

Koi Fusion's visionary founder Bo Kwon is an offspring of the great Kogi Truck. While Kogi and its founder Roy Choi was his inspiration, Bo fashioned his own path to food truck and then restaurant success. As the oldest kid in a family of first-generation Korean immigrants, Bo was raised combining delicious ingredients for his after-school meals. He could only use what was in his house, which lead him to experiment with items such as Kimchi Grilled Cheese, leftover Pasta with Bulgogi & Kimchi. As he explains it, "just whatever was in our fridge when I was hungry; left side was the parents' side and right was our side."

While the desire and homegrown talent was there, Bo didn't have a platform nor a business. He just had his parents' entrepreneurial spirit as an example. Bo got a job working in a bar in downtown Portland, and he regularly would visit a food cart nearby. While he waited in line or ate his food, he would talk with the cart owners. He became knowledgeable about what it took to operate a food business in Portland. At the time,

Portland's food scene was just developing and Bo saw opportunity. His dad was the one who came up with the idea for opening a food business, specifically a traditional Korean BBQ restaurant. But Bo saw things differently, he said "Dad, no one likes smelling like Korean food!" One day he was watching a Korean news segment while sitting on the couch, and it was all about LA's Kogi BBQ food truck. He thought to himself, I got it; this would work in Portland. Eventually Bo decided to head to Los Angeles and speak to Kogi founder Roy Choi. At first, he wanted to expand Kogi to Portland, but "Roy didn't have the ability to expand to the Portland area at the time." However, Roy offered his blessing and support, saying, "he loved the idea of us [Bo] developing our own concept and running with it." Bo decided to break out on his own, and he purchased a local Mexican food truck and learned more about operating a mobile food business. As he explains, "I literally walked up to this lady and said, 'I want to buy this cart from you, but only if you let me work for free for six months and teach me everything you know.'" And that's how it went down. The lady taught Bo the ins and outs of operating in Portland and within months he was serving Korean fusion food and tacos on the PSU campus. It was a family affair, his mom, aunt, and brother helped him out, and word spread like wildfire.

Today, he has five traditional restaurant locations. Bo and his creation, Koi Fusion, are now icons of the Portland's food truck scene. On top of the restaurants, he and his family have an amazing catering business, and the mobile truck business continues to thrive with multiple locations in the greater Portland area. Bo continues to be an inspiring entrepreneur because he pays homage to his inspirations while paving a path that is completely his own. Bravo Bo!

Index

Numbers

5 Napkin Burger, 166
51 percenters, 28, 150
110-percent employee, 28

A

AA Cater Truck, 58
Açai Hut, 240
Adams, Nate, 11
administrative expenses, 88
Airbnb, 216
Airstream trailers, 56
Aloha (POS system), 143
Amazon, 49
America's first viral eatery, 6
Ansel, Dominique, 216
anti-establishment coffee
   retailer, 35
Apple, 116
Armenco, 58
Armstrong, Govind, 242
The Art of War, 182
aspirational experience, 3
aspirational story, 223
assembly line, creating, 24–25

auction sites, 257
Austin Daily Press, 241
authentic concept, 22
Authorize.net, 144
auto insurance (commercial),
   113
average cover, 36
average sales, estimating, 18–19

B

Baby's Badass Burgers, 11
Balthazar, 218
Behance, 117
Ben & Jerry's Ice Cream, 35
Bezos, Jeff, 49
bill-and-hold service (supplier),
   171
Bill's, 215
Bing, 119
bloggers, 122–123
Bon Appetit, 6
Borough Market (London), 13
Bowien, Danny, 177
brand
   content, 219
   equity, 103

logo design, 116–118
trusted, 231–232
brand creation, 46–52
   brand definition, 49–52
   concept definition, 46–48
Branson, Richard, 49
breakeven point, 88–89
bricks-and-mortar location,
   254–255
building your spots, 75–77
BurgerFi, 215
businesses, incorporation, 90
business model, 17–21
   average sales, estimating,
      18–19
   commissary costs, 21
   food and labor costs, 17–18
   labor costs, estimating, 19
   passing the test, 20
   production time, 20
   revenue streams, 21
business plan, 81–91
   breakeven point, 88–89
   business structure, 89–91
      corporation, 90–91
      limited partnership, 90
      partnership, 90
      sole proprietorship,
         89–90

competition, 85
expense forecasting, 87–88
identity, 83–84
importance of, 82–83
market, 84–85
profits, estimating, 89
sales forecasting, 85–87

C

California Heritage Museum,
240
calls to action, 213
Campbell's, 49
Cannone Cucina Italiana, 240
capital
gains, 100
operating, 95
start-up, 22–23
cash flow analysis, 198–199
cash registers, old-fashioned,
142
catering, 21
Cajun Creole Gambino's
Gourmet Exchange, 240
Chang, David, 178
Chang, Jerome, 9
*Charlie and the Chocolate
Factory*, 15
chef qualifications, 180
Chefs-a-Go-Go, 104
Chen, Chris, 9
Chernow, Michael, 14
Chevy Step-Vans, 56–58
Chicago's All Fired Up, 146
Child, Julia, 88, 240
Chirba Chirba, 11
Choi, Roy, 5
choice, appearance of, 14
clientele, 36–38, 203–213
criticism and praise, 207
employee feedback, 208

expectations, exceeding,
210–213
feedback, 204–206
understanding your
customers, 208–210
cloud storage service, 129
Clover, 144
Coca-Cola, 116
college buildings, 70
Collins, James, 15, 150, 248
comfort food, 7
commercial auto insurance,
113
commissary costs, 21
communication
hub, 130–131
marketing, 217
motivating staff, 162
trusted, 217
community
awareness (food truck lots),
239
building, 244
relationships, 68, 74–75
competition, 85
marketing plans and, 116
price-value relationship and,
42
concepts, 31–54
authentic, 22
average cover, 36
brand creation, 46–52
brand definition, 49–52
clientele, 36–38
cultural perspective, 35–36
focus group, 52–54
mantra, 32
menu, 39–41
presentation, 40–41
selections, 39–40
niche, 33–34
pricing, 41–42
downplaying the price,
42

price-value relationship,
41–42
profitability, 42
purpose definition, 42–46
example, 43–44
exercise, 44–45
lack of purpose, 43
self-discovery Q&A, 45
statement, 45–46
ultimate question, 44
testing and promoting, 244
truck categories, 33
consistency, achieving, 26–28
food sampling, 27
hiring employees, 28
recipe perfection, 26
staff training, 27
taking charge, 27–28
ConstantContact.com, 76
contribution (financing), 96
Cookie Confessionals, 227
Coolhaus Truck, 10
Copenhagen's Noma, 177
corporation, 90–91
Cost of Goods Sold (COGS)
report, 201
county health department, 108
crafting of story, 222–223
redemption, 223
relatable or aspirational, 223
repeatability, 222
simplicity and positivity,
222
struggle, 223
Craig, Nick, 44
Craigslist, 143
craigslist.com, 155, 257
craigslist.org, 59
creative element (marketing),
219
credit cards, 144–145
Crepes Bonaparte, 241
Cronut, 216
cuisine trucks, 33

cultural perspective, 35–36
culture (food truck
  revolution), 7
Cupcake Stop, 10
Curry, Steph, 17
customer service policies, 161

D

Dane, Philip, 236
decisions, early, 15
delivery, 21
department of health (DOH)
  food safety guidelines, 161
Depot letter, 110
DessertTruck, 242
Devilicious, 98
distribution element
  (marketing), 219–220
    channels, 220
      earned distribution
        channels, 220
      message reinforcement,
        220
      owned distribution
        channels, 220
      paid distribution
        channels, 220
      shared distribution
        channels, 220
    digital content, 219
    user standpoint, 220
distribution of payroll, 132
domain name, 114
dorms and college buildings,
  70
Dunkin' Donuts, 35

E

Eataly, 243
Eater.com, 8, 235
eBay, 59
eBay.com, 257
Edmunds (guide to valuing
  automobiles), 256
El Gallito chain, 8
email list sign-up, 118
emotional attachment, 29
emotional labor, 17
employee(s), *see also* hiring and
  managing staff, 149–164
    agreement form, 162
    feedback, 208
    hygiene, 108
    training, 27
enflyer.com, 76
Entourage, 9
equipment, 59, 109
events and opportunities,
  235–245
    festivals, 236–238
      combo meals, 237
      contact information,
        gathering of, 237
      getting noticed, 237
      music, 237
      organization and
        planning, 236
      parking problems, 236
      samples, 237
      signage, 237
      specialty items, 237
    food truck lots, 238–240
      city locations, 239
      description, 239
      developers, 240
      examples, 239–240
      health department
        requirements, 240

location, 239
traffic, 239
future expectations,
  243–245
    community building,
      244
    concept testing and
      promoting, 244
    food halls, 243
    generation 2.0, 243
    leading incubators, 243
    school programs, 245
  television opportunities,
    240–242
Excel, 129
expansion, 247–259
  benefits, 255
  bricks-and-mortar location,
    254–255
  capital resources, 253
  decline, 251
  determination, 247–249
    dilemma, 249
    important considerations,
      248
    location, 248
    measured pace, 248
    questions, 247
    simplicity, 248
    talent, 248
  growth, 250
  market introduction,
    249–250
  maturity, 250
  myth of success, 258–259
  pitfalls, 256
  selling your business,
    256–258
expenses
  administrative, 88
  daily, 195–197
  forecasting, 87–88
  inventory, 88

marketing, 88
payroll, 88
utilities, 88
experiential element
(marketing), 221
experiential follow through,
116

F

Facebook, 7, 119, 206, 219,
228
Business Manager, 220
marketing, 120–121
Fatburger, 215
fax, 131
fear, nature of, 16
feedback, 204–206
festivals, 236–238
combo meals, 237
contact information,
gathering of, 237
getting noticed, 237
music, 237
organization and planning,
236
parking problems, 236
samples, 237
signage, 237
specialty items, 237
financial reviews, 194–199
breakeven report, 194–195
cash flow analysis, 198–199
daily sales and expenses,
195–197
income statement, 197
numbers, 194
financing, 93–104
contribution (financing), 96
investment structure,
99–100

investors, 97–98
family and friends, 98
potential partners, 97–98
silent partners, 98
loans, 100–102
operating capital, 95
sponsorships, 103–104
start-up costs, 94–95
supplier credit, 102–103
Five Guys, 215
Flay, Bobby, 242
Florence, Tyler, 8, 241
focus group, 52–54
food blogs, 8, 235
Food Cart USA, 58
food costs, 17–18
Food and Drug Administration
(FDA), 108
food halls, 243
Food Network, 11, 98, 240
food preparation and safety,
177–189
chef, 179–181
kitchen cleanliness, 181–189
responsibilities, 178–179
Food Protection Manager
Identification, 109–110
food sampling, 27
food truck lots, 71, 238–240
city locations, 239
description, 239
developers, 240
examples, 239–240
health department
requirements, 240
location, 239
traffic, 239
food trucks, 3–12
aspirational experience, 3
comfort food, 7
emotional connection, 4
gourmet food trucks, 7
inspection, 110

insurance, 112–113
lots, 71, 238–240
city locations, 239
description, 239
developers, 240
examples, 239–240
health department
requirements, 240
location, 239
traffic, 239
matching food concept to,
40
personality, 83
responsibilities, 178–179
trend, 4
types, 8
food trucks (selection), 55–63
Chevy Step-Vans, 56, 58
customizing, 55
locating trucks, 59–61
Craigslist, 60
customizers, 60–61
dealers and auctions, 60
eBay, 60
equipment selection,
62–63
maintenance schedule,
64
powering vehicles, 63
redesigning existing
trucks, 61
prefabricated trucks, 58
rule, 55
Sprinter vans, 58
truck cost calculations, 59
types, 56
Food & Wine, 6
Ford Motor Company, 24
four *Ps*, 37
Foursquare, 7, 119–121, 228
Freightliner (vans), 58
French Laundry, 248
fusion trucks, 8

future expectations (events and opportunities), 243–245
  community building, 244
  concept testing and promoting, 244
  food halls, 243
  generation 2.0, 243
  leading incubators, 243
  school programs, 245

G

Gambino, Kevin, 240
GastroPod, 33
general liability insurance, 113
Geopath, 140
Gmail, 219
GoDaddy.com, 114
Good to Great, 15, 150, 248
Google, 116–117, 119
Google Analytics, 220
Google Chrome, 219
Goosebeary's, 183
GoPayment, 144
Gorilla Gourmet, 70
gourmet food trucks, 7
Gramercy Tavern, 149
The Great Food Truck Race, 8
The Great Truck Race, 98
Grill 'Em All, 241
Grub Street, 235
Grumman Olsen step vans, 56

H

Harvard Business Review, 44
health codes, 108–109
health inspections, 109–111
Heins, Jim, 11
Hey Cupcake, 240

hiring and managing staff, 149–164
  filling positions, 153–156
    cashier/greeter, 154
    hiring process, 155–156
    on-truck cook, 154
    prep cook, 153–154
  motivation and retention, 162–164
  number and positions, 150–152
  policies, 160–162
  scheduling, 158–160
  training and education staff, 156–158
    customer service, 157–158
    tone, 156
    training, 156–157
Hoffman, Ingrid, 11
Holzman, Daniel, 14
Huffman, Dyann, 98

I

identity, 83–84
Ikea, 46
income statement, 197
Infatuation, 206
influence, 221
In-N-Out Burger, 31
inspections (health codes), 108
Instagram, 7, 116–117, 216
insurance, 112–113
internet services, 129, 131
inventory, 39, 171–174
  counts, 172
  expenses, 88
  list (for suppliers), 169
  minimizing waste, 173
  preventing theft, 172–173

  purchasing supplies, 166–171
  review of, 201–202
investment structure, 99–100
investors, 97–98
item trucks, 33

J

Jack's Wife Freda, 218
Jankelowitz, Maya and Dean, 218
JG Melon, 215
Jobs, Steve, 233
Johnny Rockets, 215

K

Kebabalicious, 240
Keller, Thomas, 248
Kelly Blue Book, 256
Kelvin Natural Slush Co., 58
Kim, Jae, 228
kitchen
  cleanliness, 181–189
  setup, 145–146
Kogi Korean BBQ taco food truck, 5, 37
Kooper's Chowhound Burger Wagon, 11
Korilla, 117, 236
korillabbq.com, 76

L

labor costs, 17–19
lack of purpose, 43
Lagasse, Emeril, 240

large events, 70
launch event, 121–122
layered marketing, 223
Le Cirque, 9
Legal Zoom, 114
liability insurance (general),
    113
licenses
    mobile food vending
        license, 106
    permits and, 107–108
    roadway class-A license, 110
limited partnership, 90
loans, 100–102
local laws, 106–107
locating trucks, 59–61
    Craigslist, 60
    customizers, 60–61
    dealers and auctions, 60
    eBay, 60
    equipment selection, 62–63
    maintenance schedule, 64
    powering vehicles, 63
    redesigning existing trucks,
        61
location of truck, 67–77
    building your spots, 75–77
    local businesses, 74–75
    locations to avoid, 73–74
    low-traffic areas, 74
    mobility pros and cons, 68
    parking, 69–73
        dorms and college
            buildings, 70
        food truck lots, 71
        large events, 70
        nightspots, 71
        office buildings and
            office parks, 69
        residential buildings, 69
        seasonal locations, 70–71

restaurant rows, 74
    traffic, 73
logo (exterior truck), 139
Long Island City (LIC), 239
lots (food truck), 71, 238–240
    city locations, 239
    description, 239
    developers, 240
    examples, 239–240
    health department
        requirements, 240
    location, 239
    traffic, 239
low-traffic areas, 74

M

Macy's, 104
mailchimp.com, 76, 213
mainstream press, 123–124
maintenance (truck), 174–175
mall food court, 243
Mangieri, Anthony, 252
Manguera, Mark, 5
market, 84–85
market demand, 38–39
marketing, 215–33
    belief in yourself, 232–233
    creative element, 219
    distribution element,
        219–220
    expenses, 88
    experiential element, 221
    storytelling, 222–223
        crafting of story, 222
        legend, 222
        support, 223
    strategic sharing, 217–218
        communication, 217
        community, 218
        example, 218

marketing plan creation,
    115–126
    bloggers, 122–123
    brand logo design, 116–118
    event, every day as,
        124–125
    launch event, 121–122
    mainstream press, 123–124
    online presence, 118–121
        Facebook and
            Foursquare, 120–121
        Instagram and Twitter,
            119–120
        website, 118–119
    relationships, building, 126
    social media, 125–126
    truck marketing, 116
mass email applications, 76
McDonald's, 31
McNally, Keith, 218
meal trucks, 33
menu
    description (testing), 53
    items, location-specific, 77
    mix, review of, 209
    policies, 161
    presentation, 40–41
    psychology, 40
    review, 199–201
    selections, 39–40
    theme, 83
Mercedes Benz (vans), 58
Mercedes-Freightliner Sprinter
    vans, 56
Meyer, Danny, 28, 149
Microsoft Excel, 167
Micros (POS system), 143
The Mighty Cone, 240
Minetta Tavern, 166
Mission Cantina, 177
Mission Chinese, 177
mission statement, 52

mobile food vending license, 106
Mobile-Cuisine.com, 206
Momofuku, 178
motors.ebay.com, 59
multistop trucks, 56
myth
  about food business, 216–217
  of success, 258–259

N

Nana Queens, 241
New York Food Truck Association, 72, 235
New York Post, 231–232
New York Times, 230–231, 235
Nguyen, Sara, 242
niche, 33–34
nightspots, 71
Nike, 49, 116
Nikki Beach, 242
Nom Nom Truck, 241

O

Obama, Barack, 222
office buildings and office parks, 69
office setup, 127–134
  communications hub, 130–131
    fax, 131
    internet services, 131
    telephone, 130–131
  location, 128–130
  outside help, 133–134

payroll and records, 132–133
recordkeeping, 133
online bulletin boards, 257
online presence, 118–121
on-truck sales, 21
operating capital, 95
opportunities, *see* events and opportunities, 235–245
Outdoor Advertising Magazine, 140

P

The Paradox of Choice, 14
The Picnic, 240
parking, 69–73
  dorms and college buildings, 70
  food truck lots, 71
  large events, 70
  nightspots, 71
  office buildings and office parks, 69
  problems (festivals), 236
  residential buildings, 69
  seasonal locations, 70–71
partnership, 90
payroll expenses, 88
Pera Turkish Tacos, 111
Per Se, 248
permits and licenses, 107–108
personality, 29–30
Peter Luger Steakhouse, 168
Picasso, Pablo, 232
P. J. Clarke's, 215
point-of-sale (POS) system, 142–145, 196
  Aloha, 143
  credit cards, 144–145

Micros, 143
POS Lavu, 59
Revel Systems, 59
Shopify, 144
ShopKeep, 59
Square, 144
Squirrel, 143
tablet systems, 144
Poppa & Goose food truck, 183
POS Lavu (POS system), 59
possibilities, 16
pricing, 41–42
  downplaying the price, 42
  price-value relationship, 41–42
  profitability, 42
production time, 20
profit and loss statement, 197
profits, estimating, 89
promotions, 76
propane inspection, 109
purchasing, review of, 201–202
purpose definition, 42–46
  example, 43–44
  exercise, 44–45
  lack of purpose, 43
  self-discovery Q&A, 45
  statement, 45–46
  ultimate question, 44

Q–R

QuickBooks, 129

Ragin Cajun, 241
recipe perfection, 26
recordkeeping, 133
Redzepi, René, 177
Register.com, 114

regulations and licensing,
105–114
   domain name and
      trademark, 114
   health codes, 108–109
   health inspections, 109–11
   insurance, 112–113
   local laws, 106–107
   permits and licenses,
      107–108
   regulations, 111–112
Rein, Alex, 58
relationships, building, 126
Repp, Kristina, 98
residential buildings, 69
restaurant rows, 74
Revel Systems (POS system),
   59
revenue streams, 21
risk and reward, 16
Ritz-Carlton, 49
Roadstoves, 58
roadstoves.com, 257
roadway class-A license, 110
Rockrose, 239
Roy Rogers, 29

S

sales
   cost of, 88
   forecasting, 85–87
sba.gov, 102
SBA Small Business
   Investment Company (SBIC),
   102
school programs, 245
Schwartz, Barry, 14
seasonal locations, 70–71
self-contributions (financing
   considerations), 96

self-discovery Q&A, 45
selling your business, 256–258
Setting the Table, 149
set-up process, 137–138, 147
Shake Shack, 149–150, 166
Shin, Alice, 5
Shopify, 144
ShopKeep (POS system), 59
silent partners, 98
Smashburger, 215
Smorgasburg, 243
Snapchat, 7
Snook, Scott A., 44
Snyder, Harry, 31
social media, 5, 7, 125–126,
   144
   Facebook, 7, 120, 206, 219,
      228
   Foursquare, 120
   importance of, 144
   Instagram, 119
   Snapchat, 7
   Twitter, 6–7, 75, 116, 119,
      206, 228
sole proprietorship, 89–90
Song, Edward "3D," 117
Southern California Mobile
   Food Vendors Association,
   240
Souvlaki GR, 32
Speedee Service System, 24
Spencer on the Go!, 242
sponsorships, 103–104
Spotted Pig, 166
Sprinter vans, 58
Square (POS system), 144
Squirrel (POS system), 143
staff
   core skills, 28
   hiring, 28
   hygiene, 108
   training, 27

Starbucks, 31, 35, 49
start-up capital, 22–23
start-up costs, 94–95
StartUP FIU Food, 245
statement of purpose, 45–46
Steel City Pops, 240
Step-Vans, 56
storytelling (marketing),
   222–223
   crafting of story, 222–223
      redemption, 223
      relatable or aspirational,
         223
      repeatability, 222
      simplicity and positivity,
         222
      struggle, 223
   legend, 222
   support, 223
strategic sharing (marketing),
   217–218
   communication, 217
   community, 218
   example, 218
streetvendor.org, 72
success, secrets of, 13–30
   authentic concept, 22
   business model, 17–21
      average sales, estimating,
         18–19
      catering, 21
      commissary costs, 21
      delivery, 21
      food and labor costs,
         17–18
      labor costs, estimating,
         19
      on-truck sales, 21
      passing the test, 20
      production time, 20
      revenue streams, 21

consistency, achieving, 26–28
  food sampling, 27
  hiring employees, 28
  recipe perfection, 26
  staff training, 27
  taking charge, 27–28
start-up capital, 22–23
success, 15
uncertainty and fear, 15–17
value, adding, 29–30
  emotional attachment, 29
  personality, 29–30
volume generation, 23–26
  assembly line, creating, 24–25
  identifying your spots, 23–24
  travel plan, 25–26
Sun Tzu, 182
suppliers
  bill-and-hold service, 171
  credit, 102–103
  inventory list, 169
Sweetgreen in Schools program, 44
Sweetlife Festival, 44

T

taking charge, 27–28
target market, 36
team spirit, 163
Thrillist, 37
Throwdown! with Bobby Flay, 242
Timberland, 49
Topguest, 227
trademark, 114
traffic, 73

trailers, Airstream, 56
travel plan, 25–26
truck categories, 33
Truck It Fest, 236
Trudy's, 240
Twitter, 6–7, 75, 116, 118, 120, 206, 228
types of food trucks, 8

U

ultimate question, 44
Umami Burger, 215
Una Pizza Napoletana, 252
uncertainty and fear, 15–17
Union Square Cafe, 149
Union Square Greenmarket, 13
unique value proposition (UVP), 47, 51
urban centers, 4
UrbanDaddy, 37
Urbanspace, 243
U.S. Small Business Administration (SBA), 102
utilities (expenses), 88

V

value, adding, 29–30
  emotional attachment, 29
  personality, 29–30
Van Leeuwen, Ben, 10
Van Leeuwen Ice Cream Truck, 33
Veggie Ninja, 163
vending application, 110
Virgin, 49

volume generation, 23–26
  assembly line, creating, 24–25
  identifying your spots, 23–24
  travel plan, 25–26

W–X–Y–Z

Wall Street (movie), 200
Wafels & Dinges, 242
waste, 17
websites
  ConstantContact.com, 76
  craigslist.com, 155, 257
  craigslist.org, 59
  Eater.com, 8, 235
  eBay.com, 257
  enflyer.com, 76
  GoDaddy.com, 114
  korillabbq.com, 76
  legalzoom.com, 114
  mailchimp.com, 76, 213
  motors.ebay.com, 59
  nycfoodtrucks.org, 72
  Register.com, 114
  roadstoves.com, 257
  sba.gov, 102
WeWork, 245
White Castle, 29, 215
Wilcox, Tre, 242
workflow, 147
Wozniak, Steve, 222
Wu, Tiger, 163
Wu-Tang Clan, 16

Yelp, 228